Lafcadio Hearn's

JAPAN

Lafcadio Hearn's

JAPAN

An Anthology
of His Writings
on the Country
and Its People

*Edited and
with an Introduction
by*
Donald Richie

CHARLES E. TUTTLE COMPANY
Rutland, Vermont & Tokyo, Japan

Published by Charles E. Tuttle Publishing,
an imprint of Periplus Editions (HK) Ltd.

©1997 by Charles E. Tuttle Publishing Co., Inc.

LCC Card No. 96-60931
ISBN 0-8048-2096-1

First edition, 1997

Printed in Singapore

Distributed by:

USA **Charles E. Tuttle Co., Inc.**
Airport Industrial Park
RR1 Box 231-5
North Clarendon, VT 05759
Tel: (802) 773-8930
Fax: (802) 773-6993

Japan **Tuttle Shokai Inc.**
1-21-13 Seki
Tama-ku, Kawasaki-shi
Kanagawa-ken 214, Japan
Tel: (81) (44) 833-0225
Fax: (81) (44) 822-0413

Southeast Asia
Berkeley Books Pte Ltd.
5 Little Road #08-01
Singapore 536983
Tel: (65) 280 3320
Fax: (65) 280 6290

Tokyo Editorial Office:
2-6, Suido 1-chome,
Bunkyo-ku, Tokyo 112, Japan

Boston Editorial Office:
153 Milk Street, 5th Floor
Boston, MA 02109, USA

Singapore Editorial Office:
5 Little Road #08-01
Singapore 536983

Visit Tuttle Web on the Internet at:
http://www2.gol.com/users/tuttle/

Contents

Preface

Lafcadio Hearn (1850–1904) spent fourteen years in Japan—he arrived in Yokohama in April 1890 and died in Tokyo in September 1904.

If this span seems somehow short, it is because his reputation is based upon his writings on this country and because these are voluminous. Even now he remains somehow representative of Japan, and his books about the country and its people—not counting his collected letters and his uncollected articles—amount to over four thousand printed pages.

Attempting a single-volume anthology thus means leaving out much: over nine-tenths. At the same time it offers the opportunity to create a kind of narrative that reflects Hearn's expatriate life and what he saw and felt.

My choices for this anthology are determined by my belief that Hearn, besides being an occasional romancer, was also a reliable observer who has preserved for us a detailed account of turn-of-the-century Japan.

To indicate this and at the same time to illustrate the changes in attitude that informed his later writings, I

have decided upon an anthology in two parts, purposely patterned after those of his time, dealing with place
and people. The first half of the book is a description,
Hearn's vision of Japan during the early years of his stay.
The second half is devoted to his coming to terms with
the further realities of the place, the Japanese themselves.
Such a structure shows Hearn subjectively describing the
look of the country, and then objectively dramatizing
the people he met—and the many he didn't . . . those
ghosts that so people his landscape.

Everything selected is given in its entirety except for
one section, "Three Popular Ballads," where I include
the setting and leave out the ballads. I have also retained
Hearn's original punctuation, his inconsistent spelling of
place names, his treatment of Japanese words, and most
of his footnotes, which often contain further information.

—D. R.

Introduction

In the spring of 1890 the forty-year-old Lafcadio Hearn was offered a trip to Japan by *Harper's Magazine.* He was to write about his experiences and thus inform his readers about this land then already famous for being thought quaint and picturesque.

Just a year earlier Sir Edwin Arnold had written that if the reader wanted to know what Japan looked like, he or she should just "look at the nearest Japanese fan," which argues for an abundance of such in England and other countries where the fad for *japonaiserie* continued. There were indeed so many quaint and picturesque curios loose in the West that Amy Lowell could later report that the interest in Japanese poetry which so distinguished her own verse began in the rooms of her childhood—crammed with Japanese objects that her brother Percival had shipped back while representing the United States government.

In accepting the magazine's terms, Hearn wrote that in a country already so well trodden as Japan he could not be expected to discover anything completely new.

Rather, what he hoped to do was "to create, in the minds of the readers, a vivid impression of [his emphasis] *living* in Japan . . . as one taking part in the daily existence of the common people, and *thinking with their thoughts.*"

The reason that he believed anything this unlikely possible was that he had long nurtured feelings about the place. He had wandered enthusiastically through the Japanese section of the New Orleans World Exposition, read the effusions of Pierre Loti with attention, found Sir Edwin Arnold's *Light of Asia* profound, and pondered Percival Lowell's *The Soul of the Far East.* Later he even said that he had been born Japanese, had accidentally appeared in the wrong place, but had now finally found his way home.

What one usually discovers upon a return to longed-for origins is a utopia. Hearn consequently found in Japan surpassing beauty, an extraordinary charm, a lovable picturesqueness, and a place for himself. He was an aesthete and so, he thought, were the Japanese. He worshiped beauty and, therefore, so did they. He was tired of ugly commonplace and here was an extraordinary prettiness.

In this Hearn was a man of his times. The movement of art for art's sake was coming to a climax, there was a growing protest against such ideals as progress and respectability, there was also a definite move toward the politics of the aesthetic; and while the teachings of Whistler and Wilde might seem too close for comfort in London, similar teachings by Hearn in far Japan were acceptable.

Lafcadio could hold that Buddhism was superior to both Christianity and Science, and that Japan offered an Oriental refinement that London or Boston could barely even imagine. But such assertions came from a safe distance. As Earl Miner has remarked: "He offered aestheticism and unorthodoxy to his large audience at an easy remove, and flights into the strange or the exotic which were a welcome escape from the strenuous life of the late nineteenth century in England and America."

Also, finally, Hearn was also a short man and the Japanese were then a short people. And, though he was not in the Western sense an attractive-looking person, in Japan few knew how foreigners were supposed to look, and his unsightly eye and the odd twist it gave to his features remained uncommented upon.

Arriving, bent upon discovering an unspoiled utopia, he found that Yokohama and Tokyo were, from his point of view, already contaminated by the West and were thus no longer the Japan that he had hoped to find. But fortunately, a place more fitting was awaiting him. This was a small castle town on the Japan Sea coast, the provincial capital of Matsue.

Off the tourist path, as yet unused to foreigners and their ways, it seemed to represent all the best of that Old Japan now so swiftly disappearing. Though Hearn was in Matsue only a little over a year, it became for him a true paradise. There he found everything he wanted: his work, his wife, his home, and there he began to discover the Lafcadio Hearn we now know.

In the process—searching out beauty imperiled by change, chronicling traditional lives so soon to disappear—he became a witness. Hearn's is one of the few descriptions we have of what existed everywhere a century ago and is now nowhere.

* * *

At the same time, those eyes through which Hearn viewed Meiji Japan were singular—he had only one. Basil Hall Chamberlain, early mentor and friend, later recalled that he "saw details very distinctly while incapable of understanding them as a whole. Not only was this the case mentally but also physically. Blind of one eye, he was extremely short-sighted of the other. On entering a room his habit was to grope all around, closely examining wallpaper, the backs of books, pictures, curios, and other ornaments. Of these he could have drawn up an exact catalogue: but he had never properly seen either the horizon or the stars."

This was, however, a late evaluation, after Hearn had found reason to quarrel with Chamberlain—as indeed this highly irascible author did with a majority of his friends. Earlier, before the break, Chamberlain had written more generously: "Never perhaps was scientific accuracy of detail married to such tender and exquisite brilliancy of style."

Both descriptions are accurate in that they indicate that Hearn, while reflecting the reality of the country around him, was also constructing his own version of that land—he was creating what Roland Barthes was later to call a "fictive nation," a national system of one's own devising.

This need to construct one's very own Japan is common—all visitors must have experienced the urge. The Orient has long been perceived as difficult for the Occidental. Even now, long after picturesqueness has been tamed, there is still talk of "culture shock," some yet describe living there as "coping," guides still speak of "travel survival." To devise one's own land is thus a way of controlling it.

At the same time, the Orient has long seemed a haven

for Westerners seeking more intense spiritual and sensual experience—something Hearn was certainly attempting. In Japan there is much that initially seems enigmatic and there is thus the tantalizing promise of something beyond our common ken. For those not daunted by difficulty, an initial reaction is that a kind of paradise has been found, a land where whatever one desires seems possible.

There is, however unfortunately, no such place and after a time the foreigner discovers this. Initially, though, enchanted, he seeks to "understand" this attractive land, to insist upon the inscrutable, to find enigma where there is none, and to view change as destruction.

Chamberlain offers an example of these attitudes in a letter written to Hearn in 1892 "about the variability of one's feeling toward Japan being like the oscillation of a pendulum: one day swinging toward pessimism and next to optimism." He had these feelings often, "but the pessimistic feeling is generally consistent with some experience of new Japan and the optimistic with something of old Japan." This was in accord with Hearn's own initial findings. If Matsue was heaven, then Tokyo had to be hell.

In this he provides us with an early example of the classical Western attitudes toward Japan. Three stages have been observed. The first of these is an unreasoning infatuation, the second is an equally heedless dislike, and the third is when one accepts the country as it is—a state more like a marriage than a love affair. If one hears much less nowadays about the three classical stages it is because there is now so much less to infatuate and, consequently, to later abominate.

For well over a century, however, it was common for folks to fall in love with the place and, in the early stages of the affair, to compare all other countries unfavorably. During Hearn's first years in the country such ideas were so visible in his writings that a later author, John Paris (Frank Ashton-Gwatkin), could write that Hearn's books were mere visions of a land where everything was "kind, gentle, small, neat, artistic and spotlessly clean," the reverse of "our own poor vexed continent where the monstrous and the hideous multiply daily."

That the new Japan could not live up to the utopia that Hearn was constructing is quite true. Yet this fact does not affect the fidelity of his partial vision, and if an understanding of the impossibility of paradise undercut his early infatuation, it at the same time gave a kind of energy to his thoughts about the country.

* * *

This energy is reflected in the evolution of Hearn's style. When he arrived in Japan he wrote in the heightened, sensitive style typical of his *fin-de-siècle* times. For him the formative influences had been the florid Shelley, his favorite poet; the romantic Poe (in his student days Hearn called himself "The Raven"); the Gothic novelist and connoisseur of bizarre cultures, William Beckford; and George Borrow, the man who traveled with the exotic gypsies and coined a style to fit his Romany encounters.

In Japan Hearn had initially admired the writings of Pierre Loti and attempted to emulate what he took to be the French writer's technique: "On visiting a new country he always used to take notes of every fresh and powerful impression,—a landscape,—a sunset-blaze,—an architectural eccentricity,—a bit of picturesqueness in custom. . . ."

In elucidating this admired style, Hearn imitates it with his rhapsodic periods, his incantations, and his punctuation. The use of dashes with commas is a typical effusion—even more so is a lavish use of another mark of punctuation which lent the author the name of "Old Semi-Colon."

This emotive use of punctuation was matched by a word choice that sought to create an aura of general emotion rather than to give a precise meaning. The result included a number of Japanese words as well—used entirely for atmosphere rather than for precise information.

This practice was criticized by both Hearn's publisher, Harper's, and his friend Chamberlain. In his defense he wrote, typically, that "for me words have color, form, character; they have faces . . . moods, humours, eccentricities. . . . That they are unintelligible makes no difference at all."

They were truly unintelligible to him. He never learned properly to read or write, much less speak. Japanese remained a delightfully alien tongue to him, though in time he and his wife evolved a kind of baby-talk combined from both languages, and eventually he mastered the *kana* syllabary and could send her notes.

His wife read to him the stories which he, like a child, transcribed; and it was she who provided him with much of the information that became the basis of his work. It is thus quite true, as Marius Jansen writes, that Hearn "never made great progress in spoken or written Japanese . . . and he committed errors that would have been impossible had he possessed command of the language."

This incapacity in language can be defended. Words, as Roland Barthes later emphasized, are arbitrary. They are symbols that seek to capture the real, they are not that reality itself. Indeed, that they are notoriously ill-fitting to the object intended is common knowledge. Hence, to describe something is often to destroy it. Writers are aware of this, or should be, and consequently attempt to try out new combinations which they hope will more precisely describe the intended. To *not* know a language, then, is to be free of its imprecision, and to retain the ability to approach afresh.

In addition, this lack of knowledge seems appropriate to someone who saw himself as so set apart. Ignorance was like a vaccination against a general contagion—one did not come down with that general inattention to reality that language inevitably breeds. Hearn was thus not only blind in Japan, he was deaf as well. Both of these qualities contributed to his happiness.

By 1893, however, the author was changing. Romancing about things he had seen (or been told of) was not enough; something more precise was called for. The flaccid Loti was no longer an inspiration. Instead, Hearn found in Rudyard Kipling—a writer who had also been to Japan—a much more muscular model. There was also the example of Hans Christian Andersen. Later he would have his publisher send him the collected stories of the Danish author. "How great the art of the man!—the immense volume of fancy,—the magical simplicity. . . ."

Simplicity . . . after the heightened, the complicated, the curious, Hearn had learned from Japan itself the virtues of the spare. As he wrote to Chamberlain: "After years of studying poetical prose, I am forced now to study simplicity. After attempting my utmost at ornamentation, I am converted by my own mistakes. The great point is to touch with simple words. And I feel my style is not yet fixed—too artificial. By another year of study or two, I think I shall be able to do better."

One of the reasons for this evolving style was his own changing impressions of the country—stage two of the classical trinity was being reached. Again writing to Chamberlain, he stated, "As for changing my conclusions—well, I have had to change a good many. The tone [of my first book] is true in being the feeling of a place and time. Since then I've seen how thoroughly detestable [the] Japanese can be, and the revelation assisted in illuminating things."

As for the writing itself, Lafcadio told Chamberlain that for every page he wrote, ten were suppressed. He would begin by arranging notes and writing down ideas, then correcting the manuscript. The following day he would rewrite everything. Then he would begin the final copy, which would be done twice. He knew the work was finished, he said, when a kind of focusing occurred. This happened when the process was completed, the original length cut in about half, and the first impression returned ever the more strongly.

To an old friend, Elwood Hendrick, he wrote that "the best work is done the way ants do things—by tiny tireless and regular additions." He added that he never worked "without painfully forcing myself to do it." His method was to "let the thought develop itself," which led to "four or five rewritings and at least two final copies."

This meant, in effect, a kind of description new to Hearn—one no longer concerned with preference and judgment but with precision; one much less concerned with places and much more concerned with people. It meant also being more clear about the person doing the writing—himself.

Indeed, as Albert Mordell has written, it is true that in this sense "it is a mistake to think of Hearn as a 'writer on Japan.' Japan gave him nothing. He himself, not Japan, is the interesting subject."

* * *

The solitary Hearn, seeking to lose himself in Japan, became gradually aware of individuality—theirs and his. While he had never wholly succumbed to those comforting generalizations about the Japanese that even now continue to clutter the literature, he had nonetheless done his bit toward the creating of a peaceful, beauty-loving public, invariably given to quoting haiku.

Now, however, he saw more and more clearly that "the Japanese" were in reality individuals as varied as any in Cincinnati or New Orleans. By 1894 he was writing Chamberlain: "Lowell says the Japanese have no individuality. I wish he had to teach here for a year, and he would discover some of the most extraordinary individualities he ever saw."

He was now far distanced from Edwin Arnold, who had so praised quaint Japan and not once mentioned the miles of new railroad tracks. Hearn may not have liked the tracks but he wrote about them. This was because he was more and more writing about what he saw rather than about what he had wanted and expected to see.

Hearn's evocative and occasionally indulgent landscaping of Japan was succeeded by a penetrating and sometimes sentimental description of its people. These contributed to and led toward an attempt at interpretation, as he called it, in which his fictive country merged, finally, with the real.

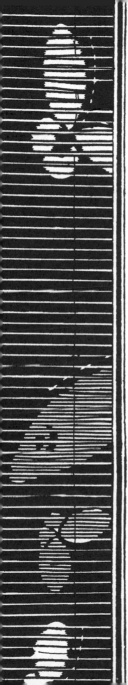

PART ONE

The Land

Note: As noted in the Introduction, Japanese was always "a delightfully alien tongue" for Hearn. His original manuscripts include Japanese terms that are dialect variations and other renderings that are simply mistakes.

Japanese words within this volume follow Hearn's original Romanized spelling, which can differ from modern Romanization. In addition, Hearn's spelling sometimes differed from essay to essay. This text retains Hearn's original spelling of all Japanese and English words and Hearn's original punctuation.

"There is some charm unutterable in the morning air, cool with the coolness of Japanese spring and wind-waves from the snowy cone of Fuji; a charm perhaps due rather to softest lucidity than to any positive tone,—an atmospheric limpidity extraordinary, with only a suggestion of blue in it, through which the most distant objects appear focused with amazing sharpness . . ." Thus did Hearn write in "My First Day in the Orient," the essay that he chose to open his first book on Japan.

It reads like an announcement of intention—paradise regained. And Hearn would continue in this vein for many hundreds of pages. His delight is manifest and his enthusiasm is infectious. These writings still retain the emotions that created them.

What such emotions meant, however, was to be learned only after some years in the country. For this reason, the section "Strangeness and Charm" from one of Hearn's last books on the country seems most fitting to open this anthology. It gives a thoughtful account of the emotional impact of Japan upon an emotional person—including a more tempered memory of that first day in the country.

Hearn's finest description of the strangeness and charm of turn-of-the-century Japan is contained in his essay on Matsue, his own personal paradise, "The Chief City of the Province of the Gods." In this detailed, decorated, and embellished essay, he clearly tells us that he adopted the place forever: It came to represent for him all the promise of Japan—in 1904, the year of his death, he was still wanting to return.

He first went to Matsue in August 1890, having arrived in Japan less than six months before, and a month later was contentedly teaching at the local middle and high schools, having obtained the position through the kindness of Professor Basil Hall Chamberlain, then at the Tokyo Imperial University.

The professor, already a famous man, living in Japan since 1873, was a distinguished scholar in the country; had mastered Japanese and was an authority on the language; had translated the oldest Japanese document, the *Kojiki;* had written on Japanese classical poetry; and had edited the still popular book about Japanese customs called *Things Japanese.* Consequently, he was also in a position to find friends jobs.

For Hearn, living in Matsue was a defining experience. In earlier places—Martinique, New Orleans, Cincinnati—he had learned to cultivate the occasionally exotic, but in this isolated city on the Japan Sea the exotic became for him a daily experience. So exotic that he, not knowing the language, understanding little of the culture, was at some disadvantage in his everyday life—shopping and cooking, for example.

The solution was a common one, reached by many men in similar circumstances: he must get married. Indeed, Hearn's beloved mentor, Sir Edwin Arnold, was to marry a Japanese. Accordingly Lafcadio submitted to an arranged marriage—with Setsuko Koizumi, the young daughter of a local déclassé samurai household.

This marriage was a success (his first, to a Cincinnati mulatto had not been) and it was to Setsuko that Hearn owed much of the felicity of his later years. Without her, Lafcadio could not have gathered all the information he needed, and certainly without her he could not have had the four children who so delighted his declining years.

He also could not have gotten the house that they moved into in June 1891. It still stands. This is the small dwelling opening up onto its small garden which is shown visitors to Matsue—Hearn's glasses still on an open page, his pipe still in its tray. His delight both in the house and in the marriage is seen in one of his best essays from this period, "In a Japanese Garden."

During this enchanted Matsue year Hearn and his wife made a number of excursions to nearby places, and from these outings came some of his most memorable early writings. He traveled up and down the coast, went to Izumo, "home of the gods," even went (as a kind of belated honeymoon trip) to the distant Oki islands.

Here included are two of the finest of these early descriptions of Japan—one that has been forgotten and one that is rightfully famous. The first is an account of an excursion Hearn made to a nearby community of outcasts—that group now known as *burakumin* and then locally known as *yama no mono*. The second is a description of a boat trip to the Kuikedo—a place he calls "The Cave of the Children's Ghosts."

Eventually, however, paradise was lost. In the fall of

1891, his contract with the Matsue schools ran out and again through the always helpful Chamberlain, he and Setsu moved to Kumamoto, where he was to teach at the local higher middle school. From the first he disliked the place—though after Matsue he would probably have disliked any place at all.

Kumamoto, on the farther side of the southernmost island, Kyushu, had been much damaged in the civil wars attending the Meiji Restoration. The castle had been burned down, whole sections of the old city destroyed, and the new buildings were all Western and badly built at that. He might have been in St. Louis. Old Japan was that far away.

Nonetheless, Kumamoto gave Hearn the time he needed to complete his first book on the country, *Glimpses of Unfamiliar Japan.* In it he kept his promise to his publisher "to give a vivid impression of living in Japan." It is still his most popular collection.

Whether it also gives the impression of "one taking part in the daily existence of the common people, and thinking with their thoughts" (the rest of the promise) is a matter of opinion. Mine is that the worth of this book—the worth of all his Japan writings—lies in Hearn's ability to show us the common (as differentiated from the quaint, the fanciful, the picturesque) face of Japan; to retain for us the feel of the ordinary scene with ordinary people in it.

This he does in a late piece, the 1904 "Letter from Japan," written in Tokyo and devoted to the daily life of the people and what they were thinking about. These thoughts were largely political, a concern that Hearn had hitherto avoided.

When he had arrived in 1890, Japan's first constitutional government was sitting, however unhappily, in

Tokyo but he, in old Matsue, could ignore it. By 1894, however, political reality was intruding itself. Japan had gone to war with China and many—among them some of his former students—died in the resulting battles. Now, in 1904, the Japanese were defeating the Russians, and these victories would ensure that the country became even more modern even faster.

This new feeling he reflects in his 1904 letter—a description of the country in all ways different from that in "My First Day in the Orient," of nearly fifteen years before. The fairy-tale atmosphere has evaporated and enchantment has metamorphosed itself into reality.

Just before this, however, Hearn had—Prospero closing his book—utilized the trappings of enchantment for one final time to fashion an extraordinarily prescient piece called "Hōrai," which, though it pretends to be a description of an old painting of the ancient Taoist isle, is actually an allegory of the modern archipelago of Japan.

> "Evil winds from the West are blowing over Hōrai; and the magical atmosphere, alas! is shrinking away before them . . . never again to appear save in pictures and poems and dreams. . . ."

Hearn, the one-eyed, saw well what was happening to his Japan.

Strangeness and Charm

The majority of the first impressions of Japan recorded by travellers are pleasurable impressions. Indeed, there must be something lacking, or something very harsh, in the nature to which Japan can make no emotional appeal. The appeal itself is the clue to a problem; and that problem is the character of a race and of its civilization.

My own first impressions of Japan,—Japan as seen in the white sunshine of a perfect spring day,—had doubtless much in common with the average of such experiences. I remember especially the wonder and the delight of the vision. The wonder and the delight have never passed away: they are often revived for me even now, by some chance happening, after fourteen years of sojourn. But the reason of these feelings was difficult to learn,—or at least to guess; for I cannot yet claim to know much about Japan. . . . Long ago the best and dearest Japanese friend I ever had said to me, a little before his death: "When you find, in four or five years more, that you cannot understand the Japanese at all, then you will begin to know something about them." After having realized the truth of my friend's

26

prediction,—after having discovered that I cannot understand the Japanese at all,—I feel better qualified to attempt this essay.

As first perceived, the outward strangeness of things in Japan produces (in certain minds, at least) a queer thrill impossible to describe,—a feeling of weirdness which comes to us only with the perception of the totally unfamiliar. You find yourself moving through queer small streets full of odd small people, wearing robes and sandals of extraordinary shapes; and you can scarcely distinguish the sexes at sight. The houses are constructed and furnished in ways alien to all your experience; and you are astonished to find that you cannot conceive the use or meaning of numberless things on display in the shops. Food-stuffs of unimaginable derivation; utensils of enigmatic forms; emblems incomprehensible of some mysterious belief; strange masks and toys that commemorate legends of gods or demons; odd figures, too, of the gods themselves, with monstrous ears and smiling faces,—all these you may perceive as you wander about; though you must also notice telegraph-poles and type-writers, electric lamps and sewing machines. Everywhere on signs and hangings, and on the backs of people passing by, you will observe wonderful Chinese characters; and the wizardry of all these texts makes the dominant tone of the spectacle.

Further acquaintance with this fantastic world will in nowise diminish the sense of strangeness evoked by the first vision of it. You will soon observe that even the physical actions of the people are unfamiliar,—that their work is done in ways the opposite of Western ways. Tools are of surprising shapes, and are handled after surprising methods: the blacksmith squats at his anvil, wielding a hammer such as no Western smith could use without long practice; the carpenter pulls, instead of pushing, his extraordinary plane and saw. Always the left is the right side, and the right side the wrong; and keys must be turned, to open or close a lock, in what we are accustomed to think the wrong direction. Mr. Percival Lowell has truthfully observed that the Japanese speak backwards, read backwards, write backwards,—and that this is "only the abc of their contrariety." For the habit of writing backwards there are obvious evolutional reasons; and the requirements of Japanese calligraphy sufficiently explain why the artist pushes his brush or pencil instead of pulling it. But why, instead of putting the thread through the eye of the needle, should the Japanese maiden slip the eye of the needle over the point of the thread? Perhaps the most remarkable, out of a hundred possible examples of antipodal action, is furnished by the Japanese art of fencing. The swordsman, delivering his blow with both hands, does not pull the blade towards him in the moment of striking, but pushes it from him. He uses it, indeed, as other Asiatics do, not on the principle of the wedge, but of the saw; yet there is a pushing motion where we should expect a pulling motion in the stroke. . . . These and other forms of unfamiliar action are strange enough to suggest the notion of a humanity even physically as little related to us as might be the population of another planet,—the notion of some anatomical unlikeness. No such unlikeness, however, appears to exist; and all this oppositeness probably implies, not so much the outcome of a human experience entirely independent of Aryan experience, as the outcome of an experience evolutionally younger than our own.

Yet that experience has been one of no mean order. Its manifestations do not merely startle: they also delight. The delicate perfection of workmanship, the light strength and grace of objects, the power manifest to obtain the best results with the least material, the achieving of mechanical ends by the simplest possible means, the comprehension of irregularity as æsthetic value, the shapeliness and perfect taste of everything, the sense displayed of harmony in tints or colours,—all this must convince you at once that our Occident has much to learn from this remote civilization, not only in matters of art and taste, but in matters likewise of economy and utility. It is no barbarian fancy that appeals to you in those amazing porcelains, those astonishing embroideries, those wonders of lacquer and ivory and bronze, which educate imagination in unfamiliar ways. No: these are the products of a civilization which became, within its own limits, so exquisite that none but an artist is capable of judging its manufactures,—a civilization that can be termed imperfect only by those who would also term imperfect the Greek civilization of three thousand years ago.

But the underlying strangeness of this world,—the psychological strangeness,—is much more startling than the visible and superficial. You begin to suspect the range of it after having discovered that no adult Occidental can perfectly master the language. East and West the fundamental parts of human nature—the emotional bases of it—are much the same: the mental difference between a Japanese and a European child is mainly potential. But with growth the difference rapidly develops and widens, till it becomes, in adult life, inexpressible. The whole of the Japanese mental superstructure evolves into forms having nothing in common with Western psychological development: the expression of thought becomes regulated, and the expression of emotion inhibited in ways that bewilder and astound. The ideas of this people are not our ideas; their sentiments are not our sentiments; their ethical life represents for us regions of thought and emotion yet unexplored, or perhaps long forgotten. Any one of their ordinary phrases, translated into Western speech, makes hopeless nonsense; and the literal rendering into Japanese of the simplest English sentence would scarcely be comprehended by any Japanese who had never studied a European tongue. Could you learn all the words in a Japanese dictionary, your acquisition would not help you in the least to make yourself understood in speaking, unless you had learned also to think like a Japanese,—that is to say, to think backwards, to think upside-down and inside-out, to think in directions totally foreign to Aryan habit. Experience in the acquisition of European languages can help you to learn Japanese about as much as it could help you to acquire the language spoken by the inhabitants of Mars. To be able to use the Japanese tongue as a Japanese uses it, one would need to be born again, and to have one's mind completely reconstructed, from the foundation upwards. It is possible that a person of European parentage, born in Japan, and accustomed from infancy to use the vernacular, might retain in after-life that instinctive knowledge which could alone enable him to adapt his mental relations to the relations of any Japanese environment. There is actually an Englishman named Black, born in Japan, whose proficiency in the language is proved by the fact that he is able to earn a fair income as a professional storyteller *(hanashika)*. But this is an extraordinary case. . . . As for the literary language, I need only observe that to make acquaintance with it requires very much more than a knowledge of several thousand Chinese characters. It is safe to say that no Occidental can undertake to render at sight any literary text laid before him—indeed the number of native scholars able to do so is very small;—and although the learning displayed in this direction by various Euro-peans may justly compel our admiration, the work of none could have been given to the world without Japanese help.

But as the outward strangeness of Japan proves to be full of beauty, so the inward strangeness appears to have its charm,—an ethical charm reflected in the common life of the people. The attractive aspects of that life do not indeed imply, to the ordinary observer, a psychological differentiation measurable by scores of centuries: only a scientific mind, like that of Mr. Percival Lowell, immediately perceives the problem presented. The less gifted stranger, if naturally sympathetic, is merely pleased and puzzled, and

tries to explain, by his own experience of happy life on the
other side of the world, the social conditions that charm
him. Let us suppose that he has the good fortune of being
able to live for six months or a year in some old-fashioned
town of the interior. From the beginning of this sojourn he
can scarcely fail to be impressed by the apparent kindliness
and joyousness of the existence about him. In the relations
of the people to each other, as well as in all their relations
to himself, he will find a constant amenity, a tact, a good-
nature such as he will elsewhere have met with only in the
friendship of exclusive circles. Everybody greets everybody
with happy looks and pleasant words; faces are always smiling; the commonest incidents of everyday life are transfigured by a courtesy at once so artless and so faultless that it
appears to spring directly from the heart, without any
teaching. Under all circumstances a certain outward cheer-
fulness never fails: no matter what troubles may come,—
storm or fire, flood or earthquake,—the laughter of greeting voices, the bright smile and graceful bow, the kindly
inquiry and the wish to please, continue to make existence
beautiful. Religion brings no gloom into this sunshine:
before the Buddhas and the gods folk smile as they pray;
the temple courts are playgrounds for the children; and
within the enclosure of the great public shrines—which are
places of festivity rather than of solemnity—dancing-plat-
forms are erected. Family existence would seem to be everywhere characterized by gentleness: there is no visible quar-
relling, no loud harshness, no tears and reproaches.
Cruelty, even to animals, appears to be unknown: one sees
farmers, coming to town, trudging patiently beside their
horses or oxen, aiding their dumb companions to bear the
burden, and using no whips or goads. Drivers or pullers of
carts will turn out of their way, under the most provoking
circumstances, rather than overrun a lazy dog or a stupid
chicken. . . . For no inconsiderable time one may live in the
midst of appearances like these, and perceive nothing to
spoil the pleasure of the experience.

Of course the conditions of which I speak are now passing away; but they are still to be found in the remoter districts. I have lived in districts where no case of theft had
occurred for hundreds of years,—where the newly-built
prisons of Meiji remained empty and useless,—where the
people left their doors unfastened by night as well as by
day. These facts are familiar to every Japanese. In such a
district, you might recognize that the kindness shown to
you, as a stranger, is the consequence of official command;
but how explain the goodness of the people to each other?
When you discover no harshness, no rudeness, no dishon-
esty, no breaking of laws, and learn that this social condition has been the same for centuries, you are tempted to
believe that you have entered into the domain of a morally
superior humanity. All this soft urbanity, impeccable hon-
esty, ingenuous kindliness of speech and act, you might
naturally interpret as conduct directed by perfect goodness
of heart. And the simplicity that delights you is no simplicity of barbarism. Here every one has been taught; every
one knows how to write and speak beautifully, how to
compose poetry, how to behave politely; there is everywhere cleanliness and good taste; interiors are bright and
pure; the daily use of the hot bath is universal. How refuse
to be charmed by a civilization in which every relation
appears to be governed by altruism, every action directed
by duty, and every object shaped by art? You cannot help
being delighted by such conditions, or feeling indignant at
hearing them denounced as "heathen." And according to
the degree of altruism within yourself, these good folk will
be able, without any apparent effort, to make you happy.
The mere sensation of the milieu is a placid happiness: it is
like the sensation of a dream in which people greet us
exactly as we like to be greeted, and say to us all that we like
to hear, and do for us all that we wish to have done,—
people moving soundlessly through spaces of perfect
repose, all bathed in vapoury light. Yes—for no little time
these fairy folk can give you all the soft bliss of sleep. But

sooner or later, if you dwell long with them, your contentment will prove to have much in common with the happiness of dreams. You will never forget the dream,—never;
but it will lift at last, like those vapours of spring which
lend preternatural loveliness to a Japanese landscape in the
forenoon of radiant days. Really you are happy because you
have entered bodily into Fairyland,—into a world that is
not, and never could be your own. You have been trans-
ported out of your own century—over spaces enormous of
perished time—into an era forgotten, into a vanished
age,—back to something ancient as Egypt or Nineveh.
That is the secret of the strangeness and beauty of
things,—the secret of the thrill they give,—the secret of the
elfish charm of the people and their ways. Fortunate mortal! the tide of Time has turned for you! But remember that
here all is enchantment,—that you have fallen under the
spell of the dead,—that the lights and the colours and the
voices must fade away at last into emptiness and silence.

* * *

Some of us, at least, have often wished that it were possible to live for a season in the beautiful vanished world of
Greek culture. Inspired by our first acquaintance with the
charm of Greek art and thought, this wish comes to us even
before we are capable of imagining the true conditions of
the antique civilization. If the wish could be realized, we
should certainly find it impossible to accommodate ourselves to those conditions,—not so much because of the
difficulty of learning the environment, as because of the
much greater difficulty of feeling just as people used to feel
some thirty centuries ago. In spite of all that has been done
for Greek studies since the Renaissance, we are still unable
to understand many aspects of the old Greek life: no modern mind can really feel, for example, those sentiments and
emotions to which the great tragedy of Œdipus made
appeal. Nevertheless we are much in advance of our fore-

fathers of the eighteenth century, as regards the knowledge of Greek civilization. In the time of the French revolution, it was thought possible to reëstablish in France the conditions of a Greek republic, and to educate children according to the system of Sparta. To-day we are well aware that no mind developed by modern civilization could find happiness under any of those socialistic despotisms which existed in all the cities of the ancient world before the Roman conquest. We could no more mingle with the old Greek life, if it were resurrected for us,—no more become a part of it,—than we could change our mental identities. But how much would we not give for the delight of beholding it,—for the joy of attending one festival in Corinth, or of witnessing the Pan-Hellenic games ? . . .

And yet, to witness the revival of some perished Greek civilization,—to walk about the very Crotona of Pythagoras,—to wander through the Syracuse of Theocritus,—were not any more of privilege than is the opportunity actually afforded us to study Japanese life. Indeed, from the evolutional point of view, it were less of a privilege,—since Japan offers us the living spectacle of conditions older, and psychologically much farther away from us, than those of any Greek period with which art and literature have made us closely acquainted.

The reader scarcely needs to be reminded that a civilization less evolved than our own, and intellectually remote from us, is not on that account to be regarded as necessarily inferior in all respects. Hellenic civilization at its best represented an early stage of sociological evolution; yet the arts which it developed still furnish our supreme and unapproachable ideals of beauty. So, too, this much more archaic civilization of Old Japan attained an average of æsthetic and moral culture well worthy of our wonder and praise. Only a shallow mind—a very shallow mind—will pronounce the best of that culture inferior. But Japanese civilization is peculiar to a degree for which there is perhaps no

Western parallel, since it offers us the spectacle of many successive layers of alien culture superimposed above the simple indigenous basis, and forming a very bewilderment of complexity. Most of this alien culture is Chinese, and bears but an indirect relation to the real subject of these studies. The peculiar and surprising fact is that, in spite of all superimposition, the original character of the people and of their society should still remain recognizable. The wonder of Japan is not to be sought in the countless borrowings with which she has clothed herself,—much as a princess of the olden time would don twelve ceremonial robes, of divers colours and qualities, folded one upon the other so as to show their many-tinted edges at throat and sleeves and skirt;—no, the real wonder is the Wearer. For the interest of the costume is much less in its beauty of form and tint than in its significance as idea, as representing something of the mind that devised or adopted it. And the supreme interest of the old Japanese civilization lies in what it expresses of the race-character,—that character which yet remains essentially unchanged by all the changes of Meiji.

"Suggests" were perhaps a better word than "expresses," for this race-character is rather to be divined than recognized. Our comprehension of it might be helped by some definite knowledge of origins; but such knowledge we do not yet possess. Ethnologists are agreed that the Japanese race has been formed by a mingling of peoples, and that the dominant element is Mongolian; but this dominant element is represented in two very different types,—one slender and almost feminine of aspect; the other, squat and powerful. Chinese and Korean elements are known to exist in the populations of certain districts; and there appears to have been a large infusion of Aino blood. Whether there be any Malay or Polynesian element also has not been decided. Thus much only can be safely affirmed,—that the race, like all good races, is a mixed one; and that the peoples who originally united to form it have been so blended together as to develop, under long social discipline, a tolerably uniform type of character. This character, though immediately recognizable in some of its aspects, presents us with many enigmas that are very difficult to explain.

Nevertheless, to understand it better has become a matter of importance. Japan has entered into the world's competitive struggle; and the worth of any people in that struggle depends upon character quite as much as upon force. We can learn something about Japanese character if we are able to ascertain the nature of the conditions which shaped it,—the great general facts of the moral experience of the race. And these facts we should find expressed or suggested in the history of the national beliefs, and in the history of those social institutions derived from and developed by religion.

The Chief City of
the Province of the Gods

I

The first of the noises of a Matsue day comes to the sleeper like the throbbing of a slow, enormous pulse exactly under his ear. It is a great, soft, dull buffet of sound—like a heartbeat in its regularity, in its muffled depth, in the way it quakes up through one's pillow as to be felt rather than heard. It is simply the pounding of the ponderous pestle of the kometsuki, the cleaner of rice,—a sort of colossal wooden mallet with a handle about fifteen feet long horizontally balanced on a pivot. By treading with all his force on the end of the handle, the naked kometsuki elevates the pestle, which is then allowed to fall back by its own weight into the rice tub. The measured muffled echoing of its fall seems to me the most pathetic of all sounds of Japanese life; it is the beating, indeed, of the Pulse of the Land.

Then the boom of the great bell of Tōkōji, the Zenshū temple, shakes over the town; then come melancholy echoes of drumming from the tiny little temple of Jizō in the street Zaimokuchō, near my house, signaling the

Buddhist hour of morning prayer. And finally the cries of
the earliest itinerant venders begin,—*"Daikoyai! kabuya-
kabu!"*—the sellers of daikon and other strange vegetables.
"Moyaya-moya!"—the plaintive call of the women who sell
little thin slips of kindling-wood for the lighting of charcoal fires.

II

Roused thus by these earliest sounds of the city's wak-
ening life, I slide open my little Japanese paper window to
look out upon the morning over a soft green cloud of
spring foliage rising from the river-bounded garden below.
Before me, tremulously mirroring everything upon its farther side, glimmers the broad glassy mouth of the
Ōhashigawa, opening into the grand Shinji Lake, which
spreads out broadly to the right in a dim gray frame of
peaks. Just opposite to me, across the stream, the blue-
pointed Japanese dwellings have their to[1] all closed; they
are still shut up like boxes, for it is not yet sunrise, although
it is day.

But oh, the charm of the vision,—those first ghostly
love-colors of a morning steeped in mist soft as sleep itself
resolved into a visible exhalation. Long reaches of faintly-
tinted vapor cloud the far lake verge,—long nebulous
bands, such as you may have seen in old Japanese picture-
books, and must have deemed only artistic whimsicalities
unless you had previously looked upon the real phenome-
na. All the bases of the mountains are veiled by them, and
they stretch athwart the loftier peaks at different heights
like immeasurable lengths of gauze (this singular appearance the Japanese term "shelving"),[2] so that the lake appears
incomparably larger than it really is, and not an actual lake,
but a beautiful spectral sea of the same tint as the dawn sky
and mixing with it, while peak-tips rise like islands from
the brume, and visionary strips of hill-ranges figure as
league-long causeways stretching out of sight,—an exquis-

ite chaos, ever changing aspect as the delicate fogs rise, slowly, very slowly. As the sun's yellow rim comes into sight, fine thin lines of warmer tone—spectral violets and opalines—shoot across the flood, treetops take tender fire, and the unpainted façades of high edifices across the water change their wood-color to vapory gold through the delicious haze.

Looking sunward, up the long Ōhashigawa, beyond the many-pillared wooden bridge, one high-pooped junk, just hoisting sail, seems to me the most fantastically beautiful craft I ever saw,—a dream of Orient seas, so idealized by the vapor is it; the ghost of a junk, but a ghost that catches the light as clouds do; a shape of gold mist, seemingly semi-diaphanous, and suspended in pale blue light.

III

And now from the river-front touching my garden there rises to me a sound of clapping of hands,—one, two, three, four claps,—but the owner of the hands is screened from view by the shrubbery. At the same time, however, I see men and women descending the stone steps of the wharves on the opposite side of the Ōhashigawa, all with little blue towels tucked into their girdles. They wash their faces and hands and rinse their mouths,—the customary ablution preliminary to Shintō prayer. Then they turn their faces to the sunrise and clap their hands four times and pray. From the long high white bridge come other clappings, like echoes, and others again from far light graceful craft, curved like new moons,—extraordinary boats, in which I see bare-limbed fishermen standing with foreheads bowed to the golden East. Now the clappings multiply,—multiply at last into an almost continuous volleying of sharp sounds. For all the population are saluting the rising sun,—O-Hi-San, the Lady of Fire, Ama-terasu-oho-mi-Kami, the Lady of the Great Light.[3] "*Konnichi-Sama!* Hail this day to thee, divinest Day-Maker! Thanks unutterable unto thee, for this thy sweet light, making beautiful the world!" So, doubtless, the thought, if not the utterance, of countless hearts. Some turn to the sun only, clapping their hands; yet many turn also to the West, to holy Kitzuki, the immemorial shrine; and not a few turn their faces successively to all the points of heaven; murmuring the names of a hundred gods; and others, again, after having saluted the Lady of Fire, look toward high Ichibata, toward the place of the great temple of Yakushi-Nyorai, who giveth sight to the blind,—not clapping their hands as in Shintō worship, but only rubbing the palms softly together after the Buddhist manner. But all—for in this most antique province of Japan all Buddhists are Shintōists likewise—utter the archaic words of Shintō prayer: *"Harai tamai kiyome tamai to Kami imi tami."*

Prayer to the most ancient gods who reigned before the coming of the Buddha, and who still reign here in their own Izumo-land,—in the Land of Reed Plains, in the Place of the Issuing of Clouds; prayer to the deities of primal chaos and primeval sea and of the beginnings of the world,—strange gods with long weird names, kindred of U-hiji-ni-no-Kami, the First Mud-Lord, kindred of Su-hiji-ni-no-Kami, the First Sand-Lady; prayer to those who came after them,—the gods of strength and beauty, the world-fashioners, makers of the mountains and the isles, ancestors of these sovereigns whose lineage still is named "The Sun's Succession;" prayer to the Three Thousand Gods "residing within the provinces," and to the Eight Hundred Myriads who dwell in the azure Takama-no-hara,—in the blue Plain of High Heaven. *"Nippon-koku-chū-yaoyorozu-no-Kami-gami-sama!"*

IV

"Ho-ke-kyō!"

My uguisu is awake at last, and utters his morning prayer. You do not know what an uguisu is? An uguisu is a holy little bird that professes Buddhism. All uguisu have professed Buddhism from time immemorial; all uguisu preach alike to men the excellence of the divine Sutra.

"Ho-ke-kyō!"

In the Japanese tongue, Ho-ke-kyō; in Sanscrit, Saddharma-Pundarika: "The Sutra of the Lotus of the Good Law," the divine book of the Nichiren sect. Very brief, indeed, is my little feathered Buddhist's confession of faith,—only the sacred name reiterated over and over again like a litany, with liquid bursts of twittering between.

"Ho-ke-kyō!"

Only this one phrase, but how deliciously he utters it! With what slow amorous ecstasy he dwells upon its golden syllables!

It hath been written: "He who shall keep, read, teach, or write this Sutra shall obtain eight hundred good qualities of the Eye. He shall see the whole Triple Universe down to the great hell Aviki, and up to the extremity of existence. He shall obtain twelve hundred good qualities of the Ear. He shall hear all sounds in the Triple Universe,—sounds of gods, goblins, demons, and beings not human."

"Ho-ke-kyō!"

A single word only. But it is also written: "He who shall joyfully accept but a single word from this Sutra, incalculably greater shall be his merit than the merit of one who should supply all beings in the four hundred thousand Asankhyeyas of worlds with all the necessaries for happiness."

"Ho-ke-kyō!"

Always he makes a reverent little pause after uttering it and before shrilling out his ecstatic warble, his bird-hymn of praise. First the warble; then a pause of about five seconds; then a slow, sweet, solemn utterance of the holy name in a tone as of meditative wonder; then another pause; then another wild, rich, passionate warble. Could you see him, you would marvel how so powerful and penetrating a soprano could ripple from so minute a throat; for he is one of the very tiniest of all feathered singers, yet his chant can be heard far across the broad river, and children going to school pause daily on the bridge, a whole cho away, to listen to his song. And uncomely withal: a neutral-tinted mite, almost lost in his immense box-cage of hinoki wood, darkened with paper screens over its little wire-grated windows, for he loves the gloom.

Delicate he is and exacting even to tyranny. All his diet must be laboriously triturated and weighed in scales, and measured out to him at precisely the same hour each day. It demands all possible care and attention merely to keep him alive. He is precious, nevertheless. "Far and from the uttermost coasts is the price of him," so rare he is. Indeed, I could not have afforded to buy him. He was sent to me by one of the sweetest ladies in Japan, daughter of the governor of Izumo, who, thinking the foreign teacher might feel lonesome during a brief illness, made him the exquisite gift of this dainty creature.

V

The clapping of hands has ceased; the toil of the day begins; continually louder and louder the pattering of geta over the bridge. It is a sound never to be forgotten, this pattering of geta over the Ōhashi,—rapid, merry, musical, like the sound of an enormous dance; and a dance it veritably is. The whole population is moving on tiptoe, and the multitudinous twinkling of feet over the verge of the sunlit roadway is an astonishment. All those feet are small, symmetrical,—light as the feet of figures painted on Greek vases,—and the step is always taken toes first; indeed, with geta it could be taken no other way, for the heel touches neither the geta nor the ground, and the foot is tilted forward by the wedge-shaped wooden sole. Merely to stand upon a pair of geta is difficult for one unaccustomed to their use, yet you see Japanese children running at full speed in geta with soles at least three inches high, held to the foot only by a forestrap fastened between the great toe and the other toes, and they never trip and the geta never falls off. Still more curious is the spectacle of men walking in bokkuri or takageta, a wooden sole with wooden supports at least five inches high fitted underneath it so as to make the whole structure seem the lacquered model of a wooden bench. But the wearers stride as freely as if they had nothing upon their feet.

Now children begin to appear, hurrying to school The undulation of the wide sleeves of their pretty speckled robes, as they run, looks precisely like a fluttering of extraordinary butterflies. The junks spread their great white or yellow wings, and the funnels of the little steamers which have been slumbering all night by the wharves begin to smoke.

One of the tiny lake steamers lying at the opposite wharf has just opened its steam-throat to utter the most unimaginable, piercing, desperate, furious howl. When that cry is heard everybody laughs. The other little steamboats utter only plaintive mooings, but unto this particular vessel— newly built and launched by a rival company—there has been given a voice expressive to the most amazing degree of reckless hostility and savage defiance. The good people of Matsue, upon hearing its voice for the first time, gave it forthwith a new and just name,—Ōkami-Maru. "Maru" signifies a steamship. "Ōkami" signifies a wolf.

VI

A very curious little object now comes slowly floating down the river, and I do not think that you could possibly guess what it is.

The Hotoke, or Buddhas, and the beneficent Kami are not the only divinities worshiped by the Japanese of the poorer classes. The deities of evil, or least some of them, are duly propitiated upon certain occasions, and requited by offerings whenever they graciously vouchsafe to inflict a temporary ill instead of an irremediable misfortune.[4] (After all, this is no more irrational than the thanksgiving prayer at the close of the hurricane season in the West Indies, after the destruction by storm of twenty-two thousand lives.) So men sometimes pray to Ekibiogami, the God of Pestilence, and to Kaze-no-Kami, the God of Wind and of Bad Colds, and to Hoso-no-Kami, the God of Smallpox, and to divers evil genii.

Now when a person is certainly going to get well of smallpox a feast is given to the Hoso-no-Kami, much as a feast is given to the Fox-God when a possessing fox has promised to allow himself to be cast out. Upon a sando-wara, or small straw mat, such as is used to close the end of a rice-bale, one or more kawarake, or small earthenware vessels, are placed. These are filled with a preparation of rice and red beans, called adzukimeshi, whereof both Inari-Sama and Hoso-no-Kami are supposed to be very fond. Little bamboo wands with gohei (paper cuttings) fastened to them are then planted either in the mat or in the adzukimeshi, and the color of these gohei must be red. (Be it observed that the gohei of other Kami are always white.) This offering is then either suspended to a tree, or set afloat in some running stream at a considerable distance from the home of the convalescent. This is called "seeing the God off."

VII

The long white bridge with its pillars of iron is recognizably modern. It was, in fact, opened to the public only last spring with great ceremony. According to some most ancient custom, when a new bridge has been built the first persons to pass over it must be the happiest of the community. So the authorities of Matsue sought for the happiest folk, and selected two aged men who had both been married for more than half a century, and who had had not less than twelve children, and had never lost any of them. These good patriarchs first crossed the bridge, accompanied by their venerable wives, and followed by their grown-up children, grandchildren, and great grandchildren, amidst a great clamor of rejoicing, the showering of fireworks, and the firing of cannon.

But the ancient bridge so recently replaced by this structure was much more picturesque, curving across the flood and supported upon multitudinous feet, like a long-legged centipede of the innocuous kind. For three hundred years it had stood over the stream firmly and well, and it had its particular tradition.

When Horiō Yoshiharu, the great general who became daimyō of Izumo in the Keichō era, first undertook to put a bridge over the mouth of this river, the builders labored in vain; for there appeared to be no solid bottom for the pillars of the bridge to rest upon. Millions of great stones were cast into the river to no purpose, for the work constructed by day was swept away or swallowed up by night. Nevertheless, at last the bridge was built, but the pillars began to sink soon after it was finished; then a flood carried half of it away, and as often as it was repaired so often it was wrecked. Then a human sacrifice was made to appease the vexed spirits of the flood. A man was buried alive in the river-bed below the place of the middle pillar, where the current is most treacherous, and thereafter the bridge remained immovable for three hundred years.

This victim was one Gensuke, who had lived in the street Saikamachi; for it had been determined that the first man who should cross the bridge wearing hakama without a machi[5] should be put under the bridge; and Gensuke sought to pass over not having a machi in his hakama, so they sacrificed him. Wherefore the midmost pillar of the bridge was for three hundred years called by his name,—Gensuke-bashira. It is averred that upon moonless nights a ghostly fire flitted about that pillar,—always in the dead watch hour between two and three; and the color of the light was red, though I am assured that in Japan, as in other lands, the fires of the dead are most often blue.

VIII

Now some say that Gensuke was not the name of a man, but the name of an era, corrupted by local dialect into the semblance of a personal appellation. Yet so profoundly is the legend believed, that when the new bridge was being built thousands of country-folk were afraid to come to town; for a rumor arose that a new victim was needed, who was to be chosen from among them, and that it had been determined to make the choice from those who still wore their hair in queues after the ancient manner. Wherefore hundreds of aged men cut off their queues. Then another rumor was circulated to the effect that the police had been secretly instructed to seize the one thousandth person of those who crossed the new bridge the first day, and to treat him after the manner of Gensuke. And at the time of the great festival of the Rice-God, when the city is usually thronged by farmers coming to worship at the many shrines of Inari, this year there came but few; and the loss to local commerce was estimated at several thousand yen.

IX

The vapors have vanished, sharply revealing a beautiful little islet in the lake, lying scarcely half a mile away,—a low, narrow strip of land with a Shintō shrine upon it, shadowed by giant pines; not pines like ours, but huge, gnarled, shaggy, tortuous shapes, vast-reaching like ancient oaks. Through a glass one can easily discern a torii, and before it two symbolic lions of stone *(Kara-shishi),* one with its head broken off, doubtless by its having been over-turned and dashed about by heavy waves during some great storm. This islet is sacred to Benten, the Goddess of

Eloquence and Beauty, wherefore it is called Benten-no-shima But it is more commonly called Yome-ga-shima, or "The Island of the Young Wife," by reason of a legend. It is said that it arose in one night, noiselessly as a dream, bearing up from the depths of the lake the body of a drowned woman who had been very lovely, very pious, and very unhappy. The people, deeming this a sign from heaven, consecrated the islet to Benten, and thereon built a shrine unto her, planted trees about it, set a torii before it, and made a rampart about it with great curiously-shaped stones; and there they buried the drowned woman.

Now the sky is blue down to the horizon, the air is a caress of spring. I go forth to wander through the queer old city.

X

I perceive that upon the sliding doors, or immediately above the principal entrance of nearly every house, are pasted oblong white papers bearing ideographic inscriptions; and overhanging every threshold I see the sacred emblem of Shintō, the little rice straw rope with its long fringe of pendent stalks. The white papers at once interest me; for they are ofuda, or holy texts and charms, of which I am a devout collector. Nearly all are from temples in Matsue or its vicinity; and the Buddhist ones indicate by the sacred words upon them to what particular shū, or sect, the family belongs,—for nearly every soul in this community professes some form of Buddhism as well as the all-dominant and more ancient faith of Shintō. And even one quite ignorant of Japanese ideographs can nearly always distinguish at a glance the formula of the great Nichiren sect from the peculiar appearance of the column of characters composing it, all bristling with long sharp points and banneret zigzags, like an army; the famous text *Namu-myō-hō-ren-ge-kyō*, inscribed of old upon the flag of the great captain Kato Kiyomasa, the extirpator of Spanish

Christianity, the glorious *vir ter execrandus* of the Jesuits. Any pilgrim belonging to this sect has the right to call at whatever door bears the above formula and ask for alms or food.

But by far the greater number of the ofuda are Shintō. Upon almost every door there is one ofuda especially likely to attract the attention of a stranger, because at the foot of the column of ideographs composing its text there are two small figures of foxes, a black and a white fox, facing each other in a sitting posture, each with a little bunch of rice-straw in its mouth, instead of the more usual emblematic key. These ofuda are from the great Inari temple of Oshiroyama[6], within the castle grounds, and are charms against fire. They represent, indeed, the only form of assurance against fire yet known in Matsue,—so far, at least, as wooden dwellings are concerned. And although a single spark and a high wind are sufficient in combination to obliterate a larger city in one day, great fires are unknown in Matsue, and small ones are of rare occurrence.

The charm is peculiar to the city; and of the Inari in question this tradition exists:—

> When Naomasu, the grandson of Iyeyasu, first came to Matsue to rule the province, there entered into his presence a beautiful boy, who said: "I came hither from the home of your august father in Echizen, to protect you from all harm. But I have no dwelling-place, and am staying therefore at the Buddhist temple of Fu-mon-in. Now if you will make for me a dwelling within the castle grounds, I will protect from fire the buildings there and the houses of the city, and your other residence likewise which is in the capital. For I am Inari Shinyemon." With these words he vanished from sight. Therefore Naomasu dedicated to him the great temple which still stands in the castle grounds, surrounded by one thousand foxes of stone.

XI

I now turn into a narrow little street, which, although so ancient that its dwarfed two-story houses have the look of things grown up from the ground, is called the Street of the New Timber. New the timber may have been one hundred and fifty years ago; but the tints of the structures would ravish an artist,—the sombre ashen tones of the wood-work, the furry browns of old thatch, ribbed and patched and edged with the warm soft green of those velvety herbs and mosses which flourish upon Japanese roofs.

However, the perspective of the street frames in a vision more surprising than any details of its mouldering homes. Between very lofty bamboo poles, higher than any of the dwellings, and planted on both sides of the street in lines, extraordinary black nets are stretched, like prodigious cob-webs against the sky, evoking sudden memories of those monster spiders which figure in Japanese mythology and in the picture-books of the old artists. But these are only fish-ing-nets of silken thread; and this is the street of the fish-ermen. I take my way to the great bridge.

XII

A stupendous ghost!

Looking eastward from the great bridge over those sharply beautiful mountains, green and blue, which tooth the horizon, I see a glorious spectre towering to the sky. Its base is effaced by far mists: out of the air the thing would seem to have shaped itself,—a phantom cone, diaphanous-ly gray below, vaporously white above, with a dream of per-petual snow,—the mighty mountain of Daisen.

At the first approach of winter it will in one night become all blanched from foot to crest; and then its snowy pyramid so much resembles that Sacred Mountain, often compared by poets to a white inverted fan, half opened, hanging in the sky, that it is called Izumo-Fuji, "the Fuji of

Izumo." But it is really in Hōki, not in Izumo, though it cannot be seen from any part of Hōki to such advantage as from here. It is the one sublime spectacle of this charming land; but it is visible only when the air is very pure. Many are the marvelous legends related concerning it, and somewhere upon its mysterious summit the Tengu are believed to dwell.

XIII

At the farther end of the bridge, close to the wharf where the little steamboats are, is a very small Jizō temple (Jizō-dō). Here are kept many bronze drags; and whenever any one has been drowned and the body not recovered, these are borrowed from the little temple and the river is dragged. If the body be thus found, a new drag must be presented to the temple.

From here, half a mile southward to the great Shintō temple of Tenjin, deity of scholarship and calligraphy, broadly stretches Tenjinmachi, the Street of the Rich Merchants, all draped on either side with dark blue hangings, over which undulate with every windy palpitation from the lake while wondrous ideographs, which are names and signs, while down the wide way, in white perspective, diminishes a long line of telegraph poles.

Beyond the temple of Tenjin the city is again divided by a river, the Shindotegawa, over which arches the bridge Tenjin-bashi. Again beyond this other large quarters extend to the hills and curve along the lake shore. But in the space between the two rivers is the richest and busiest life of the city, and also the vast and curious quarter of the temples. In this islanded district are likewise the theatres, and the place where wrestling-matches are held, and most of the resorts of pleasure.

Parallel with Tenjinmachi runs the great street of the Buddhist temples, or Teramachi, of which the eastern side is one unbroken succession of temples,—a solid front of court walls tile-capped, with imposing gateways at regular intervals. Above this long stretch of tile-capped wall rise the beautiful tilted massive lines of gray-blue temple roofs against the sky. Here all the sects dwell side by side in harmony,—Nichiren-shū, Shingon-shū, Zen-shū, Tendai-shū, even that Shin-shū, unpopular in Izumo because those who follow its teaching strictly must not worship the Kami. Behind each temple court there is a cemetery, or hakaba; and eastward beyond these are other temples, and beyond them yet others,—masses of Buddhist architecture mixed with shreds of gardens and miniature homesteads, a huge labyrinth of mouldering courts and fragments of streets.

To-day, as usual, I find I can pass a few hours very profitably in visiting the temples; in looking at the ancient images seated within the cups of golden lotus-flowers under their aureoles of gold; in buying curious mamori; in examining the sculptures of the cemeteries, where I can nearly always find some dreaming Kwannon or smiling Jizō well worth the visit.

The great courts of Buddhist temples are places of rare interest for one who loves to watch the life of the people; for these have been for unremembered centuries the playing-places of the children. Generations of happy infants have been amused in them. All the nurses, and little girls who carry tiny brothers or sisters upon their backs, go thither every morning that the sun shines; hundreds of children join them; and they play at strange, funny games,—"Oni-gokko," or the game of Devil, "Kage-Oni," which signifies the Shadow and the Demon, and "Mekusan-gokko," which is a sort of "blindman's buff."

Also, during the long summer evenings, these temples are wrestling-grounds, free to all who love wrestling; and in many of them there is a dohyō-ba, or wrestling-ring. Robust young laborers and sinewy artisans come to these courts to test their strength after the day's tasks are done, and here the fame of more than one now noted wrestler was first made. When a youth has shown himself able to overmatch at wrestling all others in his own district, he is challenged by champions of other districts; and if he can overcome these also, he may hope eventually to become a skilled and popular professional wrestler.

It is also in the temple courts that the sacred dances are performed and that public speeches are made. It is in the temple courts, too, that the most curious toys are sold, on the occasion of the great holidays,—toys most of which have a religious signification. There are grand old trees, and ponds full of tame fish, which put up their heads to beg for food when your shadow falls upon the water. The holy lotus is cultivated therein.

"Though growing in the foulest slime, the lotus remains pure and undefiled.

"And the soul of him who remains ever pure in the midst of temptation is likened unto the lotus.

"Therefore is the lotus carven or painted upon the furniture of temples; therefore also does it appear in all the representations of our Lord Buddha.

"In Paradise the blessed shall sit at ease enthroned upon the cups of golden lotus-flowers."[7]

A bugle-call rings through the quaint street; and round the corner of the last temple come marching a troop of handsome young riflemen, uniformed somewhat like French light infantry, marching by fours so perfectly that all the gaitered legs move as if belonging to a single body, and every sword-bayonet catches the sun at exactly the same angle, as the column wheels into view. These are the students of the Shihan-Gakkō, the College of Teachers, performing their daily military exercises. Their professors give them lectures upon the microscopic study of cellular tissues, upon the segregation of developing nerve structure, upon spectrum analysis, upon the evolution of the color sense, and upon the cultivation of bacteria in glycerine infusions. And they are none the less modest and knightly in manner for all their modern knowledge, nor the less reverentially devoted to their dear old fathers and mothers whose ideas were shaped in the era of feudalism.

XIV

Here come a band of pilgrims, with yellow straw over-coats, "rain-coats" *(mino),* and enormous yellow straw hats, mushroom-shaped, of which the down-curving rim partly hides the face. All carry staffs, and wear their robes well girded up so as to leave free the lower limbs, which are inclosed in white cotton leggings of a peculiar and inde-scribable kind. Precisely the same sort of costume was worn by the same class of travelers many centuries ago; and just as you now see them trooping by,—whole families wan-dering together, the pilgrim child clinging to the father's hand,—so may you see them pass in quaint procession across the faded pages of Japanese picture-books a hundred years old.

At intervals they halt before some shop-front to look at the many curious things which they greatly enjoy seeing, but which they have no money to buy.

I myself have become so accustomed to surprises, to interesting or extraordinary sights, that when a day hap-pens to pass during which nothing remarkable has been heard or seen I feel vaguely discontented. But such blank days are rare: they occur in my own case only when the weather is too detestable to permit of going out-of-doors. For with ever so little money one can always obtain the pleasure of looking at curious things. And this has been one of the chief pleasures of the people in Japan for centuries and centuries, for the nation has passed its generations of lives in making or seeking such things. To divert one's self seems, indeed, the main purpose of Japanese existence, beginning with the opening of the baby's wondering eyes. The faces of the people have an indescribable look of patient expectancy,—the air of waiting for something interesting to make its appearance. If it fail to appear, they will travel to find it: they are astonishing pedestrians and tireless pilgrims, and I think they make pilgrimages not more for the sake of pleasing the gods than of pleasing themselves by the sight of rare and pretty things. For every temple is a museum, and every hill and valley throughout the land has its temple and its wonders.

Even the poorest farmer, one so poor that he cannot afford to eat a grain of his own rice, can afford to make a pilgrimage of a month's duration; and during that season when the growing rice needs least attention hundreds of thousands of the poorest go on pilgrimages. This is possible, because from ancient times it has been the custom for everybody to help pilgrims a little; and they can always find rest and shelter at particular inns *(kichinyado)* which receive pilgrims only, and where they are charged merely the cost of the wood used to cook their food.

But multitudes of the poor undertake pilgrimages requiring much more than a month to perform, such as the pilgrimage to the thirty-three great temples of Kwannon, or that to the eighty-eight temples of Kōbōdaishi; and these, though years be needed to accomplish them, are as nothing compared to the enormous Sengaji, the pilgrimage to the thousand temples of the Nichiren sect. The time of a generation may pass ere this can be made. One may begin it in early youth, and complete it only when youth is long past. Yet there are several in Matsue, men and women, who have made this tremendous pilgrimage, seeing all Japan, and supporting themselves not merely by begging, but by some kinds of itinerant peddling.

The pilgrim who desires to perform this pilgrimage carries on his shoulders a small box, shaped like a Buddhist shrine, in which he keeps his spare clothes and food. He also carries a little brazen gong, which he constantly sounds while passing through a city or village, at the same time chanting the Namu-myō-hō-ren-ge-kyō; and he always bears with him a little blank book, in which the priest of every temple visited stamps the temple seal in red ink. The pilgrimage over, this book with its one thousand seal impressions becomes an heirloom in the family of the pilgrim.

XV

I too must make divers pilgrimages, for all about the city, beyond the waters or beyond the hills, lie holy places immemorially old.

Kitzuki, founded by the ancient gods, who "made stout the pillars upon the nethermost rock bottom, and made high the cross-beams to the Plain of High Heaven,"— Kitzuki, the Holy of Holies, whose high priest claims descent from the Goddess of the Sun; and Ichibata, famed shrine of Yakushi-Nyorai, who giveth sight to the blind,— Ichibata-no-Yakushi, whose lofty temple is approached by six hundred and forty steps of stone; and Kiomidzu, shrine of Kwannon of the Eleven Faces, before whose altar the sacred fire has burned without ceasing for a thousand years; and Sada, where the Sacred Snake lies coiled forever on the sambo of the gods; and Oba, with its temples of Izanami and Izanagi, parents of gods and men, the makers of the world; and Yaegaki, whither lovers go to pray for unions with the beloved; and Kaka, Kaka-ura, Kaka-no-Kukedo San,—all these I hope to see.

But of all places, Kaka-ura! I assuredly I must go to Kaka.

Few pilgrims go thither by sea, and boatmen are forbidden to go there if there be even wind enough "to move three hairs." So that whosoever wishes to visit Kaka must either wait for a period of dead calm—very rare upon the coast of the Japanese Sea—or journey thereunto by land; and by land the way is difficult and wearisome. But I must see Kaka. For at Kaka, in a great cavern by the sea, there is a famous Jizō of stone; and each night, it is said, the ghosts of little children climb to the high cavern and pile up

before the statue small heaps of pebbles; and every morning, in the soft sand, there may be seen the fresh prints of
tiny naked feet, the feet of the infant ghosts. It is also said
that in the cavern there is a rock out of which comes a
stream of milk, as from a woman's breast; and the white
stream flows forever, and the phantom children drink of it.
Pilgrims bring with them gifts of small straw sandals,—the
zōri that children wear,—and leave them before the cavern,
that the feet of the little ghosts may not be wounded by the
sharp rocks. And the pilgrim treads with caution, lest he
should overturn any of the many heaps of stones; for if this
be done the children cry.

XVI

The city proper is as level as a table, but is bounded on
two sides by low demilunes of charming hills shadowed
with evergreen foliage and crowned with temples or
shrines. There are thirty-five thousand souls dwelling in ten
thousand houses forming thirty-three principal and many
smaller streets; and from each end of almost every street,
beyond the hills, the lake, or the eastern rice-fields, a
mountain summit is always visible,—green, blue, or gray
according to distance. One may ride, walk, or go by boat
to any quarter of the town; for it is not only divided by two
rivers, but is also intersected by numbers of canals crossed
by queer little bridges curved like a well-bent bow.
Architecturally (despite such constructions in European
style as the College of Teachers, the great public school, the
Kenchō, the new post-office) it is much like other quaint
Japanese towns; the structure of its temples, taverns, shops,
and private dwellings is the same as in other cities of the
western coast. But doubtless owing to the fact that Matsue
remained a feudal stronghold until a time within the memory of thousands still living, those feudal distinctions of
caste so sharply drawn in ancient times are yet indicated
with singular exactness by the varying architecture of dif-

ferent districts. The city can be definitely divided into three architectural quarters: the district of the merchants and shop-keepers, forming the heart of the settlement, where all the houses are two stories high; the district of the temples, including nearly the whole southeastern part of the town; and the district or districts of the shizoku (formerly called samurai) comprising a vast number of large, roomy, garden-girt, one-story dwellings. From these elegant homes in feudal days, could be summoned at a moment's notice five thousand "two-sworded men" with their armed retainers, making a fighting total for the city alone of probably not less than thirteen thousand warriors. More than one third of all the city's buildings were then samurai homes; for Matsue was the military centre of the most ancient province of Japan. At both ends of the town, which curves in a crescent along the lake shore, were the two main settlements of samurai; but just as some of the most important temples are situated outside of the temple districts, so were many of the finest homesteads of this knightly caste situated in other quarters. They mustered most thickly, however, about the castle, which stands to-day on the summit of its citadel hill—the Oshiroyama—solid as when first built long centuries ago; a vast and sinister shape, all iron gray, rising against the sky from a cyclopean foundation of stone. Fantastically grim the thing is, and grotesquely complex in detail; looking somewhat like a huge pagoda, of which the second, third, and fourth stories have been squeezed down and telescoped into one another by their own weight. Crested at its summit, like a feudal helmet, with two colossal fishes of bronze lifting their curved bodies skyward from either angle of the roof, and bristling with horned gables and gargoyled eaves and tilted puzzles of tiled roofing at every story, the creation is a veritable architectural dragon, made up of magnificent monstrosities,—a dragon, moreover, full of eyes set at all conceivable angles, above, below, and on every side. From under the black scowl of the loftiest eaves, looking east and south, the whole city can be seen at a single glance, as in the vision of a soaring hawk; and from the northern angle the view plunges down three hundred feet to the castle road, where walking figures of men appear no larger than flies.

XVII

The grim castle has its legend.

It is related that, in accordance with some primitive and barbarous custom, precisely like that of which so terrible a souvenir has been preserved for us in the most pathetic of Serbian ballads, "The Foundation of Skadra," a maiden of Matsue was interred alive under the walls of the castle at the time of its erection, as a sacrifice to some forgotten gods. Her name has never been recorded; nothing concerning her is remembered except that she was beautiful and very fond of dancing.

Now after the castle had been built, it is said that a law had to be passed forbidding that any girl should dance in the streets of Matsue. For whenever any maiden danced the hill Oshiroyama would shudder, and the great castle quiver from basement to summit.

XVIII

One may still sometimes hear in the streets a very humorous song, which every one in town formerly knew by heart, celebrating the Seven Wonders of Matsue. For Matsue was formerly divided into seven quarters, in each of which some extraordinary object or person was to be seen. It is now divided into five religious districts, each containing a temple of the state religion. People living within those districts are called ujiko, and the temple the ujigami, or dwelling place of the tutelary god. The ujiko must support the ujigami. (Every village and town has at least one ujigami.)

There is probably not one of the multitudinous temples

of Matsue which has not some marvelous tradition attached to it; each of the districts has many legends; and I think that each of the thirty-three streets has its own special ghost story. Of these ghost stories I cite two specimens: they are quite representative of one variety of Japanese folklore.

Near to the Fu-mon-in temple, which is in the northeastern quarter, there is a bridge called Adzuki-togi-bashi, or The Bridge of the Washing of Peas. For it was said in other years that nightly a phantom woman sat beneath that bridge washing phantom peas. There is an exquisite Japanese iris-flower, of rainbow-violet color, which flower is named kaki-tsubata; and there is a song about that flower called kaki-tsubata-no-uta. Now this song must never be sung near the Adzuki-togi-bashi, because, for some strange reason, which seems to have been forgotten, the ghosts haunting that place become so angry upon hearing it that to sing it there is to expose one's self to the most frightful calamities. There was once a samurai who feared nothing, who one night went to that bridge and loudly sang the song. No ghost appearing, he laughed and went home. At the gate of his house he met a beautiful tall woman whom he had never seen before, and who, bowing, presented him with a lacquered box—fumi-bako—such as women keep their letters in. He bowed to her in his knightly way; but she said, "I am only the servant,—this is my mistress's gift," and vanished out of his sight. Opening the box, he saw the bleeding head of a young child. Entering his house, he found upon the floor of the guest-room the dead body of his own infant son with the head torn off.

Of the cemetery Dai-Oji, which is in the street called Nakabaramachi, this story is told:—

> In Nakabaramachi there is an ameya, or little shop in which midzu-ame is sold,—the amber-tinted syrup, made of malt, which is given to children when milk cannot be obtained for them. Every night at a late

hour there came to that shop a very pale woman, all in white, to buy one rin[8] worth of midzu-ame. The ame-seller wondered that she was so thin and pale, and often questioned her kindly; but she answered nothing. At last one night he followed her, out of curiosity. She went to the cemetery; and he became afraid and returned.

The next night the woman came again, but bought no midzu-ame, and only beckoned to the man to go with her. He followed her, with friends, into the cemetery. She walked to a certain tomb, and there disappeared; and they heard, under the ground, the crying of a child. Opening the tomb, they saw within it the corpse of the woman who nightly visited the ameya, with a living infant, laughing to see the lantern light, and beside the infant a little cup of midzu-ame. For the mother had been prematurely buried; the child was born in the tomb, and the ghost of the mother had thus provided for it,—love being stronger than death.

XIX

Over the Tenjin-bashi, or Bridge of Tenjin, and through small streets and narrow of densely populated districts, and past many a tenantless and mouldering feudal homestead, I make my way to the extreme southwestern end of the city, to watch the sunset from a little sobaya[9] facing the lake. For to see the sun sink from this sobaya is one of the delights of Matsue.

There are no such sunsets in Japan as in the tropics: the light is gentle as a light of dreams; they are no furies of color; there are no chromatic violences in nature in this Orient. All in sea or sky is tint rather than color, and tint vapor-toned. I think that the exquisite taste of the race in the matter of colors and of tints, as exemplified in the dyes of their wonderful textures, is largely attributable to the sober and delicate beauty of nature's tones in this all-temperate world where nothing is garish.

Before me the fair vast lake sleeps, softly luminous, far-ringed with chains of blue volcanic hills shaped like a sierra. On my right, at its eastern end, the most ancient quarter of the city spreads its roofs of blue-gray tile; the houses crowd thickly down to the shore, to dip their wooden feet into the flood. With a glass I can see my own windows and the far spreading of the roofs beyond, and above all else the green citadel with its grim castle, grotesquely peaked. The sun begins to set, and exquisite astonishments of tinting appear in water and sky.

Dead rich purples cloud broadly behind and above the indigo blackness of the serrated hills—mist purples, fading upward smokily into faint vermilions and dim gold, which again melt up through ghostliest greens into the blue. The deeper waters of the lake, far away, take a tender violet indescribable, and the silhouette of the pine-shadowed island seems to float in that sea of soft sweet color. But the shallower and nearer is cut from the deeper water by the current as sharply as by a line drawn, and all the surface on this side of that line is a shimmering bronze,—old rich ruddy gold-bronze.

All the fainter colors change every five minutes,—wondrously change and shift like tones and shades of fine shot-silks.

XX

Often in the streets at night, especially on the nights of sacred festivals *(matsuri),* one's attention will be attracted to some small booth by the spectacle of an admiring and perfectly silent crowd pressing before it. As soon as one can get a chance to look one finds there is nothing to look at but a few vases containing sprays of flowers, or perhaps some light gracious branches freshly cut from a blossoming tree. It is simply a little flower-show, or, more correctly, a free exhibition of master skill in the arrangement of flowers. For the Japanese do not brutally chop off flower-heads to work them up into meaningless masses of color, as we barbarians do: they love nature too well for that; they know how much the natural charm of the flower depends upon its setting and mounting, its relation to leaf and stem, and they select a single graceful branch or spray just as nature made it. At first you will not, as a Western stranger, comprehend such an exhibition at all: you are yet a savage in such matters compared with the commonest coolies about you. But even while you are still wondering at popular interest in this simple little show, the charm of it will begin to grow upon you, will become a revelation to you; and, despite your Occidental idea of self-superiority, you will feel humbled by the discovery that all flower displays you have ever seen abroad were only monstrosities in comparison with the natural beauty of those few simple sprays. You will also observe how much the white or pale blue screen behind the flowers enhances the effect by lamp or lantern light. For the screen has been arranged with the special purpose of showing the exquisiteness of plant shadows; and the sharp silhouettes of sprays and blossoms cast thereon are beautiful beyond the imagining of any Western decorative artist.

XXI

It is still the season of mists in this land whose most ancient name signifies the Place of the Issuing of Clouds. With the passing of twilight a faint ghostly brume rises over lake and landscape, spectrally veiling surfaces, slowly obliterating distances. As I lean over the parapet of the Tenjin-bashi, on my homeward way, to take one last look eastward, I find that the mountains have already been effaced. Before me there is only a shadowy flood far vanishing into vagueness without a horizon—the phantom of a sea. And I become suddenly aware that little white things are fluttering slowly down into it from the fingers of a woman standing upon the bridge beside me, and murmuring something in a low sweet voice. She is praying for her dead child. Each of those little papers she is dropping into the current bears a tiny picture of Jizō, and perhaps a little inscription. For when a child dies the mother buys a small woodcut *(hanko)* of Jizō, and with it prints the image of the divinity upon one hundred little papers. And she sometimes also writes upon the papers words signifying "For the sake of . . . ,"—inscribing never the living, but the kaimyō or soul-name only, which the Buddhist priest has given to the dead, and which is written also upon the little commemorative tablet kept within the Buddhist household shrine, or *butsuma*. Then, upon a fixed day (most commonly the forty-ninth day after the burial), she goes to some place of running water and drops the little papers therein one by one; repeating, as each slips through her fingers, the holy invocation, *"Namu Jizō, Dai Bosatsu!"*

Doubtless this pious little woman, praying beside me in the dusk, is very poor. Were she not, she would hire a boat and scatter her tiny papers far away upon the bosom of the lake. (It is now only after dark that this may be done; for the police—I know not why—have been instructed to prevent the pretty rite, just as in the open ports they have been instructed to prohibit the launching of the little straw boats of the dead, the shōryōbune).

But why should the papers be cast into running water? A good old Tendai priest tells me that originally the rite was only for the souls of the drowned. But now these gentle hearts believe that all waters flow downward to the Shadow-world and through the Sai-no-Kawara, where Jizō is.

XXII

At home again I slide open once more my little paper window, and look out upon the night. I see the paper lanterns flitting over the bridge, like a long shimmering of fireflies. I see the spectres of a hundred lights trembling upon the black flood. I see the broad shōji of dwellings beyond the river suffused with the soft yellow radiance of invisible lamps; and upon those lighted spaces I can discern slender moving shadows, silhouettes of graceful women. Devoutly do I pray that glass may never become universally adopted in Japan,—there would be no more delicious shadows.

I listen to the voices of the city awhile. I hear the great bell of Tōkōji rolling its soft Buddhist thunder across the dark, and the songs of the night-walkers whose hearts have been made merry with wine, and the long sonorous chanting of the night-peddlers.

"*U-mu-don-yai-soba-yai!*" It is the seller of hot soba, Japanese buckwheat, making his last round.

"*Umai handan, machibito endan, usemono ninsō kasō kichikyō no urainai!*" The cry of the itinerant fortune-teller.

"*Ame-yu!*" The musical cry of the seller of midzu-ame, the sweet amber syrup which children love.

"*Amai!*" The shrilling call of the seller of ama-zaké, sweet rice wine.

"*Kawachi-no-kuni-hiotan-yama-koi-no-tsuji-ura!*" The peddler of love-papers, of divining-papers, pretty tinted things with little shadowy pictures upon them. When held near a fire or a lamp, words written upon them with invisible ink begin to appear. These are always about sweethearts, and sometimes tell one what he does not wish to know. The fortunate ones who read them believe themselves still more fortunate; the unlucky abandon all hope; the jealous become even more jealous than they were before.

From all over the city there rises into the night a sound like the bubbling and booming of great frogs in a marsh,— the echoing of the tiny drums of the dancing girls, of the charming geisha. Like the rolling of a waterfall continually reverberates the multitudinous pattering of geta upon the bridge. A new light rises in the east; the moon is wheeling up from behind the peaks, very large and weird and wan through the white vapors. Again I hear the sounds of the clapping of many hands. For the wayfarers are paying obeisance to O-Tsuki-San: from the long bridge they are saluting the coming of the White Moon-Lady.[10]

I sleep, to dream of little children, in some mouldering mossy temple court, playing at the game of Shadows and of Demons.

In a Japanese Garden

I

My little two-story house by the Ōhashigawa, although dainty as a bird-cage, proved much too small for comfort at the approach of the hot season,—the rooms being scarcely higher than steamship cabins, and so narrow that an ordinary mosquito-net could not be suspended in them. I was sorry to lose the beautiful lake view, but I found it necessary to remove to the northern quarter of the city, into a very quiet street behind the mouldering castle. My new home is a katchiū-yashiki, the ancient residence of some samurai of high rank. It is shut off from the street, or rather roadway, skirting the castle moat by a long, high wall coped with tiles. One ascends to the gateway, which is almost as large as that of a temple court, by a low broad flight of stone steps; and projecting from the wall, to the right of the gate, is a lookout window, heavily barred, like a big wooden cage. Thence, in feudal days, armed retainers kept keen watch on all who passed by,—invisible watch, for the bars are set so closely that a face behind them cannot be seen from the roadway. Inside the gate the approach to the dwelling is also walled in on both sides, so that the visitor, unless privileged, could see before him only the house entrance, always closed with white shōji. Like all samurai homes, the residence itself is but one story high, but there are fourteen rooms within, and these are lofty, spacious, and beautiful. There is, alas, no lake view nor any charming prospect. Part of the O-Shiroyama, with the castle on its summit, half concealed by a park of pines, may be seen above the coping of the front wall, but only a part; and scarcely a hundred yards behind the house rise densely wooded heights, cutting off not only the horizon, but a large slice of the sky as well. For this immurement, however, there exists fair compensation in the shape of a very pretty garden, or rather a series of garden spaces, which surround the dwelling on three sides. Broad verandas overlook these, and from a certain veranda angle I can enjoy the sight of two gardens at once. Screens of bamboos and woven rushes, with wide gateless openings in their midst, mark the boundaries of the three divisions of the pleasure grounds. But these structures are not intended to serve as true fences; they are ornamental, and only indicate where one style of landscape gardening ends and another begins.

II

Now a few words upon Japanese gardens in general.

After having learned—merely by seeing, for the practical knowledge of the art requires years of study and experience, besides a natural, instinctive sense of beauty—something about the Japanese manner of arranging flowers, one can thereafter consider European ideas of floral decoration only as vulgarities. This observation is not the result of any hasty enthusiasm, but a conviction settled by long residence in the interior. I have come to understand the unspeakable loneliness of a solitary spray of blossoms arranged as only a Japanese expert knows how to arrange

it,—not by simply poking the spray into a vase, but by perhaps one whole hour's labor of trimming and posing and
daintiest manipulation,—and therefore I cannot think now
of what we Occidentals call a "bouquet" as anything but a
vulgar murdering of flowers, an outrage upon the color-
sense, a brutality, an abomination. Somewhat in the same
way, and for similar reasons, after having learned what an
old Japanese garden is, I can remember our costliest gardens at home only as ignorant displays of what wealth can
accomplish in the creation of incongruities that violate
nature.

Now a Japanese garden is not a flower garden; neither is
it made for the purpose of cultivating plants. In nine cases
out of ten there is nothing in it resembling a flower-bed.
Some gardens may contain scarcely a sprig of green; some
have nothing green at all, and consist entirely of rocks and
pebbles and sand, although these are exceptional.[1] As a
rule, a Japanese garden is a landscape garden, yet its existence does not depend upon any fixed allowance of space.
It may cover one acre or many acres. It may also be only ten
feet square. It may, in extreme cages, be much less; for a
certain kind of Japanese garden can be contrived small
enough to put in a tokonoma. Such a garden, in a vessel no
larger than a fruit-dish, is called koniwa or toko-niwa, and
may occasionally be seen in the tokonoma of humble little
dwellings so closely squeezed between other structures as to
possess no ground in which to cultivate an outdoor garden.
(I say "an outdoor garden," because there are indoor gardens, both upstairs and downstairs, in some large Japanese
houses.) The toko-niwa is usually made in some curious
bowl, or shallow carved box, or quaintly shaped vessel
impossible to describe by any English word. Therein are
created minuscule hills with minuscule houses upon them,
and microscopic ponds and rivulets spanned by tiny
humped bridges; and queer wee plants do duty for trees,
and curiously formed pebbles stand for rocks, and there are

tiny tōrō, perhaps a tiny torii as well,—in short, a charming and living model of a Japanese landscape.

Another fact of prime importance to remember is that, in order to comprehend the beauty of a Japanese garden, it is necessary to understand—or at least to learn to understood—the beauty of stones. Not of stones quarried by the hand of man, but of stones shaped by nature only. Until you can feel, and keenly feel, that stones have character, that stones have tones and values, the whole artistic meaning of a Japanese garden cannot be revealed to you. In the foreigner, however æsthetic he may be, this feeling needs to be cultivated by study. It is inborn in the Japanese; the soul of the race comprehends Nature infinitely better than we do, at least in her visible forms. But although, being an Occidental, the true sense of the beauty of stones can be reached by you only through long familiarity with the Japanese use and choice of them, the characters of the lessons to be acquired exist everywhere about you, if your life be in the interior. You cannot walk through a street without observing tasks and problems in the æsthetics of stones for you to master. At the approaches to temples, by the side of roads, before holy groves, and in all parks and pleasure-grounds, as well as in all cemeteries, you will notice large, irregular, flat slabs of natural rock—mostly from the river beds and water-worn—sculptured with ideographs, but unhewn. These have been set up as votive tablets, as commemorative monuments, as tombstones, and are much more costly than the ordinary cut-stone columns and haka chiseled with the figures of divinities in relief. Again, you will see before most of the shrines, nay, even in the grounds of nearly all large homesteads, great irregular blocks of granite or other hard rocks, worn by the action of torrents, and converted into water-basins *(chodzu-bachi)* by cutting a circular hollow in the top. Such are but common examples of the utilization of stones even in the poorest villages; and if you have any natural artistic sentiment, you cannot fail to discover, sooner or later, how much more beautiful are these natural forms than any shapes from the hand of the stone-cutter. It is probable, too, that you will become so habituated at last to the sight of inscriptions cut upon rock surfaces, especially if you travel much through the country, that you will often find yourself involuntarily looking for texts or other chiselings where there are none, and could not possibly be, as if ideographs belonged by natural law to rock formation. And stones will begin, perhaps, to assume for you a certain individual or physiognomical aspect,—to suggest moods and sensations, as they do to the Japanese. Indeed, Japan is particularly a land of suggestive shapes in stone; as high volcanic lands are apt to be; and such shapes doubtless addressed themselves to the imagination of the race at a time long prior to the date of that archaic text which tells of demons in Izumo "who made rocks, and the roots of trees, and leaves, and the foam of the green waters to speak."

As might be expected in a country where the suggestiveness of natural forms is thus recognized, there are in Japan many curious beliefs and superstitions concerning stones. In almost every province there are famous stones supposed to be sacred or haunted, or to possess miraculous powers, such as the Women's Stone at the temple of Hachiman at Kamakura, and the Sessho-seki, or Death Stone of Nasu, and the Wealth-giving Stone at Enoshima, to which pilgrims pay reverence. There are even legends of stones having manifested sensibility, like the tradition of the Nodding Stones which bowed down before the monk Daita when he preached unto them the word of Buddha; or the ancient story from the Kojiki, that the Emperor O-Jin, being augustly intoxicated, smote with his august staff a great stone in the middle of the Ohosaka road, *whereupon the stone ran away!*"[2]

Now stones are valued for their beauty; and large stones selected for their shape may have an æsthetic worth of hundreds of dollars. And large stones form the skeleton, or framework, in the design of old Japanese gardens. Not only is every stone chosen with a view to its particular expressiveness of form but every stone in the garden or about the premises has its separate and individual name, indicating its purpose or its decorative duty. But I can tell you only a little, a very little, of the folk-lore of a Japanese garden; and if you want to know more about stones and their names, and about the philosophy of gardens, read the unique essay of Mr. Conder on The Art of Landscape Gardening in Japan,[3] and his beautiful book on the Japanese Art of Floral Decoration; and also the brief but charming chapter on Gardens, in Morse's Japanese Homes.[4]

III

No effort to create an impossible or purely ideal landscape is made in the Japanese garden. Its artistic purpose is to copy faithfully the attractions of a veritable landscape, and to convey the real impression that a real landscape communicates. It is therefore at once a picture and a poem; perhaps even more a poem than a picture. For as nature's scenery, in its varying aspects, affects us with sensations of joy or of solemnity, of grimness or of sweetness, of force or of peace, so must the true reflection of it in the labor of the landscape gardener create not merely an impression of beauty, but a mood in the soul. The grand old landscape gardeners, those Buddhist monks who first introduced the art into Japan, and subsequently developed it into an almost occult science, carried their theory yet farther than this. They held it possible to express moral lessons in the design of a garden, and abstract ideas, such as Chastity, Faith, Piety, Content, Calm, and Connubial Bliss. Therefore were gardens contrived according to the character of the owner, whether poet, warrior, philosopher, or priest. In those ancient gardens (the art, alas, is passing away under the withering influence of the utterly com-

monplace Western taste) there were expressed both a mood
of nature and some rare Oriental conception of a mood of
man.

I do not know what human sentiment the principal
division of my garden was intended to reflect; and there is
none to tell me. Those by whom it was made passed away
long generations ago, in the eternal transmigration of souls.
But as a poem of nature it requires no interpreter. It occupies the front portion of the grounds, facing south; and it
also extends west to the verge of the northern division of
the garden, from which it is partly separated by a curious
screen-fence structure. There are large rocks in it, heavily
mossed; and divers fantastic basins of stone for holding
water; and stone lamps green with years; and a shachihoko,
such as one sees at the peaked angles of castle roofs,—a
great stone fish, an idealized porpoise, with its nose in the
ground and its tail in the air.[5] There are miniature hills,
with old trees upon them; and there are long slopes of
green, shadowed by flowering shrubs, like river banks; and
there are green knolls like islets. All these verdant elevations
rise from spaces of pale yellow sand, smooth as a surface of
silk and miming the curves and meanderings of a river
course. These sanded spaces are not to be trodden upon;
they are much too beautiful for that. The least speck of dirt
would mar their effect; and it requires the trained skill of
an experienced native gardener—a delightful old man he
is—to keep them in perfect form. But they are traversed in
various directions by lines of flat unhewn rock slabs, placed
at slightly irregular distances from one another, exactly like
stepping-stones across a brook. The whole effect is that of
the shores of a still stream in some lovely, lonesome, drowsy
place.

There is nothing to break the illusion, so secluded the
garden is. High walls and fences shut out streets and con-
tiguous things; and the shrubs and the trees, heightening
and thickening toward the boundaries, conceal from view
even the roofs of the neighboring katchiū-yashiki. Softly

beautiful are the tremulous shadows of leaves on the sunned sand; and the scent of flowers comes thinly sweet with every waft of tepid air; and there is a humming of bees.

IV

By Buddhism all existences are divided into *Hijō,* things without desire, such as stones and trees; and *Ujō,* things having desire, such as men and animals. This division does not, so far as I know, find expression in the written philosophy of gardens; but it is a convenient one. The folk-lore of my little domain relates both to the inanimate and the animate. In natural order, the Hijō may be considered first, beginning with a singular shrub near the entrance of the yashiki, and close to the gate of the first garden.

Within the front gateway of almost every old samurai house, and usually near the entrance of the dwelling itself, there is to be seen a small tree with large and peculiar leaves. The name of this tree in Izumo is tegashiwa, and there is one beside my door. What the scientific name of it is I do not know; nor am I quite sure of the etymology of the Japanese name. However, there is a word tegashi, meaning a bond for the hands; and the shape of the leaves of the tegashiwa somewhat resembles the shape of a hand.

Now, in old days, when the samurai retainer was obliged to leave his home in order to accompany his daimyō to Yedo, it was customary, just before his departure, to set before him a baked tai[6] served up on a tegashiwa leaf. After this farewell repast, the leaf upon which the tai had been served was hung up above the door as a charm to bring the departed knight safely back again. This pretty superstition about the leaves of the tegashiwa had its origin not only in their shape but in their movement. Stirred by a wind they seemed to beckon,—not indeed after our Occidental manner, but in the way that a Japanese signs to his friend to come, by gently waving his hand up and down with the palm towards the ground.

Another shrub to be found in most Japanese gardens is the nanten,[7] about which a very curious belief exists. If you have an evil dream, a dream which bodes ill luck, you should whisper it to the nanten early in the morning, and then it will never come true.[8] There are two varieties of this graceful plant: one which bears red berries, and one which bears white. The latter is rare. Both kinds grow in my garden. The common variety is placed close to the veranda (perhaps for the convenience of dreamers); the other occupies a little flower-bed in the middle of the garden, together with a small citron-tree. This most dainty citron-tree is called "Buddha's fingers,"[9] because of the wonderful shape of its fragrant fruits. Near it stands a kind of laurel, with lanciform leaves glossy as bronze; it is called by the Japanese yuzuri-ha,[10] and is almost as common in the gardens of old samurai homes as the tegashiwa itself. It is held to be a tree of good omen, because no one of its old leaves ever falls off before a new one, growing behind it, has well developed. For thus the yuzuri-ha symbolizes hope that the father will not pass away before his son has become a vigorous man, well able to succeed him as the head of the family. Therefore, on every New Year's Day the leaves of the yuzuri-ha, mingled with fronds of fern, are attached to the shimenawa which is then suspended before every Izumo home.

V

The trees, like the shrubs, have their curious poetry and legends. Like the stones, each tree has its special landscape name according to its position and purpose in the composition. Just as rocks and stones form the skeleton of the ground-plan of a garden, so pines form the framework of its foliage design. They give body to the whole. In this garden there are five pines,—not pines tormented into fantasticalities, but pines made wondrously picturesque by long and tireless care and judicious trimming. The object of the gardener has been to develop to the utmost possible degree their natural tendency to rugged line and massings of foliage,—that spiny sombre-green foliage which Japanese art is never weary of imitating in metal inlay or golden lacquer. The pine is a symbolic tree in this land of symbolism. Ever green, it is at once the emblem of unflinching purpose and of vigorous old age; and its needle-shaped leaves are credited with the power of driving demons away.

There are two sakuranoki,[11] Japanese cherry-trees— those trees whose blossoms, as Professor Chamberlain so justly observes, are "beyond comparison more lovely than anything Europe has to show." Many varieties are cultivated and loved; those in my garden bear blossoms of the most ethereal pink, a flushed white. When, in spring, the trees flower, it is as though fleeciest masses of cloud faintly tinged by sunset had floated down from the highest sky to fold themselves about the branches. This comparison is no poetical exaggeration; neither is it original: it is an ancient Japanese description of the most marvelous floral exhibition which nature is capable of making. The reader who has never seen a cherry-tree blossoming in Japan cannot possibly imagine the delight of the spectacle. There are no green leaves; these come later: there is only one glorious burst of blossoms, veiling every twig and bough in their delicate mist; and the soil beneath each tree is covered deep out of sight by fallen petals as by a drift of pink snow.

But these are cultivated cherry-trees. There are others which put forth their leaves before their blossoms, such as the yamazakura, or mountain cherry.[12] This too, however, has its poetry of beauty and of symbolism. Sang the great Shintō writer and poet, Motowori:—

> *Shikishima no*
> *Yamato-gokoro wo*
> *Hito-towaba,*
> *Asa-hi ni niou*
> *Yamazakura-bana.*[13]

Whether cultivated or uncultivated, the Japanese cherry-trees are emblems. Those planted in old samurai gardens were not cherished for their loveliness alone. Their spotless blossoms were regarded as symbolizing that delicacy of sentiment and blamelessness of life belonging to high courtesy and true knightliness. "As the cherry flower is first among flowers," says an old proverb, "so should the warrior be first among men."

Shadowing the western end of this garden, and projecting its smooth dark limbs above the awning of the veranda, is a superb umenoki, Japanese plum-tree, very old, and originally planted here, no doubt, as in other gardens, for the sake of the sight of its blossoming. The flowering of the umenoki,[14] in the earliest spring, is scarcely less astonishing than that of the cherry-tree, which does not bloom for a full month later; and the blossoming of both is celebrated by popular holidays. Nor are these, although the most famed, the only flowers thus loved. The wistaria, the convolvulus, the peony, each in its season, form displays of efflorescence lovely enough to draw whole populations out of the cities into the country to see them. In Izumo, the blossoming of the peony is especially marvelous. The most famous place for this spectacle is the little island of Daikonshima, in the grand Naka-umi lagoon, about an hour's sail from Matsue. In May the whole island flames crimson with peonies; and even the boys and girls of the public schools are given a holiday, in order that they may enjoy the sight.

Though the plum flower is certainly a rival in beauty of the sakura-no-hana, the Japanese compare woman's beauty—physical beauty—to the cherry flower, never to the plum flower. But womanly virtue and sweetness, on the other hand, are compared to the ume-no-hana, never to the cherry blossom. It is a great mistake to affirm, as some writers have done, that the Japanese never think of comparing a woman to trees and flowers. For grace, a maiden is likened to a slender willow;[15] for youthful charm, to the cherry-tree in flower; for sweetness of heart, to the blossoming plum-tree. Nay, the old Japanese poets have compared woman to all beautiful things. They have even sought similes from flowers for her various poses, for her movements, as in the verse,—

> *Tateba shakuyaku;* [16]
> *Suwareba botan;*
> *Aruku sugatawa*
> *Himeyuri* [17] *no hana.* [18]

Why, even the names of the humblest country girls are often those of beautiful trees or flowers prefixed by the honorific *O:* [19] O-Matsu (Pine), O-Také (Bamboo), O-Ume (Plum), O-Hana (Blossom), O-Ine (Ear-of-Young-Rice), not to speak of the professional flower-names of dancing-girls and of jorō. It has been argued with considerable force that the origin of certain tree-names borne by girls must be sought in the folk-conception of the tree as an emblem of longevity, or happiness, or good fortune, rather than in any popular idea of the beauty of the tree in itself. But however this may be, proverb, poem, song, and popular speech to-day yield ample proof that the Japanese comparisons of women to trees and flowers are in no wise inferior to our own in æsthetic sentiment.

VI

That trees, at least Japanese trees, have souls cannot seem an unnatural fancy to one who has seen the blossoming of the umenoki and the sakuranoki. This is a popular belief in Izumo and elsewhere. It is not in accord with Buddhist philosophy, and yet in a certain sense it strikes one as being much closer to cosmic truth than the old Western orthodox notion of trees as "things created for the use of man." Furthermore, there exist several odd superstitions about particular trees, not unlike certain West Indian beliefs which have had a good influence in checking the destruction of valuable timber. Japan, like the tropical world, has its goblin trees. Of these, the enoki *(Celtis Willdenowiana)* and the yanagi (drooping willow) are deemed especially ghostly, and are rarely now to be found in old Japanese gardens. Both are believed to have the power of haunting. *"Enoki ga bakeru,"* the Izumo saying is. You will find in a Japanese dictionary the word "bakeru" translated by such terms as "to be transformed," "to be metamorphosed," "to be changed," etc.; but the belief about these trees is very singular, and cannot be explained by any such rendering of the verb "bakeru." The tree itself does not change form or place, but a spectre called "Ki-no o-baké" disengages itself from the tree and walks about in various guises.[20] Most often the shape assumed by the phantom is that of a beautiful woman. The tree spectre seldom speaks, and seldom ventures to go very far away from its tree. If approached, it immediately shrinks back into the trunk or the foliage. It is said that if either an old yanagi or a young enoki be cut blood will flow from the gash. When such trees are very young it is not believed that they have supernatural habits, but they become more dangerous the older they grow.

There is a rather pretty legend—recalling the old Greek dream of dryads—about a willow-tree which grew in the garden of a samurai of Kyōto. Owing to its weird reputation, the tenant of the homestead desired to cut it down; but another samurai dissuaded him, saying: "Rather sell it to me, that I may plant it in my garden. That tree has a soul; it were cruel to destroy its life." Thus purchased and transplanted, the yanagi flourished well in its new home, and its spirit, out of gratitude, took the form of a beautiful woman, and became the wife of the samurai who had befriended it. A charming boy was the result of this union. A few years later, the daimyō to whom the ground belonged gave orders that the tree should be cut down. Then the wife wept bitterly, and for the first time revealed to her husband the whole story. "And now," she added, "I know that I must die; but our child will live, and you will always love him. This thought is my only solace." Vainly the astonished and terrified husband sought to retain her. Bidding him farewell forever, she vanished into the tree. Needless to say that the samurai did everything in his power to persuade the daimyō to forego his purpose. The prince wanted the tree for the reparation of a great Buddhist temple, the San-jiu-san-gen-dō.[21] The tree was felled, but, having fallen, it suddenly became so heavy that three hundred men could not move it. Then the child, taking a branch in his little hand, said, "Come," and the tree followed him, gliding along the ground to the court of the temple.

Although said to be a bakemono-ki, the enoki sometimes receives highest religious honors; for the spirit of the god Kōjin, to whom old dolls are dedicated, is supposed to dwell within certain very ancient enoki trees, and before these are placed shrines whereat people make prayers.

VII

The second garden, on the north side, is my favorite. It contains no large growths. It is paved with blue pebbles, and its centre is occupied by a pondlet,—a miniature lake fringed with rare plants, and containing a tiny island, with tiny mountains and dwarf peach-trees and pines and azaleas, some of which are perhaps more than a century old, though scarcely more than a foot high. Nevertheless, this work, seen as it was intended to be seen, does not appear to the eye in miniature at all. From a certain angle of the guest-room looking out upon it, the appearance is that of a real lake shore with a real island beyond it, a stone's throw away. So cunning the art of the ancient gardener who contrived all this, and who has been sleeping for a hundred years under the cedars of Gesshoji, that the illusion can be detected only from the zashiki by the presence of an ishidōrō, or stone lamp, upon the island. The size of the ishidōrō betrays the false perspective, and I do not think it was placed there when the garden was made.

Here and there at the edge of the pond, and almost level with the water, are placed large flat stones, on which one may either stand or squat, to watch the lacustrine population or to tend the water-plants. There are beautiful water-lilies, whose bright green leaf-disks float oilily upon the surface *(Nuphar Japonica),* and many lotus plants of two kinds, those which bear pink and those which bear pure white flowers. There are iris plants growing along the bank, whose blossoms are prismatic violet, and there are various ornamental grasses and ferns and mosses. But the pond is essentially a lotus pond; the lotus plants make its greatest charm. It is a delight to watch every phase of their marvelous growth, from the first unrolling of the leaf to the fall of the last flower. On rainy days, especially, the lotus plants are worth observing. Their great cup-shaped leaves, swaying high above the pond, catch the rain and hold it a while; but always after the water in the leaf reaches a certain level the stem bends, and empties the leaf with a loud plash, and then straightens again. Rain-water upon a lotus-leaf is a favorite subject with Japanese metal-workers, and metal-work only can reproduce the effect, for the motion and color of water moving upon the green oleaginous surface are exactly those of quicksilver.

VIII

The third garden, which is very large, extends beyond the inclosure containing the lotus pond to the foot of the wooded hills which form the northern and northeastern boundary of this old samurai quarter. Formerly all this broad level space was occupied by a bamboo grove; but it is now little more than a waste of grasses and wild flowers. In the northeast corner there is a magnificent well, from which ice-cold water is brought into the house through a most ingenious little aqueduct of bamboo pipes; and in the northwestern end, veiled by tall weeds, there stands a very small stone shrine of Inari, with two proportionately small stone foxes sitting before it. Shrine and images are chipped and broken, and thickly patched with dark green moss. But on the east side of the house one little square of soil belonging to this large division of the garden is still cultivated. It is devoted entirely to chrysanthemum plants, which are shielded from heavy rain and strong sun by slanting frames of light wood fashioned like shōji, with panes of white paper, and supported like awnings upon thin posts of bamboo. I can venture to add nothing to what has already been written about these marvelous products of Japanese floriculture considered in themselves; but there is a little story relating to chrysanthemums which I may presume to tell.

There is one place in Japan where it is thought unlucky to cultivate chrysanthemums, for reasons which shall presently appear; and that place is in the pretty little city of Himeji, in the province of Harima. Himeji contains the ruins of a great castle of thirty turrets; and a daimyō used to dwell therein whose revenue was one hundred and fifty-six thousand koku of rice. Now, in the house of one of that daimyō's chief retainers there was a maid-servant, of good family, whose name was O-Kiku; and the name "Kiku" signifies a chrysanthemum flower. Many precious things were intrusted to her charge, and among others ten costly dishes of gold. One of these was suddenly missed, and could not be found; and the girl, being responsible therefor, and knowing not how otherwise to prove her innocence, drowned herself in a well. But ever thereafter her ghost, returning nightly, could be heard counting the dishes slowly, with sobs:—

Ichi-mai,
Ni-mai,
San-mai,

Yo-mai,
Go-mai,
Roku-mai,
Shichi-mai,
Hachi-mai,
Ku-mai—

Then would be heard a despairing cry and a loud burst of weeping; and again the girl's voice counting the dishes plaintively: "One—two—three—four—five—six—seven—eight—*nine*"—

Her spirit passed into the body of a strange little insect, whose head faintly resembles that of a ghost with long disheveled hair; and it is called O-Kiku mushi, or "the fly of O-Kiku;" and it is found, they say, nowhere save in Himeji. A famous play was written about O-Kiku, which is still acted in all the popular theatres, entitled Banshu-O-Kiku-no-Sara-ya shiki; or, The Manor of the Dish of O-Kiku of Banshu.

Some declare that Banshu is only the corruption of the name of an ancient quarter of Tōkyō (Yedo), where the story should have been laid. But the people of Himeji say that part of their city now called Go-Ken-Yashiki is identical with the site of the ancient manor. What is certainly true is that to cultivate chrysanthemum flowers in the part of Himeji called Go-Ken-Yashiki is deemed unlucky, because the name of O-Kiku signifies "chrysanthemum." Therefore, nobody, I am told, ever cultivates chrysanthemums there.

IX

Now of the ujō, or things having desire, which inhabit these gardens.

There are four species of frogs: three that dwell in the lotus pond, and one that lives in the trees. The tree frog is a very pretty little creature, exquisitely green; it has a shrill cry, almost like the note of *semi;* and it is called amagaeru, or the "rain frog," because, like its kindred in other countries, its croaking is an omen of rain. The pond frogs are called babagaeru, shinagaeru, and Tono-san-gaeru. Of these, the first named variety is the largest and the ugliest: its color is very disagreeable, and its full name ("babagaeru" being a decent abbreviation) is quite as offensive as its hue. The shinagaeru, or "striped frog," is not handsome, except by comparison with the previously mentioned creature. But the Tono-san-gaeru, so called after a famed daimyō who left behind him a memory of great splendor, is beautiful: its color is a fine bronze-red.

Besides these varieties. of frogs there lives in the garden a huge uncouth goggle-eyed thing which, although called here hikigaeru, I take to be a toad. "Hikigaeru" is the name ordinarily used for a bullfrog. This creature enters the house almost daily to be fed, and seems to have no fear even of strangers. My people consider it a luck-bringing visitor; and it is credited with the power of drawing all the mosquitoes out of a room into its mouth by simply sucking its breath in. Much as it is cherished by gardeners and others, there is a legend about a goblin toad of old times, which, by sucking in its breath, drew into its mouth, not insects, but men.

The pond is inhabited also by many small fish; imori, or newts, with bright red bellies; and multitudes of little water-beetles, called maimaimushi, which pass their whole time in gyrating upon the surface of the water so rapidly that it is almost impossible to distinguish their shape clearly. A man who runs about aimlessly to and fro, under the influence of excitement, is compared to a maimaimushi. And there are some beautiful snails, with yellow stripes on their shells. Japanese children have a charm song which is supposed to have power to make the snail put out its horns:—

Daidaimushi,[22] *daidaimushi, tsuno chitto dashare!*
Ame kaze fuku kara tsuno chitto dashare![23]

The playground of the children of the better classes has always been the family garden, as that of the children of the poor is the temple court. It is in the garden that the little ones first learn something of the wonderful life of plants and the marvels of the insect-world; and there, also, they are first taught those pretty legends and songs about birds and flowers which form so charming a part of Japanese folk-lore. As the home training of the child is left mostly to the mother, lessons of kindness to animals are early inculcated; and the results are strongly marked in after life. It is true, Japanese children are not entirely free from that unconscious tendency to cruelty characteristic of children in all countries, as a survival of primitive instincts. But in this regard the great moral difference between the sexes is strongly marked from the earliest years. The tenderness of the woman-soul appears even in the child. Little Japanese girls who play with insects or small animals rarely hurt them, and generally set them free after they have afforded a reasonable amount of amusement. Little boys are not nearly so good, when out of sight of parents or guardians. But if seen doing anything cruel, a child is made to feel ashamed of the act, and hears the Buddhist warning, "Thy future birth will be unhappy, if thou dost cruel things."

Somewhere among the rocks in the pond lives a small tortoise,—left in the garden, probably, by the previous tenants of the house. It is very pretty, but manages to remain invisible for weeks at a time. In popular mythology, the tortoise is the servant of the divinity Kompira;[24] and if a pious fisherman finds a tortoise, he writes upon his back characters signifying "Servant of the Deity Kompira," and then gives it a drink of saké and sets it free. It is supposed to be very fond of saké.

Some say that the land tortoise, or "stone tortoise," only, is the servant of Kompira, and the sea tortoise, or turtle, the servant of the Dragon Empire beneath the sea. The turtle is said to have the power to create, with its breath, a cloud, a fog, or a magnificent palace. It figures in the beautiful old folk-tale of Urashima.[25] All tortoises are supposed to live for a thousand years, wherefore one of the most frequent symbols of longevity in Japanese art is a tortoise. But the tortoise most commonly represented by native painters and metal-workers has a peculiar tail, or rather a multitude of small tails, extending behind it like the fringes of a straw rain-coat, mino, whence it is called minogamé. Now, some of the tortoises kept in the sacred tanks of Buddhist temples attain a prodigious age, and certain water-plants attach themselves to the creatures' shells and stream behind them when they walk. The myth of the minogamé is supposed to have had its origin in old artistic efforts to represent the appearance of such tortoises with confervæ fastened upon their shells.

X

Early in summer the frogs are surprisingly numerous, and, after dark, are noisy beyond description; but week by week their nightly clamor grows feebler, as their numbers diminish under the attacks of many enemies. A large family of snakes, some fully three feet long, make occasional inroads into the colony. The victims often utter piteous cries, which are promptly responded to, whenever possible, by some inmate of the house, and many a frog has been saved by my servant-girl, who, by a gentle tap with a bamboo rod, compels the snake to let its prey go. These snakes are beautiful swimmers. They make themselves quite free about the garden; but they come out only on hot days; None of my people would think of injuring or killing one of them. Indeed, in Izumo it is said that to kill a snake is unlucky. "If you kill a snake without provocation," a peasant assured me, "you will afterwards find its head in the komebitsu [the box in which cooked rice is kept] when you take off the lid."

But the snakes devour comparatively few frogs. Impudent kites and crows are their most implacable destroyers; and there is a very pretty weasel which lives under the kura (godown), and which does not hesitate to take either fish or frogs out of the pond, even when the lord of the manor is watching. There is also a cat which poaches in my preserves, a gaunt outlaw, a master thief, which I have made sundry vain attempts to reclaim from vagabondage. Partly because of the immorality of this cat, and partly be cause it happens to have a long tail, it has the evil reputation of being a nekomata, or goblin cat.

It is true that in Izumo some kittens are born with long tails; but it is very seldom that they are suffered to grow up with long tails. For the natural tendency of cats is to become goblins; and this tendency to metamorphosis can be checked only by cutting off their tails in kittenhood. Cats are magicians, tails or no tails, and have the power of making corpses dance. Cats are ungrateful. "Feed a dog for three days," says a Japanese proverb, "and he will remember your kindness for three years; feed a cat for three years and she will forget your kindness in three days." Cats are mischievous: they tear the mattings, and make holes in the shōji, and sharpen their claws upon the pillars of tokonoma. Cats are under a curse: only the cat and the venomous serpent wept not at the death of Buddha; and these shall never enter into the bliss of the Gokuraku. For all these reasons, and others too numerous to relate, cats are not much loved in Izumo, and are compelled to pass the greater part of their lives out of doors.

XI

Not less than eleven varieties of butterflies have visited the neighborhood of the lotus pond within the past few days. The most common variety is snowy white. It is supposed to be especially attracted by the na, or rapeseed plant; and when little girls see it, they sing:—

Chō-chō, chō-chō, na no ha ni toware;
Na no ha ga iyenara, te ni toware.[26]

But the most interesting insects are certainly the semi
(cicadæ). These Japanese tree crickets are much more extraordinary singers than even the wonderful cicadæ of the
tropics; and they are much less tiresome, for there is a different species of semi, with a totally different song, for
almost every month during the whole warm season. There
are, I believe, seven kinds; but I have become familiar with
only four. The first to be heard in my trees is the natsuzemi, or summer semi: it makes a sound like the Japanese
monosyllable ji, beginning wheezily, slowly swelling into a
crescendo shrill as the blowing of steam, and dying away in
another wheeze. This *j-i-i-iiiiiiiii* is so deafening that
when two or three natsuzemi come close to the window I
am obliged to make them go away. Happily the natsuzemi
is soon succeeded by the minminzemi, a much finer musi-
cian, whose name is derived from its wonderful note. It is
said "to chant like a Buddhist priest reciting the kyō;" and
certainly, upon hearing it the first time, one can scarcely
believe that one is listening to a mere cicada. The minminzemi is followed, early in autumn, by a beautiful green
semi, the higurashi, which makes a singularly clear sound,
like the rapid ringing of a small bell,—*kana-kana-kana-
kana-kana.* But the most astonishing visitor of all comes
still later, the tsuku-tsuku-bōshi.[27] I fancy this creature can
have no rival in the whole world of cicadæ: its music is
exactly like the song of a bird. Its name, like that of the
minminzemi, is onomatopoetic; but in Izumo the sounds
of its chant are given thus:—

Tsuku-tsuku uisu,[28]
Tsuku-tsuki uisu,
Tsuku-tsuku-uisu;—
    Ui-ōsu,
    Ui-ōsu,

> *Ui-ōsu,*
> *Ui-ōs-s-s-s-s-s-s-su.*

However, the semi are not the only musicians of the garden. Two remarkable creatures aid their orchestra. The first
is a beautiful bright green grasshopper, known to the
Japanese by the curious name of hotoke-no-uma, or "the
horse of the dead." This insect's head really bears some
resemblance in shape to the head of a horse,—hence the
fancy. It is a queerly familiar creature, allowing itself to be
taken in the hand without struggling, and generally making itself quite at home in the house, which it often enters.
It makes a very thin sound, which the Japanese write as a
repetition of the syllables *jun-ta;* and the name junta is
sometimes given to the grasshopper itself. The other insect
is also a green grasshopper, somewhat larger, and much
shyer: it is called gisu,[29] on account of its chant:—

> *Chon,*
>   *Gisu;*
> *Chon,*
>   *Gisu;*
> *Chon,*
>   *Gisu;*
> *Chon . . . (ad libitum).*

Several lovely species of dragon-flies *(tombō)* hover
about the pondlet on hot bright days. One variety—the
most beautiful creature of the kind I ever saw, gleaming
with metallic colors indescribable, and spectrally slender—
is called Tenshi-tombō, "the Emperor's dragon-fly." There
is another, the largest of Japanese dragon-flies, but somewhat rare, which is much sought after by children as a play-
thing. Of this species it is said that there are many more
males than females; and what I can vouch for as true is
that, if you catch a female, the male can be almost immediately attracted by exposing the captive. Boys, accordingly,

try to secure a female, and when one is captured they tie it with a thread to some branch, and sing a curious little song, of which these are the original words:—

> *Konna[30] danshō Korai ō*
> *Adzuma no metō ni makete*
> *Nigeru wa haji dewa naikai?*

Which signifies, "Thou, the male, King of Korea, dost thou not feel shame to flee away from the Queen of the East?" (This taunt is an allusion to the story of the conquest of Korea by the Empress Jin-gō.) And the male comes invariably, and is also caught. In Izumo the first seven words of the original song have been corrupted into *"konna unjo Korai abura no mito;"* and the name of the male dragon-fly, unjo, and that of the female, mito, are derived from two words of the corrupted version.

XII

Of warm nights all sorts of unbidden guests invade the house in multitudes. Two varieties of mosquitoes do their utmost to make life unpleasant, and these have learned the wisdom of not approaching a lamp too closely; but hosts of curious and harmless things cannot be prevented from seeking their death in the flame. The most numerous victims of all, which come thick as a shower of rain, are called Sanemori. At least they are so called in Issue, where they do much damage to growing rice.

Now the name Sanemori is an illustrious one, that of a famous warrior of old times belonging to the Genji clan. There is a legend that while he was fighting with an enemy on horseback his own steed slipped and fell in a rice-field, and he was consequently overpowered and slain by his antagonist. He became a rice-devouring insect, which is still respectfully called, by the peasantry of Izumo, Sanemori-an. They light fires, on certain summer nights, in the rice-fields, to attract the insect, and beat gongs and sound bamboo flutes, chanting the while, "O-Sanemori, augustly deign to come hither!" A kan-nushi performs a religious rite, and a straw figure representing a horse and rider is then either burned or thrown into a neighboring river or canal. By this ceremony it is believed that the fields are cleared of the insect.

This tiny creature is almost exactly the size and color of a rice-husk. The legend concerning it may have arisen from the fact that its body, together with the wings, bears some resemblance to the helmet of a Japanese warrior.[31]

Next in number among the victims of fire are the moths, some of which are very strange and beautiful. The most remarkable is an enormous creature popularly called okori-chōchō, or the "ague moth," because there is a superstitious belief that it brings intermittent fever into any house it enters. It has a body quite as heavy and almost as powerful as that of the largest humming-bird, and its struggles, when caught in the hand, surprise by their force. It makes a very loud whirring sound while flying. The wings of one which I examined measured, outspread, five inches from tip to tip, yet seemed small in proportion to the heavy body. They were richly mottled with dusky browns and silver grays of various tones.

Many flying night-comers, however, avoid the lamp. Most fantastic of all visitors is the tōrō or kamakiri, called in Izumo kamakaké, a bright green praying mantis, extremely feared by children for its capacity to bite. It is very large. I have seen specimens over six inches long. The eyes of the kamakaké are a brilliant black at night, but by day they appear grass-colored, like the rest of the body. The mantis is very intelligent and surprisingly aggressive. I saw one attacked by a vigorous frog easily put its enemy to flight. It fell a prey subsequently to other inhabitants of the pond, but it required the combined efforts of several frogs to vanquish the monstrous insect, and even then the battle was decided only when the kamakaké had been dragged into the water.

Other visitors are beetles of divers colors, and a sort of small roach called goki-kaburi, signifying "one whose head is covered with a bowl." It is alleged that the goki-kaburi likes to eat human eyes, and is therefore the abhorred enemy of Ichibata-Sama,—Yakushi-Nyorai of Ichibata,— by whom diseases of the eye are healed. To kill the goki-kaburi is consequently thought to be a meritorious act in the sight of this Buddha. Always welcome are the beautiful fire-flies *(hotaru),* which enter quite noiselessly, and at once seek the darkest place in the house, slow-glimmering, like sparks moved by a gentle wind. They are supposed to be very fond of water; wherefore children sing to them this little song:—

> *Hotaru kōe midzu nomashō;*
> *Achi no midzu wa nigaizo;*
> *Kochi no midzu wa amaizo.*[37]

A pretty gray lizard, quite different from some which usually haunt the garden, also makes its appearance at night, and pursues its prey along the ceiling. Sometimes an extraordinarily large centipede attempts the same thing, but with less success, and has to be seized with a pair of fire-tongs and thrown into the exterior darkness. Very rarely, an enormous spider appears. This creature seems inoffensive. If captured, it will feign death until certain that it is not watched, when it will run away with surprising swiftness if it gets a chance. It is hairless, and very different from the tarantula, or fukurogumo. It is called miyamagumo, or mountain spider. There are four other kinds of spiders common in this neighborhood: tenagakumo, or "long-armed spider;" hiratakumo, or "flat spider;" jikumo, or "earth spider;" and totatekumo, or "door-shutting spider." Most spiders are considered evil beings. A spider seen anywhere at night, the people say, should be killed; for all spiders that show themselves after dark are goblins. While people are awake and watchful, such creatures make themselves small; but when everybody is fast asleep, then they assume their true goblin shape, and become monstrous.

XIII

The high wood of the hill behind the garden is full of bird life. There dwell wild uguisu, owls, wild doves, too many crows, and a queer bird that makes weird noises at night,—long deep sounds of *hoo, hoo.* It is called awamaki-dori or the "millet-sowing bird," because when the farmers hear its cry, they know that it is time to plant the millet. It is quite small and brown, extremely shy, and, so far as I can learn, altogether nocturnal in its habits.

But rarely, very rarely, a far stranger cry is heard in those trees at night, a voice as of one crying in pain the syllables *"ho-to-to-gi-su."* The cry and the name of that which utters it are one and the same, *hototogisu.*

It is a bird of which weird things are told; for they say it is not really a creature of this living world, but a night wanderer from the Land of Darkness. In the Meido its dwelling is among those sunless mountains of Shide over which all souls must pass to reach the place of judgment. Once in each year it comes; the time of its coming is the end of the fifth month, by the antique counting of moons; and the peasants, hearing its voice, say one to the other, "Now must we sow the rice; for the Shide-no-taosa is with us." The word taosa signifies the head man of a mura, or village, as villages were governed in the old days; but why the hototogisu is called the taosa of Shide I do not know. Perhaps it is deemed to be a soul from some shadowy hamlet of the Shide hills, whereat the ghosts are wont to rest on their weary way to the realm of Emma, the King of Death.

Its cry has been interpreted in various ways. Some declare that the hototogisu does not really repeat its own name, but asks, "Honzon kaketaka" (Has the honzon[33] been suspended?) Others, resting their interpretation upon the wisdom of the Chinese, aver that the bird's speech signifies, "Surely it is better to return home." This, at least, is true: that all who journey far from their native place, and hear the voice of the hototogisu in other distant provinces, are seized with the sickness of longing for home.

Only at night, the people say, is its voice heard, and most often upon the nights of great moons; and it chants while hovering high out of sight, wherefore a poet has sung of it thus:—

> *Hito koe wa*
> *Tsuki ga naitaka*
> *Hototogisu!*[34]

And another has written:—

> *Hotogisu*
> *Nakitsuru kata wo*
> *Nagamureba,—*
> *Tada ariake no*
> *Tsuki zo nokoreru.*[35]

The dweller in cities may pass a lifetime without hearing the hototogisu. Caged, the little creature will remain silent and die. Poets often wait vainly in the dew, from sunset till dawn, to hear the strange cry which has inspired so many exquisite verses. But those who have heard found it so mournful that they have likened it to the cry of one wounded suddenly to death.

> *Hototogisu*
> *Chi ni naku koe wa*
> *Ariake no*
> *Tsuki yori hokani*
> *Kiku hito mo nashi.*[36]

Concerning Izumo owls, I shall content myself with citing a composition by one of my Japanese students who wrote:

> "The Owl is a hateful bird that sees in the dark. Little children who cry are frightened by the threat that the Owl will come to take them away; for the Owl cries, *'Hō! Hō! sorōtto kōka! sorōtto koka!'* which means, 'Thou! must I enter slowly?' It also cries *'Noritsuke hose! ho! ho!'* which means, 'Do thou make the starch to use in washing to-morrow!' And when the women hear that cry, they know that to-morrow will be a fine day. It also cries, *'Tototo,'* 'The man dies,' and *'Kōtokokko,'* 'The boy dies.' So people hate it. And crows hate it so much that it is used to catch crows. The Farmer puts an Owl in the rice-field; and all the crows come to kill it, and they get caught fast in the snares. This should teach us not to give way to our dislikes for other people."

The kites which hover over the city all day do not live in the neighborhood. Their nests are far away upon the blue peaks; but they pass much of their time in catching fish, and in stealing from back yards. They pay the wood and the garden swift and sudden piratical visits; and their sinister cry—*pi-yorōyorō, pi-yorōyorō*—sounds at intervals over the town from dawn till sundown. Most insolent of all feathered creatures they certainly are,—more insolent than even their fellow-robbers, the crows. A kite will drop five miles to filch a tai out of a fish-seller's bucket, or a fried-cake out of a child's hand, and shoot back to the clouds before the victim of the theft has time to stoop for a stone. Hence the saying, "to look as surprised as if one's aburage[37] had been snatched from one's hand by a kite." There is, moreover, no telling what a kite may think proper to steal. For example, my neighbor's servant-girl went to the river the other day, wearing in her hair a string of small scarlet beads made of rice-grains prepared and dyed in a certain ingenious way. A kite lighted upon her head, and tore away and swallowed the string of beads. But it is great fun to feed these birds with dead rats or mice which have been caught in traps over night and subsequently drowned. The instant a dead rat is exposed to view a kite pounces from the sky to bear it away. Sometimes a crow may get the start of the kite, but the crow must be able to get to the woods very swiftly indeed in order to keep his prize. The children sing this song:—

> *Tobi, tobi, maute mise!*
> *Ashita no ba ni*
> *Karasu ni kakushite*
> *Nezumi yaru.*[38]

The mention of dancing refers to the beautiful balancing motion of the kite's wings in flight. By suggestion this motion is poetically compared to the graceful swaying of a maiko, or dancing-girl, extending her arms and waving the long wide sleeves of her silken robe.

Although there is a numerous sub-colony of crows in the wood behind my house, the headquarters of the corvine army are in the pine grove of the ancient castle grounds, visible from my front room. To see the crows all flying home at the same hour every evening is an interesting spectacle, and popular imagination has found an amusing comparison for it in the hurry-skurry of people running to a fire. This explains the meaning of a song which children sing to the crows returning to their nests:—

> *Ato no karasu saki ine,*
> *Ware ga iye ga yakeru ken,*
> *Hayō inde midzu kake,*
> *Midzu ga nakya yarozo,*
> *Amattara ko ni yare,*
> *Ko ga nakya modose.*[39]

Confucianism seems to have discovered virtue in the crow. There is a Japanese proverb, *"Karasu ni hampo no ko ari,"* meaning that the crow performs the filial duty of hampo, or, more literally, "the filial duty of hampo exists in the crow." "Hampo" means, literally, "to return a feeding." The young crow is said to requite its parents' care by feeding them when it becomes strong. Another example of filial piety has been furnished by the dove. *"Hato ni sanshi no rei ari,"*—the dove sits three branches below its parent; or, more literally, "has the three-branch etiquette to perform."

The cry of the wild dove *(yamabato),* which I hear almost daily from the wood, is the most sweetly plaintive sound that ever reached my ears. The Izumo peasantry say that the bird utters these words, which it certainly seems to do if one listen to it after having learned the alleged syllables:—

> *Tété*
> > *poppō*
> *Kaka*
> > *poppō*
> *Tété*
> > *poppō*
> *Kaka*
> > *poppō*
> *Tété* . . . (sudden pause)

"Tété" is the baby word for "father," and "kaka" for mother; and "poppō" signifies, in infantile speech, "the bosom."[40]

Wild uguisu also frequently sweeten my summer with their song, and sometimes come very near the house, being attracted, apparently, by the chant of my caged pet. The uguisu is very common in this province. It haunts all the woods and the sacred groves in the neighborhood of the city, and I never made a journey in Izumo during the warm season without hearing its note from some shadowy place.

But there are uguisu and uguisu. There are uguisu to be had for one or two yen, but the finely trained, cage-bred singer may command not less than a hundred.

It was at a little village temple that I first heard one curious belief about this delicate creature. In Japan, the coffin in which a corpse is borne to burial is totally unlike an Occidental coffin. It is a surprisingly small square box, wherein the dead is placed in a sitting posture. How any adult corpse can be put into so small a space may well be an enigma to foreigners. In cases of pronounced *rigor mortis* the work of getting the body into the coffin is difficult even for the professional dōshin-bozu. But the devout followers of Nichiren claim that after death their bodies will remain perfectly flexible; and the dead body of an uguisu, they affirm, likewise never stiffens, for this little bird is of their faith, and passes its life in singing praises unto the Sutra of the Lotus of the Good Law.

XIV

I have already become a little too fond of my dwelling-place. Each day, after returning from my college duties, and exchanging my teacher's uniform for the infinitely more comfortable Japanese robe, I find more than compensation for the weariness of five class-hours in the simple pleasure of squatting on the shaded veranda overlooking the gardens. Those antique garden walls, high-mossed below their ruined coping of tiles, seem to shut out even the murmur of the city's life. There are no sounds but the voices of birds, the shrilling of semi, or, at long, lazy intervals, the solitary plash of a diving frog. Nay, those walls seclude me from much more than city streets. Outside them hums the changed Japan of telegraphs and newspapers and steamships; within dwell the all-reposing peace of nature and the dreams of the sixteenth century. There is a charm of quaintness in the very air, a faint sense of something viewless and sweet all about one; perhaps the gentle haunt-

ing of dead ladies who looked like the ladies of the old picture-books, and who lived here when all this was new. Even
in the summer light—touching the gray strange shapes of
stone, thrilling through the foliage of the long-loved
trees—there is the tenderness of a phantom caress. These
are the gardens of the past. The future will know them only
as dreams, creations of a forgotten art, whose charm no
genius may reproduce.

Of the human tenants here no creature seems to be
afraid. The little frogs resting upon the lotus-leaves scarcely shrink from my touch; the lizards sun themselves within
easy reach of my hand; the water-snakes glide across my
shadow without fear; bands of semi establish their deafening orchestra on a plum branch just above my head, and a
praying mantis insolently poses on my knee. Swallows and
sparrows not only build their nests on my roof, but even
enter my rooms without concern,—one swallow has actually built its nest in the ceiling of the bath-room,—and the
weasel purloins fish under my very eyes without any scru-
ples of conscience. A wild uguisu perches on a cedar by the
window, and in a burst of savage sweetness challenges my
caged pet to a contest in song; and always through the
golden air, from the green twilight of the mountain pines,
there purls to me, the plaintive, caressing, delicious call of
the yamabato:—

> *Tété*
> > *poppō*
> *Kaka*
> > *poppō*
> *Tété*
> > *poppō*
> *Kaka*
> > *poppō*
> *Tété . . .*

No European dove has such a cry. He who can hear, for

the first time, the voice of the yamabato without feeling a new sensation at his heart little deserves to dwell in this happy world.

Yet all this—the old katchiu-yashiki and its gardens—will doubtless have vanished forever before many years. Already a multitude of gardens, more spacious and more beautiful than mine, have been converted into rice-fields or bamboo groves; and the quaint Izumo city, touched at last by some long-projected railway line,—perhaps even within the present decade,—will swell, and change, and grow commonplace, and demand these grounds for the building of factories and mills. Not from here alone, but from all the land the ancient peace and the ancient charm seem doomed to pass away. For impermanency is the nature of things, more particularly in Japan; and the changes and the changers shall also be changed until there is found no place for them,—and regret is vanity. The dead art that made the beauty of this place was the art, also, of that faith to which belongs the all-consoling text, *"Verily, even plants and trees rocks and stones, all shall enter into Nirvana."*

Three Popular Ballads[1]

During the spring of 1891, I visited the settlement in Matsué, Izumo, of an outcast people known as the *yama-no-mono*. Some results of the visit were subsequently communicated to the "Japan Mail," in a letter published June 13, 1891, and some extracts from that letter I think it may be worth while to cite here, by way of introduction to the subject of the present paper.

"The settlement is at the southern end of Matsué, in a tiny valley, or rather hollow among the hills which form a half-circle behind the city. Few Japanese of the better classes have ever visited such a village; and even the poorest of the common people shun the place as they would shun a centre of contagion; for the idea of defilement, both moral and physical, is still attached to the very name of its inhabitants. Thus, although the settlement is within half an hour's walk from the heart of the city, probably not half a dozen of the thirty-six thousand residents of Matsué have visited it.

"There are four distinct outcast classes in Matsué and its

environs: the *hachiya,* the *koya-no-mono,* the *yama-no-mono,* and the *eta* of Suguta.

"There are two settlements of *hachiya.* These were formerly the public executioners, and served under the police in various capacities. Although by ancient law the lowest class of pariahs, their intelligence was sufficiently cultivated by police service and by contact with superiors to elevate them in popular opinion above the other outcasts. They are now manufacturers of bamboo cages and baskets. They are said to be descendants of the family and retainers of Taira-no-Masakado-Heishino, the only man in Japan who ever seriously conspired to seize the imperial throne by armed force, and who was killed by the famous general Taira-no-Sadamori.

"The *koya-no-mono* are slaughterers and dealers in hides. They are never allowed to enter any house in Matsué except the shop of a dealer in *geta* and other foot-gear. Originally vagrants, they were permanently settled in Matsué by some famous daimyō, who built for them small houses—*koya*—on the bank of the canal. Hence their name. As for the *eta* proper, their condition and calling are too familiar to need comment in this connection.

"The *yama-no-mono* are so called because they live among the hills *(yama)* at the southern end of Matsué. They have a monopoly of the rag-and-waste-paper business, and are buyers of all sorts of refuse, from old bottles to broken-down machinery. Some of them are rich. Indeed, the whole class is, compared with other outcast classes, prosperous. Nevertheless, public prejudice against them is still almost as strong as in the years previous to the abrogation of the special laws concerning them. Under no conceivable circumstances could any of them obtain employment as servants. Their prettiest girls in old times often became *jorō;* but at no time could they enter a *jorō-ya* in any neighboring city, much less in their own, so they were sold to establishments in remote places. A *yama-no-mono* today could not even become a *kurumaya.* He could

not obtain employment as a common laborer in any capacity, except by going to some distant city where he could
hope to conceal his origin. But if detected under such conditions he would run serious risk of being killed by his fellow laborers. Under any circumstance it would be difficult
for a *yama-no-mono* to pass himself off for a *heimin*.
Centuries of isolation and prejudice have fixed and moulded the manners of the class in recognizable ways; and even
its language has become a special and curious dialect.

"I was anxious to see something of a class so singularly
situated and specialized; and I had the good fortune to
meet a Japanese gentleman who, although belonging to the
highest class of Matsué, was kind enough to agree to
accompany me to their village, where he had never been
himself. On the way thither he told me many curious
things about the *yama-no-mono.* In feudal times these people had been kindly treated by the *samurai;* and they were
often allowed or invited to enter the courts of *samurai*
dwellings to sing and dance, for which performances they
were paid. The songs and the dances with which they were
able to entertain even those aristocratic families were
known to no other people, and were called *Daikoku-mai.*
Singing the *Daikoku-mai* was, in fact, the special hereditary
art of the *yama-no-mono,* and represented their highest
comprehension of æsthetic and emotional matters. In former times they could not obtain admittance to a
respectable theatre; and, like the *hachiya,* had theatres of
their own. It would be interesting, my friend added, to
learn the origin of their songs and their dances; for their
songs are not in their own special dialect, but in pure
Japanese. And that they should have been able to preserve
this oral literature without deterioration is especially
remarkable from the fact that the *yama-no-mono* were
never taught to read or write. They could not even avail
themselves of those new educational opportunities which
the era of Meiji has given to the masses; prejudice is still far
too strong to allow of their children being happy in a pub-

lic school. A small special school might be possible, though there would perhaps be no small difficulty in obtaining willing teachers.[2]

"The hollow in which the village stands is immediately behind the Buddhist cemetery of Tokōji. The settlement has its own Shintō temple. I was extremely surprised at the aspect of the place; for I had expected to see a good deal of ugliness and filth. On the contrary, I saw a multitude of neat dwellings, with pretty gardens about them, and pictures on the walls of the rooms. There were many trees; the village was green with shrubs and plants, and picturesque to an extreme degree; for, owing to the irregularity of the ground, the tiny streets climbed up and down hill at all sorts of angles,—the loftiest street being fifty or sixty feet above the lower most. A large public bath-house and a public laundry bore evidence that the *yama-no-mono* liked clean linen as well as their *heimin* neighbors on the other side of the hill.

"A crowd soon gathered to look at the strangers who had come to their village,—a rare event for them. The faces I saw seemed much like the faces of the *heimin,* except that I fancied the ugly ones were uglier, making the pretty ones appear more pretty by contrast. There were one or two sinister faces, recalling faces of gypsies that I had seen; while some little girls, on the other hand, had remarkably pleasing features. There were no exchanges of civilities, as upon meeting *heimin;* a Japanese of the better class would as soon think of taking off his hat to a *yama-no-mono* as a West-Indian planter would think of bowing to a negro. The *yama-no-mono* themselves usually show by their attitude that they expect no forms. None of the men saluted us; but some of the women, on being kindly addressed, made obeisance. Other women, weaving coarse straw sandals (an inferior quality of *zōri),* would answer only 'yes' or 'no' to questions, and seemed to be suspicious of us. My friend called my attention to the fact that the women were dressed differently from Japanese women of the ordinary classes. For example, even among the very poorest *heimin* there are certain accepted laws of costume; there are certain colors which may or may not be worn, according to age. But even elderly women among these people wear *obi* of bright red or variegated hues, and *kimono* of a showy tint.

"Those of the women seen in the city streets, selling or buying, are the elders only. The younger stay at home. The elderly women always go into town with large baskets of a peculiar shape, by which the fact that they are *yama-no-mono* is at once known. Numbers of these baskets were visible, principally at the doors of the smaller dwellings. They are carried on the back, and are used to contain all that the *yama-no-mono* buy,—old paper, old wearing apparel, bottles, broken glass, and scrap-metal.

"A woman at last ventured to invite us to her house, to look at some old colored prints she wished to sell. Thither we went, and were as nicely received as in a *heimin* residence. The pictures—including a number of drawings by Hiroshige—proved to be worth buying; and my friend then asked if we could have the pleasure of hearing the *Daikoku-mai*. To my great satisfaction the proposal was well received; and on our agreeing to pay a trifle to each singer, a small band of neat-looking young girls, whom we had not seen before, made their appearance, and prepared to sing, while an old woman made ready to dance. Both the old woman and the girls provided themselves with curious instruments for the performance. Three girls had instruments shaped like mallets, made of paper and bamboo: these were intended to represent the hammer of Daikoku;[3] they were held in the left hand, a fan being waved in the right. Other girls were provided with a kind of castanets,— two flat pieces of hard dark wood, connected by a string. Six girls formed in a line before the house. The old woman took her place facing the girls, holding in her hands two little sticks, one stick being notched along a part of its length.

By drawing it across the other stick, a curious rattling noise was made.

"My friend pointed out to me that the singers formed two distinct parties, of three each. Those bearing the hammer and fan were the Daikoku band: they were to sing the ballads. Those with the castanets were the Ebisu party, and formed the chorus.

"The old woman rubbed her little sticks together, and from the throats of the Daikoku band there rang out a clear sweet burst of song, quite different from anything I had heard before in Japan, while the tapping of the castanets kept exact time to the syllabification of the words, which were very rapidly uttered. When the first three girls had sung a certain number of lines, the voices of the other three joined in, producing a very pleasant though untrained harmony; and all sang the burden together. Then the Daikoku party began another verse; and, after a certain interval, the chorus was again sung. In the mean while the old woman was dancing a very fantastic dance which provoked laughter from the crowd, occasionally chanting a few comic words.

"The song was not comic, however; it was a very pathetic ballad entitled 'Yaoya O-Shichi.' Yaoya O-Shichi was a beautiful girl, who set fire to her own house in order to obtain another meeting with her lover, an acolyte in a temple where she expected that her family would be obliged to take refuge after the fire. But being detected and convicted of arson, she was condemned by the severe law of that age to be burnt alive. The sentence was carried into effect; but the youth and beauty of the victim, and the motive of her offense, evoked a sympathy in the popular heart which found later expression in song and drama.

"None of the performers, except the old woman, lifted the feet from the ground while singing;—but all swayed their bodies in time to the melody. The singing lasted more than one hour, during which the voices never failed in their quality; and yet, so far from being weary of it, and although I could not understand a word uttered, I felt very sorry when it was all over. And with the pleasure received there came to the foreign listener also a strong sense of sympathy for the young singers, victims of a prejudice so ancient that its origin is no longer known."

In the Cave of the Children's Ghosts

I

It is forbidden to go to Kaka if there be wind enough "to move three hairs."

Now an absolutely windless day is rare on this wild western coast. Over the Japanese Sea, from Korea, or China, or boreal Siberia, some west or northwest breeze is nearly always blowing. So that I have had to wait many long months for a good chance to visit Kaka.

Taking the shortest route, one goes first to Mitsu-ura from Matsue, either by kuruma or on foot. By kuruma this little journey occupies nearly two hours and a half, though the distance is scarcely seven miles, the road being one of the worst in all Izumo. You leave Matsue to enter at once into a broad plain, level as a lake, all occupied by rice-fields and walled in by wooded hills. The path, barely wide enough for a single vehicle, traverses this green desolation, climbs the heights beyond it, and descends again into

107

another and a larger level of rice-fields, surrounded also by hills. The path over the second line of hills is much steeper; then a third rice-plain must be crossed and a third chain of green altitudes, lofty enough to merit the name of mountains. Of course one must make the ascent on foot: it is no small labor for a kurumaya to pull even an empty kuruma up to the top; and how he manages to do so without breaking the little vehicle is a mystery, for the path is stony and rough as the bed of a torrent. A tiresome climb I find it; but the landscape view from the summit is more than compensation.

Then descending, there remains a fourth and last wide level of rice-fields to traverse. The absolute flatness of the great plains between the ranges, and the singular way in which these latter "fence off" the country into sections, are matters for surprise even in a land of surprises like Japan. Beyond the fourth rice-valley there is a fourth hill chain, lower and richly wooded, on reaching the base of which the traveler must finally abandon his kuruma, and proceed over the hills on foot. Behind them lies the sea. But the very worst bit of the journey now begins. The path makes an easy winding ascent between bamboo growths and young pine and other vegetation for a shaded quarter of a mile, passing before various little shrines and pretty homesteads surrounded by high-hedged gardens. Then it suddenly breaks into steps, or rather ruins of steps—partly hewn in the rock, partly built, everywhere breached and worn—which descend, all edgeless, in a manner amazingly precipitous, to the village of Mitsu-ura. With straw sandals, which never slip, the country folk can nimbly hurry up or down such a path; but with foreign footgear one slips at nearly every step; and when you reach the bottom at last, the wonder of how you managed to get there even with the assistance of your faithful kurumaya keeps you for a moment quite unconscious of the fact that you are already in Mitsu-ura.

II

Mitsu-ura stands with its back to the mountains, at the end of a small deep bay hemmed in by very high cliffs. There is only one narrow strip of beach at the foot of the heights; and the village owes its existence to that fact, for beaches are rare on this part of the coast. Crowded between the cliffs and the sea, the houses have a painfully compressed aspect; and somehow the greater number give one the impression of things created out of wrecks of junks. The little streets, or rather alleys, are full of boats and skeletons of boats and boat timbers; and everywhere, suspended from bamboo poles much taller than the houses, immense bright brown fishing-nets are drying in the sun. The whole curve of the beach is also lined with boats, lying side by side, so that I wonder how it will be possible to get to the water's edge without climbing over them. There is no hotel; but I find hospitality in a fisherman's dwelling, while my kurumaya goes somewhere to hire a boat for Kaka-ura.

In less than ten minutes there is a crowd of several hundred people about the house, half-clad adults and perfectly naked boys. They blockade the building; they obscure the light by filling up the doorways and climbing into the windows to look at the foreigner. The aged proprietor of the cottage protests in vain, says harsh things; the crowd only thickens. Then all the sliding screens are closed. But in the paper panes there are holes; and at all the lower holes the curious take regular turns at peeping. At a higher hole I do some peeping myself. The crowd is not prepossessing: it is squalid, dull-featured, remarkably ugly. But it is gentle and silent; there are one or two pretty faces in it which seem extraordinary by reason of the general homeliness of the rest.

At last my kurumaya has succeeded in making arrangements for a boat, and I effect a sortie to the beach, followed by the kurumaya and by all my besiegers. Boats have been moved to make a passage for us, and we embark without trouble of any sort. Our crew consists of two scullers,—an old man at the stern, wearing only a rokushaku about his loins, and an old woman at the bow, fully robed and wearing an immense straw hat shaped like a mushroom. Both of course stand to their work and it would be hard to say which is the stronger or more skillful sculler. We passengers squat Oriental fashion upon a mat in the centre of the boat, where a hibachi well stocked with glowing charcoal invites us to smoke.

III

The day is clear blue to the end of the world, with a faint wind from the east, barely enough to wrinkle the sea, certainly more than enough to "move three hairs." Nevertheless the boatwoman and the boatman do not seem anxious; and I begin to wonder whether the famous prohibition is not a myth. So delightful the transparent water looks that before we have left the bay I have to yield to its temptation by plunging in and swimming after the boat. When I climb back on board we are rounding the promontory on the right; and the little vessel begins to rock. Even under this thin wind the sea is moving in long swells. And as we pass into the open, following the westward trend of the land, we find ourselves gliding over an ink-black depth, in front of one of the very grimmest coasts I ever saw.

A tremendous line of dark iron-colored cliffs, towering sheer from the sea without a beach, and with never a speck of green below their summit; and here and there along this terrible front, monstrous beetlings, breaches, fissures, earthquake rendings, and topplings-down. Enormous fractures show lines of strata pitched up skyward, or plunging down into the ocean with the long fall of cubic miles of cliff. Before fantastic gaps, prodigious masses of rock, of all nightmarish shapes, rise from profundities unfathomed. And though the wind to-day seems trying to hold its breath, white breakers are reaching far up the cliffs, and dashing their foam into the faces of the splintered crags. We are too far to hear the thunder of them; but their ominous sheet lightning fully explains to me the story of the three hairs. Along this goblin coast on a wild day there would be no possible chance for the strongest swimmer or the stoutest boat; there is no place for the foot, no hold for the hand, nothing but the sea raving against a precipice of iron. Even to-day, under the feeblest breath imaginable, great swells deluge us with spray as they splash past. And for two long hours this jagged frowning coast towers by; and, as we toil on, rocks rise around us like black teeth; and always, far away, the foam-bursts gleam at the feet of the implacable cliffs. But there are no sounds save the lapping and plashing of passing swells, and the monotonous creaking of the sculls upon their pegs.

At last, at last, a bay,—a beautiful large bay, with a demilune of soft green hills about it, overtopped by far blue mountains,—and in the very farthest point of the bay a miniature village, in front of which many junks are riding at anchor: Kaka-ura.

But we do not go to Kaka-ura yet; the Kukedo are not there. We cross the broad opening of the bay, journey along another half mile of ghastly sea-precipice, and finally make for a lofty promontory of naked Plutonic rock. We pass by its menacing foot, slip along its side, and lo! at an angle opens the arched mouth of a wonderful cavern, broad, lofty, and full of light, with no floor but the sea. Beneath us, as we slip into it, I can see rocks fully twenty feet down. The water is clear as air. This is the Shin-Kukedo, called the New Cavern, though assuredly older than human record by a hundred thousand years.

IV

A more beautiful sea-cave could scarcely be imagined. The sea, tunneling the tall promontory through and through, has also, like a great architect, ribbed and groined and polished its mighty work. The arch of the entrance is certainly twenty feet above the deep water, and fifteen wide; and trillions of wave tongues have licked the vault and walls into wondrous smoothness. As we proceed, the rock roof steadily heightens and the way widens. Then we unexpectedly glide under a heavy shower of fresh water, dripping from overhead. This spring is called the ō-chōzubachi or mitarashi[1] of Shin-Kukedo-San. From the high vault at this point it is believed that a great stone will detach itself and fall upon any evil-hearted person who should attempt to enter the cave. I safely pass through the ordeal!

Suddenly as we advance the boatwoman takes a stone from the bottom of the boat, and with it begins to rap heavily on the bow; and the hollow echoing is reiterated with thundering repercussions through all the cave. And in another instant we pass into a great burst of light, coming from the mouth of a magnificent and lofty archway on the left, opening into the cavern at right angles. This explains the singular illumination of the long vault, which at first seemed to come from beneath; for while the opening was still invisible all the water appeared to be suffused with light. Through this grand arch, between outlying rocks, a strip of beautiful green undulating coast appears, over miles of azure water. We glide on toward the third entrance to the Kukedo, opposite to that by which we came in; and enter the dwelling place of the Kami and the Hotoke, for this grotto is sacred both to Shintō and to Buddhist faith. Here the Kukedo reaches its greatest altitude and breadth. Its vault is fully forty feet above the water, and its walls thirty feet apart. Far up on the right, near the roof, is a projecting white rock, and above the rock an orifice wherefrom a slow stream drips, seeming white as the rock itself.

This is the legendary Fountain of Jizō, the fountain of milk at which the souls of dead children drink. Sometimes it flows more swiftly, sometimes more slowly; but it never ceases by night or day. And mothers suffering from want of milk come hither to pray that milk may be given unto them; and their prayer is heard. And mothers having more milk than their infants need come hither also, and pray to Jizō that so much as they can give may be taken for the dead children; and their prayer is heard, and their milk diminishes.

At least, thus the peasants of Izumo say.

And the echoing of the swells leaping against the rocks without, the rushing and rippling of the tide against the walls, the heavy rain of percolating water, sounds of lapping and gurgling and plashing, and sounds of mysterious origin coming from no visible where, make it difficult for us to hear each other speak. The cavern seems full of voices, as if a host of invisible beings were holding tumultuous converse.

Below us all the deeply lying rocks are naked to view as if seen through glass. It seems to me that nothing could be more delightful than to swim through this cave and let one's self drift with the sea-currents through all its cool shadows. But as I am on the point of jumping in, all the other occupants of the boat utter wild cries of protest. It is certain death! men who jumped in here only six months ago were never heard of again! this is sacred water, Kami-no-umi! And as if to conjure away my temptation, the boatwoman again seizes her little stone and raps fearfully upon the bow. On finding, however, that I am not sufficiently deterred by these stories of death and disappearance, she suddenly screams into my ear the magical word,

"Samé!"

Sharks! I have no longer any desire whatever to swim through the many-sounding halls of Shin-Kukedo-San. I have lived in the tropics!

And we start forthwith for Kyū-Kukedo-San, the Ancient Cavern.

V

For the ghastly fancies about the Kami-no-umi, the word "samé" afforded a satisfactory explanation. But why that long, loud, weird rapping on the bow with a stone evidently kept on board for no other purpose? There was an exaggerated earnestness about the action which gave me an uncanny sensation, something like that which moves a man while walking at night upon a lonesome road, full of queer shadows, to sing at the top of his voice. The boat-woman at first declares that the rapping was made only for the sake of the singular echo. But after some cautious further questioning, I discover a much more sinister reason for the performance. Moreover, I learn that all the seamen and seawomen of this coast do the same thing when passing through perilous places, or places believed to be haunted by the Ma. What are the Ma?

Goblins!

VI

From the caves of the Kami we retrace our course for about a quarter of a mile; then make directly for an immense perpendicular wrinkle in the long line of black cliffs. Immediately before it a huge dark rock towers from the sea, whipped by the foam of breaking swells. Rounding it, we glide behind it into still water and shadow, the shadow of a monstrous cleft in the precipice of the coast. And suddenly, at an unsuspected angle, the mouth of another cavern yawns before us; and in another moment our boat touches its threshold of stone with a little shock that sends a long sonorous echo, like the sound of a temple drum, booming through all the abysmal place. A single glance tells me whither we have come. Far within the dusk I see the face of Jizō, smiling in pale stone, and before him, and all about him, a weird congregation of gray shapes without shape,—a host of fantasticalities that strangely suggest the wreck of a cemetery. From the sea the ribbed floor of the cavern slopes high through deepening shadows back to the black mouth of a farther grotto; and all that slope is covered with hundreds and thousands of forms like shattered haka. But as the eyes grow accustomed to the gloaming it becomes manifest that these were never haka; they are only little towers of stone and pebbles deftly piled up by long and patient labor.

"*Shinda kodomo no shigoto,*" my kurumaya murmurs with a compassionate smile; "all this is the work of the dead children."

And we disembark. By counsel I take off my shoes and put on a pair of zori, or straw sandals provided for me, as the rock is extremely slippery. The others land barefoot. But how to proceed soon becomes a puzzle: the countless stone-piles stand so close together that no space for the foot seems to be left between them.

"*Mada michi ga arimasu!*" the boatwoman announces, leading the way. There is a path.

Following after her, we squeeze ourselves between the wall of the cavern on the right and some large rocks, and discover a very, very narrow passage left open between the stone-towers. But we are warned to be careful for the sake of the little ghosts: if any of their work be overturned, they will cry. So we move very cautiously and slowly across the cave to a space bare of stone-heaps, where the rocky floor is covered with a thin layer of sand, detritus of a crumbling ledge above it. And in that sand I see light prints of little feet, children's feet, tiny naked feet, only three or four inches long,—*the footprints of the infant ghosts*.

Had we come earlier, the boatwoman says, we should have seen many more. For it is at night, when the soil of the cavern is moist with dews and drippings from the roof, that They leave Their footprints upon it; but when the heat of the day comes, and the sand and the rocks dry up, the prints of the little feet vanish away.

There are only three footprints visible, but these are singularly distinct. One points toward the wall of the cavern; the others toward the sea. Here and there, upon ledges or projections of the rock, all about the cavern, tiny straw sandals—children's zori—are lying: offerings of pilgrims to the little ones, that their feet may not be wounded by the stones. But all the ghostly footprints are prints of naked feet.

Then we advance, picking our way very, very carefully between the stone-towers, toward the mouth of the inner grotto, and reach the statue of Jizō before it. A seated Jizō, carven in granite, holding in one hand the mystic jewel by virtue of which all wishes may be fulfilled; in the other his shakujō, or pilgrim's staff. Before him (strange condescension of Shintō faith!) a little torii has been erected, and a pair of gohei! Evidently this gentle divinity has no enemies; at the feet of the lover of children's ghosts, both creeds unite in tender homage.

I said feet. But this subterranean Jizō has only one foot. The carven lotus on which he reposes has been fractured and broken: two great petals are missing; and the right foot, which must have rested upon one of them, has been knocked off at the ankle. This, I learn upon inquiry, has been done by the waves. In times of great storm the billows rush into the cavern like raging Oni, and sweep all the little stone towers into shingle as they come, and dash the statues against the rocks. But always during the first still night after the tempest the work is reconstructed as before!

"Hotoke ga shimpai shite; naki-naki tsumi naoshimasu."

They make mourning, the hotoke; weeping they pile up the stones again, they rebuild their tower of prayer.

All about the black mouth of the inner grotto the bone-colored rock bears some resemblance to a vast pair of yawning jaws. Downward from this sinister portal the cavern-floor slopes into a deeper and darker aperture. And within it, as one's eyes become accustomed to the gloom, a still larger vision of stone towers is disclosed; and beyond them, in a nook of the grotto, three other statues of Jizō smile, each one with a torii before it. Here I have the misfortune to upset first one stone-pile and then another, while trying to proceed. My kurumaya, almost simultaneously, ruins a third. To atone therefor, we must build six new towers, or double the number of those which we have cast down. And while we are thus busied, the boatwoman tells of two fishermen who remained in the cavern through all one night, and heard the humming of the viewless gathering, and sounds of speech, like the speech of children murmuring in multitude.

VII

Only at night do the shadowy children come to build their little stone-heaps at the feet of Jizō; and it is said that every night the stones are changed. When I ask why they do not work by day, when there is none to see them, I am answered: "O-Hi-San[2] might see them; *the dead exceedingly fear the Lady-Sun.*"

To the question, "Why do they come from the sea?" I can get no satisfactory answer. But doubtless in the quaint imagination of this people, as also in that of many another, there lingers still the primitive idea of some communication, mysterious and awful, between the world of waters and the world of the dead. It is always over the sea, after the Feast of Souls, that the spirits pass murmuring back to their dim realm, in those elfish little ships of straw which are launched for them upon the sixteenth day of the seventh moon. Even when these are launched upon rivers, or when floating lanterns are set adrift upon lakes or canals to light the ghosts upon their way, or when a mother bereaved drops into some running stream one hundred little prints of Jizō for the sake of her lost darling, the vague idea behind the pious act is that all waters flow to the sea and the sea itself unto the "Nether-distant Land."

Some time, somewhere, this day will come back to me at night, with its visions and sounds: the dusky cavern, and its gray hosts of stone climbing back into darkness, and the faint prints of little naked feet, and the weirdly smiling images, and the broken syllables of the waters, inward-borne, multiplied by husky echoings, blending into one vast ghostly whispering, like the humming of the Sai-no-Kawara.

And over the black-blue bay we glide to the rocky beach of Kaka-ura.

VIII

As at Mitsu-ura, the water's edge is occupied by a serried line of fishing-boats, each with its nose to the sea; and behind these are ranks of others; and it is only just barely possible to squeeze one's way between them over the beach to the drowsy, pretty, quaint little streets behind them. Everybody seems to be asleep when we first land: the only living creature visible is a cat, sitting on the stern of a boat; and even that cat, according to Japanese beliefs, might not be a real cat, but an o-baké or a nekomata—in short, a goblin-cat, *for it has a long tail.* It is hard work to discover the solitary hotel: there are no signs; and every house seems a private house, either a fisherman's or a farmer's. But the little place is worth wandering about in. A kind of yellow stucco is here employed to cover the exterior of walls; and this light warm tint under the bright blue day gives to the miniature streets a more than cheerful aspect.

When we do finally discover the hotel, we have to wait quite a good while before going in; for nothing is ready; everybody is asleep or away, though all the screens and sliding doors are open. Evidently there are no thieves in Kaka-ura. The hotel is on a little hillock, and is approached from the main street (the rest are only miniature alleys) by two little flights of stone steps. Immediately across the way I see a Zen temple and a Shintō temple, almost side by side.

At last a pretty young woman, naked to the waist, with a bosom like a Naiad, comes running down the street to the hotel at a surprising speed, bowing low with a smile as she hurries by us into the house. This little person is the waiting-maid of the inn, O-Kayo-San,—a name signifying "Years of Bliss." Presently she reappears at the threshold, fully robed in a nice kimono, and gracefully invites us to enter, which we are only too glad to do. The room is neat and spacious; Shintō kakemono from Kitzuki are suspended in the toko and upon the walls; and in one corner I see a very handsome Zen-butsudan, or household shrine. (The form of the shrine, as well as the objects of worship therein, vary according to the sect of the worshipers.) Suddenly I become aware that it is growing strangely dark; and looking about me, perceive that all the doors and windows and other apertures of the inn are densely blocked up by a silent, smiling crowd which has gathered to look at me. I could not have believed there were so many people in Kaka-ura.

In a Japanese house, during the hot season, everything is thrown open to the breeze. All the shōji or sliding paper-screens, which serve for windows; and all the opaque paper-screens (*fusuma*) used in other seasons to separate apartments, are removed. There is nothing left between floor and roof save the frame or skeleton of the building; the dwelling is literally *unwalled,* and may be seen through in any direction. The landlord, finding the crowd embarrassing, closes up the building in front. The silent, smiling crowd goes to the rear. The rear is also closed. Then the crowd masses to right and left of the house; and both sides have to be closed, which makes it insufferably hot. And the crowd make gentle protest.

Wherefore our host, being displeased, rebukes the multitude with argument and reason, yet without lifting his

voice. (Never do these people lift up their voices in anger.)
And what he says I strive to translate, with emphases, as
follows:—

> "You-as-for! outrageousness doing,—*what* marvel-
>   ous is?
> *"Theatre is not!*
> *"Juggler is not!*
> *"Wrestler is not!*
> *"What amusing is?*
> "Honorable-*Guest* this is!
> "Now august-to-eat-time-is; to-look-at *evil* matter
>   is. *Honorable returning-time-in-*to-look-at-as-for-is-
>   good."

But outside, soft laughing voices continue to plead;
pleading, shrewdly enough, only with the feminine portion
of the family: the landlord's heart is less easily touched.
And these, too, have their arguments:—

> "Oba-San!
> "O-Kayo-San!
> "Shōji-to-open-condescend!—want to see!
> *"Though-we-look-at, Thing-that-by-looking-at-is-*
>   *worn-out-it-is-not!*
> "So that not-to-hinder looking-at is good.
> "Hasten therefore to open!"

As for myself, I would gladly protest against this sealing-
up, for there is nothing offensive nor even embarrassing in
the gaze of these innocent, gentle people; but as the landlord seems to be personally annoyed, I do not like to inter-
fere. The crowd, however, does not go away: it continues to
increase, waiting for my exit. And there is one high window in the rear, of which the paper-panes contain some
holes; and I see shadows of little people climbing up to get
to the holes. Presently there is an eye at every hole.

When I approach the window, the peepers drop noiselessly to the ground, with little timid bursts of laughter,
and run away. But they soon come back again. A more
charming crowd could hardly be imagined: nearly all boys

and girls, half-naked because of the heat, but fresh and clean as flower-buds. Many of the faces are surprisingly pretty; there are but very few which are not extremely pleasing. But where are the men, and the old women? Truly, this population seems not of Kaka-ura, but rather of the Sai-no-Kawara. The boys look like little Jizō.

During dinner, I amuse myself by poking pears and little pieces of radish through the holes in the shōji. At first there is much hesitation and silvery laughter; but in a little while the silhouette of a tiny hand reaches up cautiously, and a pear vanishes away. Then a second pear is taken, without snatching, as softly as if a ghost had appropriated it. Thereafter hesitation ceases, despite the effort of one elderly woman to create a panic by crying out the word *Mahōtsukai,* "wizard." By the time the dinner is over and the shōji removed, we have all become good friends. Then the crowd resumes its silent observation from the four cardinal points.

I never saw a more striking difference in the appearance of two village populations than that between the youth of Mitsu-ura and of Kaka. Yet the villages are but two hours' sailing distance apart. In remoter Japan, as in certain islands of the West Indies, particular physical types are developed apparently among communities but slightly isolated; on one side of a mountain a population may be remarkably attractive, while upon the other you may find a hamlet whose inhabitants are decidedly unprepossessing. But nowhere in this country have I seen a prettier *jeunesse* than that of Kaka-ura.

"Returning-time-in-to-look-at-as-for-is-good." As we descend to the bay, the whole of Kaka-ura, including even the long-invisible ancients of the village accompanies us; making no sound except the pattering of geta. Thus we are escorted to our boat. Into all the other craft drawn up on the beach the younger folk clamber lightly, and seat themselves on the prows and the gunwales to gaze at the mar-

velous *Thing-that-by-looking-at-worn-out-is-not.* And all smile, but say nothing, even to each other: somehow the experience gives me the sensation of being asleep; it is so soft, so gentle, and so queer withal, just like things seen in dreams. And as we glide away over the blue lucent water I look back to the people all waiting and gazing still from the great semicircle of boats; all the slender brown child-limbs dangling from the prows; all the velvety-black heads motionless in the sun; all the boy-faces smiling Jizō-smiles; all the black soft eyes still watching, tirelessly watching, the *Thing-that-by-looking-at-worn-out-is-not.* And as the scene, too swiftly receding, diminishes to the width of a kake-mono, I vainly wish that I could buy this last vision of it, to place it in my toko, and delight my soul betimes with gazing thereon. Yet another moment, and we round a rocky point; and Kaka-ura vanishes from my sight forever. So all things pass away.

Assuredly those impressions which longest haunt recollection are the most transitory: we remember many more instants than minutes, more minutes than hours; and who remembers an entire day? The sum of the remembered happiness of a lifetime is the creation of seconds. What is more fugitive than a smile? yet when does the memory of a vanished smile expire? or the soft regret which that memory may evoke?

Regret for a single individual smile is something common to normal human nature; but regret for the smile of a population, for a smile considered as an abstract quality, is certainly a rare sensation, and one to be obtained, I fancy, only in this Orient land whose people smile forever like their own gods of stone. And this precious experience is already mine; I am regretting the smile of Kaka.

Simultaneously there comes the recollection of a strangely grim Buddhist legend. Once the Buddha smiled; and by the wondrous radiance of that smile were countless worlds illuminated. But there came a Voice, saying: *"It is not real! It cannot last!"* And the light passed.

A Letter from Japan

Tōkyō, August 1, 1904.

Here, in this quiet suburb, where the green peace is broken only by the voices of children at play and the shrilling of cicadæ, it is difficult to imagine that, a few hundred miles away, there is being carried on one of the most tremendous wars of modern times, between armies aggregating more than half a million of men, or that, on the intervening sea, a hundred ships of war have been battling. This contest, between the mightiest of Western powers and a people that began to study Western science only within the recollection of many persons still in vigorous life, is, on one side at least, a struggle for national existence. It was inevitable, this struggle,—might perhaps have been delayed, but certainly not averted. Japan has boldly challenged an empire capable of threatening simultaneously the civilizations of the East and the West,—a mediæval power that, unless vigorously checked, seems destined to absorb Scandinavia and to dominate China. For all industrial civilization the contest is one of vast moment;—for Japan it is probably the supreme crisis in her national life. As to what

123

her fleets and her armies have been doing, the world is fully informed; but as to what her people are doing at home, little has been written.

To inexperienced observation they would appear to be doing nothing unusual; and this strange calm is worthy of record. At the beginning of hostilities an Imperial mandate was issued, bidding all non-combatants to pursue their avocations as usual, and to trouble themselves as little as possible about exterior events;—and this command has been obeyed to the letter. It would be natural to suppose that all the sacrifices, tragedies, and uncertainties of the contest had thrown their gloom over the life of the capital in especial; but there is really nothing whatever to indicate a condition of anxiety or depression. On the contrary, one is astonished by the joyous tone of public confidence, and the admirably restrained pride of the nation in its victories. Western tides have strewn the coast with Japanese corpses; regiments have been blown out of existence in the storming of positions defended by wire-entanglements; battleships have been lost: yet at no moment has there been the least public excitement. The people are following their daily occupations just as they did before the war; the cheery aspect of things is just the same; the theatres and flower displays are not less well patronized. The life of Tōkyō has been, to outward seeming, hardly more affected by the events of the war than the life of nature beyond it, where the flowers are blooming and the butterflies hovering as in other summers. Except after the news of some great victory,—celebrated with fireworks and lantern processions,— there are no signs of public emotion; and but for the frequent distribution of newspaper extras, by runners ringing bells, you could almost persuade yourself that the whole story of the war is an evil dream.

Yet there has been, of necessity, a vast amount of suffering—viewless and voiceless suffering—repressed by that sense of social and patriotic duty which is Japanese religion.

As a seventeen-syllable poem of the hour tells us, the news of every victory must bring pain as well as joy:—

> *Gōgwai no*
> *Tabi teki mikata*
> *Goké ga fuè.*
>
> [Each time that an extra is circulated the widows
> of foes and friends have increased in multitude.]

The great quiet and the smiling tearlessness testify to the more than Spartan discipline of the race. Anciently the people were trained, not only to conceal their emotions, but to speak in a cheerful voice and to show a pleasant face under any stress of moral suffering; and they are obedient to that teaching to-day. It would still be thought a shame to betray personal sorrow for the loss of those who die for Emperor and fatherland. The public seem to view the events of the war as they would watch the scenes of a popular play. They are interested without being excited; and their extraordinary self-control is particularly shown in various manifestations of the "Play-impulse." Everywhere the theatres are producing war dramas (based upon actual fact); the newspapers and magazines are publishing war stories and novels; the cinematograph exhibits the monstrous methods of modern warfare; and numberless industries are turning out objects of art or utility designed to commemorate the Japanese triumphs.

But the present psychological condition, the cheerful and even playful tone of public feeling, can be indicated less by any general statement than by the mention of ordinary facts,—every-day matters recorded in the writer's diary.

Never before were the photographers so busy; it is said that they have not been able to fulfill half of the demands made upon them. The hundreds of thousands of men sent to the war wished to leave photographs with their families, and also to take with them portraits of parents, children, and other beloved persons. The nation was being photographed during the past six months.

A fact of sociological interest is that photography has added something new to the poetry of the domestic faith. From the time of its first introduction, photography became popular in Japan; and none of those superstitions, which inspire fear of the camera among less civilized races, offered any obstacle to the rapid development of a new industry. It is true that there exists some queer-folk beliefs about photographs,—ideas of mysterious relation between the sun-picture and the person imaged. For example: if, in the photograph of a group, one figure appear indistinct or blurred, that is thought to be an omen of sickness or death. But this superstition has its industrial value: it has compelled photographers to be careful about their work,— especially in these days of war, when everybody wants to have a good clear portrait, because the portrait might be needed for another purpose than preservation in an album.

During the last twenty years there has gradually come into existence the custom of placing the photograph of a dead parent, brother, husband, or child, beside the mortuary tablet kept in the Buddhist household shrine. For this reason, also, the departing soldier wishes to leave at home a good likeness of himself.

The rites of domestic affection, in old samurai families, are not confined to the cult of the dead. On certain occasions, the picture of the absent parent, husband, brother, or betrothed, is placed in the alcove of the guest room, and a feast laid out before it. The photograph, in such cases, is fixed upon a little stand *(dai);* and the feast is served as if the person were present. This pretty custom of preparing a meal for the absent is probably more ancient than any art of portraiture; but the modern photograph adds to the human poetry of the rite. In feudal time it was the rule to set the repast facing the direction in which the absent person had gone—north, south, east, or west. After a brief interval the covers of the vessels containing the cooked food were lifted and examined. If the lacquered inner surface was thickly beaded with vapor, all was well; but if the surface was dry, that was an omen of death, a sign that the disembodied spirit had returned to absorb the essence of the offerings.

As might have been expected, in a country where the "play-impulse" is stronger, perhaps, than in any other part of the world, the Zeitgeist found manifestation in the flower displays of the year. I visited those in my neighborhood, which is the Quarter of the Gardeners. This quarter is famous for its azaleas *(tsutsuji);* and every spring the azalea gardens attract thousands of visitors,—not only by the wonderful exhibition then made of shrubs which look like solid masses of blossom (ranging up from snowy white, through all shades of pink, to a flamboyant purple) but also by displays of effigies: groups of figures ingeniously formed with living leaves and flowers. These figures, life-size, usually represent famous incidents of history or drama. In many cases—though not in all—the bodies and the costumes are composed of foliage and flowers trained to grow about a framework; while the faces, feet, and hands are represented by some kind of flesh-colored composition.

This year, however, a majority of the displays represented scenes of the war,—such as an engagement between Japanese infantry and mounted Cossacks, a night attack by torpedo boats, the sinking of a battleship. In the last-mentioned display, Russian bluejackets appeared, swimming for their lives in a rough sea;—the pasteboard waves and the swimming figures being made to rise and fall by the pulling of a string; while the crackling of quick firing guns was imitated by a mechanism contrived with sheets of zinc.

It is said that Admiral Tōgō sent to Tōkyō for some flowering-trees in pots—in as much as his responsibilities allowed him no chance of seeing the cherry-flowers and the plum-blossoms in their season,—and that the gardeners responded even too generously.

Almost immediately after the beginning of hostilities, thousands of "war pictures"—mostly cheap lithographs— were published. The drawing and coloring were better than those of the prints issued at the time of the war with China; but the details were to a great extent imaginary,—altogether imaginary as to the appearance of Russian troops. Pictures of the engagements with the Russian fleet were effective, despite some lurid exaggeration. The most startling things were pictures of Russian defeats in Korea, published before a single military engagement had taken place;—the artist had "flushed to anticipate the scene." In these prints the Russians were depicted as fleeing in utter rout, leaving their officers—very fine-looking officers— dead upon the field; while the Japanese infantry, with dreadfully determined faces, were coming up at a double. The propriety and the wisdom of thus pictorially predicting victory, and easy victory to boot, may be questioned. But I am told that the custom of so doing is an old one; and it is thought that to realize the common hope thus imaginatively is lucky. At all events, there is no attempt at deception in these pictorial undertakings;—they help to keep up the public courage, and they ought to be pleasing to the gods.

Some of the earlier pictures have now been realized in grim fact. The victories in China had been similarly fore-shadowed: they amply justified the faith of the artist. . . . To-day the war pictures continue to multiply; but they have changed character. The inexorable truth of the photograph, and the sketches of the war correspondent, now bring all the vividness and violence of fact to help the artist's imagination. There was something naïve and the-atrical in the drawings of anticipation; but the pictures of the hour represent the most tragic reality,—always becoming more terrible. At this writing, Japan has yet lost no single battle; but not a few of her victories have been dearly won.

To enumerate even a tenth of the various articles ornamented with designs inspired by the war—articles such as combs, clasps, fans, brooches, card-cases, purses—would require a volume. Even cakes and confectionery are stamped with naval or military designs; and the glass or paper windows of shops—not to mention the signboards—have pictures of Japanese victories painted upon them. At night the shop lanterns proclaim the pride of the nation in its fleets and armies; and a whole chapter might easily be written about the new designs in transparencies and toy lanterns. A new revolving lantern—turned by the air-current which its own flame creates—has become very popular. It represents a charge of Japanese infantry upon Russian defenses; and holes pierced in the colored paper, so as to produce a continuous vivid flashing while the transparency revolves, suggest the exploding of shells and the volleying of machine guns.

Some displays of the art-impulse, as inspired by the war, have been made in directions entirely unfamiliar to Western experience,—in the manufacture, for example, of women's hair ornaments and dress materials. Dress goods decorated with war pictures have actually become a fashion,—especially crêpe silks for underwear, and figured silk linings for cloaks and sleeves. More remarkable than these are the new hairpins;—by hairpins I mean those long double-pronged ornaments of flexible metal which are called *kanzashi,* and are more or less ornamented according to the age of the wearer. (The *kanzashi* made for young girls are highly decorative; those worn by older folk are plain, or adorned only with a ball of coral or polished stone.) The new hairpins might be called commemorative: one, of which the decoration represents a British and a Japanese flag intercrossed, celebrates the Anglo-Japanese alliance; another represents an officer's cap and sword; and the best of all is surmounted by a tiny metal model of a battleship. The battleship-pin is not merely fantastic: it is actually pretty!

As might have been expected, military and naval subjects occupy a large place among the year's designs for toweling. The towel designs celebrating naval victories have been particularly successful: they are mostly in white, on a blue ground; or in black, on a white ground. One of the best—blue and white—represented only a flock of gulls wheeling about the masthead of a sunken iron-clad, and, far away, the silhouettes of Japanese battleships passing to the horizon. . . . What especially struck me in this, and in several other designs, was the original manner in which the Japanese artist had seized upon the traits of the modern battleship,—the powerful and sinister lines of its shape,— just as he would have caught for us the typical character of a beetle or a lobster. The lines have been just enough exaggerated to convey, at one glance, the real impression made by the aspect of these iron monsters,—a vague impression of bulk and force and menace, very difficult to express by ordinary methods of drawing.

Besides towels decorated with artistic sketches of this sort, there have been placed upon the market many kinds of towels bearing comic war pictures,—caricatures or cartoons which are amusing without being malignant. It will be remembered that at the time of the first attack made upon the Port Arthur squadron, several of the Russian officers were in the Dalny Theatre,—never dreaming that the Japanese would dare to strike the first blow. This incident has been made the subject of a towel design. At one end of the towel is a comic study of the faces of the Russians, delightedly watching the gyrations of a ballet dancer. At the other end is a study of the faces of the same commanders when they find, on returning to the port, only the masts of their battleships above water. Another towel shows a procession of fish in front of a surgeon's office—waiting their turns to be relieved of sundry bayonets, swords, revolvers, and rifles, which have stuck in their throats. A third towel picture represents a Russian diver examining, with a prodigious magnifying-glass, the holes made by torpedoes in the hull of a sunken cruiser. Comic verses or legends, in cursive text, are printed beside these pictures.

The great house of Mitsui, which placed the best of these designs on the market, also produced some beautiful souvenirs of the war, in the shape of *fukusa*. (A *fukusa* is an ornamental silk covering, or wrapper, put over presents sent to friends on certain occasions, and returned after the present has been received.) These are made of the heaviest and costliest silk, and inclosed within appropriately decorated covers. Upon one *fukusa* is a colored picture of the cruisers Nisshin and Kasuga, under full steam; and upon another has been printed, in beautiful Chinese characters, the full text of the Imperial Declaration of war.

But the strangest things that I have seen in this line of production were silk dresses for baby girls,—figured stuffs which, when looked at from a little distance, appeared incomparably pretty, owing to the masterly juxtaposition of tints and colors. On closer inspection the charming design proved to be composed entirely of war pictures,— or, rather, fragments of pictures, blended into one astonishing combination: naval battles; burning warships; submarine mines exploding; torpedo boats attacking; charges of Cossacks repulsed by Japanese infantry; artillery rushing into position; storming of forts; long lines of soldiery advancing through mist. Here were colors of blood and fire, tints of morning haze and evening glow, noon-blue and starred night-purple, sea-gray and field-green,—most wonderful thing ! . . . I suppose that the child of a military or naval officer might, without impropriety, be clad in such a robe. But then—the unspeakable pity of things!

The war toys are innumerable: I can attempt to mention only a few of the more remarkable kinds.

Japanese children play many sorts of card games, some

of which are old, others quite new. There are poetical card
games, for example, played with a pack of which each card
bears the text of a poem, or part of a poem; and the player
should be able to remember the name of the author of any
quotation in the set. Then there are geographical card
games, in which each of the cards used bears the name, and
perhaps a little picture, of some famous site, town, or temple; and the player should be able to remember the district
and province in which the mentioned place is situated. The
latest novelty in this line is a pack of cards with pictures
upon them of the Russian war vessels; and the player
should be able to state what has become of every vessel
named,—whether sunk, disabled, or confined in Port
Arthur.

There is another card game in which the battleships,
cruisers, and torpedo craft of both Japan and Russia are
represented. The winner in this game destroys his "cap-
tures" by tearing the cards taken. But the shops keep pack-
ages of each class of warship cards in stock; and when all
the destroyers or cruisers of one country have been put *hors
de combat,* the defeated party can purchase new vessels
abroad. One torpedo boat costs about one farthing; but
five torpedo boats can be bought for a penny.

The toy-shops are crammed with models of battleships,—in wood, clay, porcelain, lead, and tin,—of many
sizes and prices. Some of the larger ones, moved by clock-
work, are named after Japanese battleships: Shikishima,
Fuji, Mikasa. One mechanical toy represents the sinking of
a Russian vessel by a Japanese torpedo boat. Among cheap-
er things of this class is a box of colored sand, for the rep-
resentation of naval engagements. Children arrange the
sand so as to resemble waves; and with each box of sand are
sold two fleets of tiny leaden vessels. The Japanese ships are
white, and the Russian black; and explosions of torpedoes
are to be figured by small cuttings of vermilion paper,
planted in the sand.

The children of the poorest classes make their own war toys; and I have been wondering whether those ancient feudal laws (translated by Professor Wigmore), which fixed the cost and quality of toys to be given to children, did not help to develop that ingenuity which the little folk display. Recently I saw a group of children in our neighborhood playing at the siege of Port Arthur, with fleets improvised out of scraps of wood and some rusty nails. A tub of water represented Port Arthur. Battleships were figured by bits of plank, into which chop-sticks had been fixed to represent masts, and rolls of paper to represent funnels. Little flags, appropriately colored, were fastened to the masts with rice paste. Torpedo boats were imaged by splinters, into each of which a short thick nail had been planted to indicate a smokestack. Stationary submarine mines were represented by small squares of wood, each having one long nail driven into it; and these little things, when dropped into water with the nail head downwards, would keep up a curious bobbing motion for a long time. Other squares of wood, having clusters of short nails driven into them, represented floating mines: and the mimic battleships were made to drag for these, with lines of thread. The pictures in the Japanese papers had doubtless helped the children to imagine the events of the war with tolerable accuracy.

Naval caps for children have become, of course, more in vogue than ever before. Some of the caps bear, in Chinese characters of burnished metal, the name of a battleship, or the words *Nippon Teikoku* (Empire of Japan),—disposed like the characters upon the cap of a blue-jacket. On some caps, however, the ship's name appears in English letters,— Yashima, Fuji, etc.

The play-impulse, I had almost forgotten to say, is shared by the soldiers themselves,—though most of those called to the front do not expect to return in the body. They ask only to be remembered at the Spirit Invoking

Shrine *(Shōkonsha),* where the shades of all who die for
Emperor and country are believed to gather. The men of
the regiments temporarily quartered in our suburb, on
their way to the war, found time to play at mimic war with
the small folk of the neighborhood. (At all times Japanese
soldiers are very kind to children; and the children here
march with them, join in their military songs, and correctly salute their officers, feeling sure that the gravest officer
will return the salute of a little child.) When the last regi-
ment went away, the men distributed toys among the children assembled at the station to give them a parting
cheer,—hairpins, with military symbols for ornament to
the girls; wooden infantry and tin cavalry to the boys. The
oddest present was a small clay model of a Russian soldier's
head, presented with the jocose promise: "If we come back,
we shall bring you some real ones." In the top of the head
there is a small wire loop, to which a rubber string can be
attached. At the time of the war with China, little clay
models of Chinese heads, with very long queues, were
favorite toys.

The war has also suggested a variety of new designs for
that charming object, the *toko-niwa.* Few of my readers
know what a *toko-niwa,* or "alcove-garden," is. It is a miniature garden—perhaps less than two feet square—contrived
within an ornamental shallow basin of porcelain or other
material, and placed in the alcove of a guest-room by way
of decoration. You may see there a tiny pond; a streamlet
crossed by humped bridges of Chinese pattern; dwarf trees
forming a grove, and shading the model of a Shinto temple; imitations in baked clay of stone lanterns,—perhaps
even the appearance of a hamlet of thatched cottages. If the
toko-niwa be not too small, you may see real fish swimming
in the pond, or a pet tortoise crawling among the rock-
work. Sometimes the miniature garden represents Hōrai,
and the palace of the Dragon-King.

Two new varieties have come into fashion. One is a

model of Port Arthur, showing the harbor and the forts; and with the materials for the display there is sold a little map, showing how to place certain tiny battleships, representing the imprisoned and the investing fleets. The other *toko-niwa* represents a Korean or Chinese landscape, with hill ranges and rivers and woods; and the appearance of a battle is created by masses of toy soldiers—cavalry, infantry, and artillery—in all positions of attack and defense. Minute forts of baked clay, bristling with cannon about the size of small pins, occupy elevated positions. When properly arranged the effect is panoramic. The soldiers in the foreground are about an inch long; those a little farther away about half as long; and those upon the hills are no larger than flies.

But the most remarkable novelty of this sort yet produced is a kind of *toko-niwa* recently on display at a famous shop in Ginza. A label bearing the inscription, *Kaï-téï no Ikken* (View of the Ocean-Bed) sufficiently explained the design. The *suïbon,* or "water-tray," containing the display was half filled with rocks and sand so as to resemble a sea-bottom; and little fishes appeared swarming in the foreground. A little farther back, upon an elevation, stood Otohimé, the Dragon-King's daughter, surrounded by her maiden attendants, and gazing, with just the shadow of a smile, at two men in naval uniform who were shaking hands,—dead heroes of the war: Admiral Makaroff and Commander Hirosé! . . . These had esteemed each other in life; and it was a happy thought thus to represent their friendly meeting in the world of Spirits.

Though his name is perhaps unfamiliar to English readers, Commander Takeo Hirosé has become, deservedly, one of Japan's national heroes. On the 27th of March, during the second attempt made to block the entrance to Port Arthur, he was killed while endeavoring to help a comrade,—a comrade who had formerly saved him from death. For five years Hirosé had been a naval attaché at St.

Petersburg, and had made many friends in Russian naval
and military circles. From boyhood his life had been devoted to study and duty; and it was commonly said of him
that he had no particle of selfishness in his nature. Unlike
most of his brother officers, he remained unmarried,—
holding that no man who might be called on at any
moment to lay down his life for his country had a moral
right to marry. The only amusements in which he was ever
known to indulge were physical exercises; and he was
acknowledged one of the best *jūjutsu* (wrestlers) in the
empire. The heroism of his death, at the age of thirty-six,
had much less to do with the honors paid to his memory
than the self-denying heroism of his life.

Now his picture is in thousands of homes, and his name
is celebrated in every village. It is celebrated also by the
manufacture of various souvenirs, which are sold by myriads. For example, there is a new fashion in sleeve buttons,
called *Kinen-botan,* or "Commemoration-buttons." Each
button bears a miniature portrait of the commander, with
the inscription, *Shichi-shō hōkoku,* "Even in seven successive lives—for love of country." It is recorded that Hirosé
often cited, to friends who criticised his ascetic devotion to
duty, the famous utterance of Kusunoki Masashigé, who
declared, ere laying down his life for the Emperor Go-
Daigo, that he desired to die for his sovereign in seven successive existences.

But the highest honor paid to the memory of Hirosé is
of a sort now possible only in the East, though once possible also in the West, when the Greek or Roman patriot
hero might be raised, by the common love of his people, to
the place of the Immortals. . . . Wine-cups of porcelain
have been made, decorated with his portrait; and beneath
the portrait appears, in ideographs of gold, the inscription,
Gunshin Hirosé Chūsa. The character *"gun"* signifies war;
the character *"shin,"* a god,—either in the sense of *divus* or
deus, according to circumstances; and the Chinese text,
read in the Japanese way, is *Ikusa no Kami.* Whether that

stern and valiant spirit is really invoked by the millions
who believe that no brave soul is doomed to extinction, no
well-spent life laid down in vain, no heroism cast away, I
do not know. But, in any event, human affection and gratitude can go no farther than this; and it must be confessed
that Old Japan is still able to confer honors worth dying
for.

Boys and girls in all the children's schools are now
singing the Song of Hirosé Chūsa, which is a marching
song. The words and the music are published in a little
booklet, with a portrait of the late commander upon the
cover. Everywhere, and at all hours of the day, one hears
this song being sung:—

> *He whose every word and deed gave to men an exam-*
> *ple of what the war-folk of the Empire of Nippon*
> *should be,—Commander Hirosé: is he really dead?*

> *Though the body die, the spirit dies not. He who*
> *wished to be reborn seven times into this world, for the*
> *sake of serving his country, for the sake of requiting the*
> *Imperial favor,—Commander Hirosé: has he really*
> *died?*

> *"Since I am a son of the Country of the Gods, the fire*
> *of the evil-hearted Russians cannot touch me!"—The*
> *sturdy Takeo who spoke thus: can he really be dead?. . .*

> *Nay ! that glorious war-death meant undying fame;—*
> *beyond a thousand years the valiant heart shall live;—*
> *as to a god of war shall reverence be paid to him. . . .*

Observing the playful confidence of this wonderful people in their struggle for existence against the mightiest
power of the West,—their perfect trust in the wisdom of
their leaders and the valor of their armies,—the good

humor of their irony when mocking the enemy's blun-
ders,—their strange capacity to find, in the world-stirring
events of the hour, the same amusement that they would
find in watching a melodrama,—one is tempted to ask:
"What would be the moral consequence of a national
defeat?" . . . It would depend, I think, upon circumstances.
Were Kuropatkin able to fulfill his rash threat of invading
Japan, the nation would probably rise as one man. But otherwise the knowledge of any great disaster would be bravely borne. From time unknown Japan has been a land of cat-
aclysms,—earthquakes that ruin cities in the space of a
moment; tidal waves, two hundred miles long, sweeping
whole coast populations out of existence; floods submerg-
ing hundreds of leagues of well-tilled fields; eruptions
burying provinces. Calamities like this have disciplined the
race in resignation and in patience; and it has been well
trained also to bear with courage all the misfortunes of war.
Even by the foreign peoples that have been most closely in
contact with her, the capacities of Japan remained
unguessed. Perhaps her power to resist aggression is far surpassed by her power to endure.

Hōrai

Blue vision of depth lost in height,—sea and sky interblending through luminous haze. The day is of spring, and the hour morning.

Only sky and sea,—one azure enormity. . . . In the fore, ripples are catching a silvery light, and threads of foam are swirling anything save color: dim warm blue of water widening away to melt into blue of air. Horizon there is none: only distance soaring into space,—infinite concavity hollowing before you, and hugely arching above you,—the color deepening with the height. But far in the midway blue there hangs a faint, faint vision of palace towers, with high roofs horned and curved like moons,—some shadowing of splendor strange and old, illumined by a sunshine soft as memory.

. . . What I have thus been trying to describe is a kaké-mono,—that is to say, a Japanese painting on silk, suspended to the wall of my alcove;—and the name of it is SHINKIRŌ, which signifies "Mirage." But the shapes of the mirage are unmistakable. Those are the glimmering portals of Hōrai the blest; and those are the moony roofs of the

Palace of the Dragon-King;—and the fashion of them (though limned by a Japanese brush of to-day) is the fashion of things Chinese, twenty-one hundred years ago. . . .

Thus much is told of the place in the Chinese books of that time:—

> In Hōrai there is neither death nor pain; and there is no winter. The flowers in that place never fade, and the fruits never fail; and if a man taste of those fruits even but once, he can never again feel thirst or hunger. In Hōrai grow the enchanted plants *So-rin-shi,* and *Riku-gō-aoi,* and *Ban-kon-tō,* which heal all manner of sickness;—and there grows also the magical grass *Yō-shin-shi,* that quickens the dead; and the magical grass is watered by a fairy water of which a single drink confers perpetual youth. The people of Hōrai eat their rice out of very, very small bowls; but the rice never diminishes within those bowls,—however much of it be eaten,—until the eater desires no more. And the people of Hōrai drink their wine out of very, very small cups; but no man can empty one of those cups,—however stoutly he may drink,—until there comes upon him the pleasant drowsiness of intoxication.

All this and more is told in the legends of the time of the Shin dynasty. But that the people who wrote down those legends ever saw Hōrai, even in a mirage, is not believable. For really there are no enchanted fruits which leave the eater forever satisfied,—nor any magical grass which revives the dead,—nor any fountain of fairy water,—nor any bowls which never lack rice,—nor any cups which never lack wine. It is not true that sorrow and death never enter Hōrai;—neither is it true that there is not any winter. The winter in Hōrai is cold;—and winds then bite to the bone; and the heaping of snow is monstrous on the roofs of the Dragon-King.

Nevertheless there are wonderful things in Hōrai; and the most wonderful of all has not been mentioned by any Chinese writer. I mean the atmosphere of Hōrai. It is an atmosphere peculiar to the place; and, because of it, the sunshine in Hōrai is *whiter* than any other sunshine,—a milky light that never dazzles,—astonishingly clear, but very soft. This atmosphere is not of our human period; it is enormously old,—so old that I feel afraid when I try to think how old it is;—and it is not a mixture of nitrogen and oxygen. It is not made of air at all, but of ghost,—the substance of quintillions of quintillions of generations of souls blended into one immense translucency,—souls of people who thought in ways never resembling our ways. Whatever mortal man inhales that atmosphere, he takes into his blood the thrilling of these spirits; and they change the senses within him,—reshaping his notions of Space and Time,—so that he can see only as they used to see, and feel only as they used to feel, and think only as they used to think. Soft as sleep are these changes of sense; and Hōrai, discerned across them, might thus be described:—

> *—Because in Hōrai there is no knowledge of great evil, the hearts of people never grow old. And, by reason of always being young in heart, the people of Hōrai smile from birth until death—except when the Gods send sorrow among them; and faces then are veiled until the sorrow goes away. All folk in Hōrai love and trust each other, as if all were members of a single household;—and the speech of the women is like birdsong, because the hearts of them are light as the souls of birds;—and the swaying of the sleeves of the maidens at play seems a flutter of wide, soft wings. In Hōrai nothing is hidden but grief, because there is no reason for shame;—and nothing is locked away, because there could not be any*

*theft;—and by night as well as by day all doors remain
unbarred, because there is no reason for fear. And
because the people are fairies—though mortal—all
things in Hōrai, except the Palace of the Dragon-King,
are small and quaint and queer;—and these fairy-folk
do really eat their rice out of very small bowls and drink
their wine out of very, very small cups. . . .*

—Much of this seeming would be due to the inhalation
of that ghostly atmosphere—but not all. For the spell
wrought by the dead is only the charm of an Ideal, the
glamour of an ancient hope;—and something of that hope
has found fulfillment in many hearts,—in the simple beauty of unselfish lives,—in the sweetness of Woman. . . .

—Evil winds from the West are blowing over Hōrai;—
and the magical atmosphere, alas! is shrinking away before
them. It lingers now in patches only, and bands,—like
those long bright bands of cloud that trail across the landscapes of Japanese painters. Under these shreds of elfish
vapor you still can find Hōrai—but not elsewhere. . . .
Remember that Hōrai is also called Shinkirō, which signifies Mirage,—the Vision of the Intangible. And the Vision
is fading,—never again to appear save in pictures and
poems and dreams. . . .

PART TWO

⤫

The People

Early in 1893 Hearn wrote to Chamberlain concerning his cook: "My cook wears a smiling, healthy, rather pleasing face. He is a good-looking young man. Whenever I used to think of him I thought of the smile. . . . One day I looked through a little hole in the shoji and saw him alone. The face was not the same face. It was thin and drawn and showed queer lines worn by old hardship. I thought: 'He will look just like that when he is dead.' I went in and the man was all changed—young and happy again—nor have I ever seen that look of trouble in his face since. But I knew when he is alone he wears it. He never shows his real face to me; he wears the mask of happiness as an etiquette. . . ."

In cold Kumamoto, it was the real face that Hearn became interested in—the real face of the cook, the real face of Japan. Consequently, he wrote much less about landscape and general impressions; he wrote about particulars—particular people. Japan became much less a reflection of his own feelings; rather, he took as his own the feelings of the people he met.

In 1895—now in modern, Westernized Kobe—he wrote Chamberlain that it was a day when "I felt as if I hated Japan unspeakably, and the whole world seemed not worth living in, when there came two women to the house, to sell ballads. One took her samisen and sang; and people crowded into the tiny yard to hear. Never did I listen to anything sweeter. All the sorrow and beauty, all the pain and sweetness of life thrilled and quivered in that voice; and the old first love of Japan and of things Japanese came back, and a great tenderness seemed to fill the place like a haunting. I looked at the people, and I saw they were nearly all weeping and snuffing; and though I could not understand the words, I could feel the pathos and beauty of things. Then, too, for the first time, I noticed that the singer was blind. Both women were almost surprisingly ugly, but the voice of the one that sang was indescribably beautiful; and she sang as peasants and birds and semi sing, which is nature and is divine. They were wanderers both. I called them in, and treated them well, and heard their story. It was not romantic at all,—small-pox, blindness, a sick husband (paralyzed) and children to care for. I got two copies of the ballad, and enclose one. . . ."

Hearn was in Kobe because, the Kumamoto contract lapsed, he had to make a living and he had found a job writing editorials and occasional pieces for the *Kobe Chronicle.* It was an occupation for which he was temperamentally suited. He had been a journalist in various cities in the United States, and in Martinique as well, and in Japan he had learned how to make the casual article a vehicle of observation.

He had discovered that the Japanese form of the *zui-*

hitsu fitted his talent. Indeed, most of his pieces are just such "wanderings of the brush," usually carefully formless, informal excursions, a genre which in earlier writings sometimes lent itself to effusion and in later writings often to an impressionistic precision.

His *zuihitsu* "Bits of Life and Death," probably written in 1894, is a collection of observations of domestic life in Kumamoto. In a late Matsue piece, "On Women's Hair," description is personified in a lively manner.

These are followed by some of his portraits of women, both alive or long dead: "A Street Singer," "Kimiko," and "Yuko: A Reminiscence." After these, three small stories have been included: "On a Bridge," "The Case of O-Dai," and "Drifting," the last, one of Hearn's few adventure stories.

"Diplomacy" reflects the author's continued interest in the past, in the dead, and in ghosts—though with a sardonic quality not usually encountered. The full-fledged Hearn ghost story is seen in "A Passional Karma," one of his very finest but one not often reprinted, perhaps because of its length.

As Lafcadio's final word on the people he lived among, and as a summing up of this extraordinary experience, I include a chapter, "Survivals," from his last completed book, *Japan: An Attempt at Interpretation,* which indicates his belief in the survival of much he had known and loved—though in some other form.

The informal, *zuihitsu*-like essay fit Hearn's needs precisely because his methods were not suited to sustained writing—as the strained and laborious structure of his last book, his only treatment of a single subject at length, indicates. Hearn's vehicle was usually a single picture, or a reflection, or an impression of some sort.

Like many of his fellow *fin-de-siècle* artists in distant

Europe, Hearn was, indeed, an impressionist. This quality has been described by Earl Miner as a belief that
"truth is made up of varying perceptions and is relative
to the perceiver." Hearn was forced to rely on the perceptions and intuitions of impressionism both because
he had no other means and because it was his only way
of reaching his distant readers.

If he could render the impressions made by Japan
upon him, then he could create those same impressions
upon the reader. This is the method of artists as otherwise dissimilar as Flaubert (one of Hearn's enthusiasms)
and the much later Ernest Hemingway, and it was the
one that most suited Hearn's purposes.

These ("to create, in the minds, of the readers, a vivid
impression of living in Japan") were enforced by what
Hearn was at the time learning, as differentiated from
feeling. He became a student not only of fancy and folk-
lore but also of those elements upon which they are
based: religion and history. The longer he lived in the
country the more seriously he studied Buddhism, and
the closer he moved to that other, unreachable goal, so
confidently expressed before he had even come to
Japan—to become "as one taking part in the daily existence of the common people, and *thinking with their
thoughts.*"

In 1895 he made a big step in that direction by
becoming a Japanese citizen. His reasons were various,
and perhaps a more or less enthusiastic empathy was
among them. Yet, he already knew—and had written—
that the possibility of actually becoming one with the
Japanese was unlikely, and there were possibly other reasons as well.

One certainly was that he had a family to support. If
Setsuko became British (Hearn's actual nationality) she

would have to give up her legal rights including her land holdings. Even as the wife of a foreigner these were imperiled. So part of the reason behind the move was economic.

The result was Hearn as Japanese: Yakumo Koizumi—Setsuko's family name and a wonderfully fanciful given-name reference to beloved Matsue, the land of the eight clouds. This transformation was accompanied by a new job. Writing every day in Kobe had proved too much for the remaining eye and so the ever helpful Chamberlain found Hearn a position at the Tokyo Imperial University's College of Literature.

So there Hearn finally was—back in Tokyo. Setsuko was delighted, a country woman triumphantly in the capital, but to Lafcadio Tokyo was "the most horrible place in Japan." In fact, as he wrote Chamberlain, "there is no Japan in it," only "dirty shoes,—absurd fashions,—wickedly expensive living,—airs, vanities,—gossip."

In this horrible place he lived, first, in Ushigome, near a temple he much liked. After the authorities had cut down all of its beautiful trees to make room for modernization, he moved out to Nishi-Ogikubo, the suburbs mentioned in the 1904 "Letter." There he wrote his last books, quarreled with his friend and benefactor Chamberlain (over something so slight it is not even recorded), and became thoroughly disillusioned with the Tokyo Imperial University.

In 1903, when his contract was due for renewal, he was told that his pay was to be docked, that since he was now Japanese he would be paid as a Japanese. Indeed, he was not entitled to a foreigner's salary, but, in fact, the new president wanted to get rid of foreigners. Hearn later often repeated the "painful remark" this president had made to him: If he could not live upon the reduced salary, he should learn, like any other Japanese, to eat rice.

While this may seem only sensible to us, Hearn was of the generation that believed that the white man deserved a bit of respect. Though he disliked the imperialistic foreigner (another reason for leaving Kobe was that he found it was filled with little else), he himself embodied a number of such qualities.

To insist, as he early did, upon a picturesque country and a childlike people is to prepare the way for forces that will modernize the old, render practical the pretty, and form the simple people into something more economically profitable. Indeed, to Orientalize is to take advantage.

Hearn would have been horrified by this thought but there it is. And it is among the reasons that after the Pacific War Hearn's scholarly standing so declined. No postwar Japanologist could have quoted Hearn with approval. In addition, there was the idea that he was an amateur in a field fast becoming professional, that he had been popular—always anathema to academe—and that he was somehow a spokesman for a Japan which had been, after all, the enemy.

This latter is, of course, not true. Whatever else, even in his most smitten days, Hearn was never a spokesman for Japan. He always retained an independence of thought and this grew stronger the longer he lived in the country. Indeed, his is the first objective voice we hear above the clamor of the Orientalists seeking to love or to hate.

In his last completed book, *Japan: An Attempt at Interpretation,* Hearn attempted to sum up his experience and finally give a structure to his thoughts. It should not be surprising that these are largely metaphysical. Of the book's twenty-two chapters, thirteen deal with religion or subjects involved with traditional religious issues.

While the Japanese are actually one of the least notably religious of peoples (if one of the most superstitious) Hearn's traditionalism sits well because Japan is one of the countries most consumed with its past. While it cuts down old forests and knocks down venerable buildings it is also entirely concerned with its own Japaneseness and this is predicated upon its history. Hence what the West miscalls ancestor worship, hence the various appeals to Japanese authenticity, the *yamato-damashii,* the *yamato-kotoba*—these qualities the pursuit of which remains a national passion. Hence too the national regard for Yakumo Koizumi. Though the Tokyo Imperial University failed to appreciate him, later generations have taken this critical and honest man and turned him into the spokesman he never was.

Which perhaps led to the often heard opinion that Hearn died disillusioned with the country. This is not true. The final book, an attempt at interpretation, is no more critical and no more disillusioned than any of the writings after that wonderful year in Matsue. When he died he was satisfied—in the bosom of his family, his measured assessment of his adopted land safely sent to the publishers. He saw Japan fairly and clearly, his view now undisturbed by the vapors and passions of earlier years.

Of this early, sustaining vision of the Japanese he was to write in his final book: "Sooner or later, if you dwell long with them, your contentment will prove to have much in common with the happiness of dreams. You will never forget the dream—never: but it will lift at last."

But it did not lift to disillusion; rather it lifted, like a veil, to disclose a reality he had much earlier begun to discover, to reveal a people much like any other, and as different as any other. He reported what he saw. It is for this reason that we read him now.

Bits of Life and Death

I

July 25. Three extraordinary visits have been made to my house this week.

The first was that of the professional well-cleaners. For once every year all wells must be emptied and cleansed, lest the God of Wells, Suijin-Sama, be wroth. On this occasion I learned some things relating to Japanese wells and the tutelar deity of them, who has two names, being also called Mizuha-nome-no-mikoto.

Suijin-Sama protects all wells, keeping their water sweet and cool, provided that house-owners observe his laws of cleanliness, which are rigid. To those who break them sickness comes, and death. Rarely the god manifests himself, taking the form of a serpent. I have never seen any temple dedicated to him. But once each month a Shintō priest visits the homes of pious families having wells, and he repeats certain ancient prayers to the Well-God, and plants nobori, little paper flags, which are symbols, at the edge of the well. After the well has been cleaned, also, this is done. Then the first bucket of the new water must be drawn up by a man; for if a woman first draw water, the well will always thereafter remain muddy.

The god has little servants to help him in his work. These are the small fishes the Japanese call funa.[1] One or two funa are kept in every well, to clear the water of larvæ. When a well is cleaned, great care is taken of the little fish. It was on the occasion of the coming of the well-cleaners that I first learned of the existence of a pair of funa in my own well. They were placed in a tub of cool water while the well was refilling, and thereafter were replunged into their solitude.

The water of my well is clear and ice-cold. But now I can never drink of it without a thought of those two small white lives circling always in darkness, and startled through untold years by the descent of plashing buckets.

The second curious visit was that of the district firemen, in full costume, with their hand-engines. According to ancient custom, they make a round of all their district once a year during the dry spell, and throw water over the hot roofs, and receive some small perquisite from each wealthy householder. There is a belief that when it has not rained for a long time roofs may be ignited by the mere heat of the sun. The firemen played with their hose upon my roofs, trees, and garden, producing considerable refreshment; and in return I bestowed on them wherewith to buy saké.

The third visit was that of a deputation of children asking for some help to celebrate fittingly the festival of Jizō, who has a shrine on the other side of the street, exactly opposite my house. I was very glad to contribute to their fund, for I love the gentle god, and I knew the festival would be delightful. Early next morning, I saw that the shrine had already been decked with flowers and votive lanterns. A new bib had been put about Jizō's neck, and a Buddhist repast set before him. Later on, carpenters con-

structed a dancing-platform in the temple court for the
children to dance upon; and before sundown the toy-sell-
ers had erected and stocked a small street of booths inside
the precincts. After dark I went out into a great glory of
lantern fires to see the children dance; and I found,
perched before my gate, an enormous dragonfly more than
three feet long. It was a token of the children's gratitude for
the little help I had given them,—a kazari, a decoration. I
was startled for the moment by the realism of the thing;
but upon close examination I discovered that the body was
a pine branch wrapped with colored paper, the four wings
were four fire-shovels, and the gleaming head was a little
teapot. The whole was lighted by a candle so placed as to
make extraordinary shadows, which formed part of the
design. It was a wonderful instance of art sense working
without a speck of artistic material, yet it was all the labor
of a poor little child only eight years old!

II

July 30. The next house to mine, on the south side,—a
low, dingy structure,—is that of a dyer. You can always tell
where a Japanese dyer is by the long pieces of silk or cotton
stretched between bamboo poles before his door to dry in
the sun,—broad bands of rich azure, of purple, of rose, pale
blue, pearl gray. Yesterday my neighbor coaxed me to pay
the family a visit; and after having been led through the
front part of their little dwelling, I was surprised to find
myself looking from a rear veranda at a garden worthy of
some old Kyōto palace. There was a dainty landscape in
miniature, and a pond of clear water peopled by goldfish
having wonderfully compound tails.

When I had enjoyed this spectacle awhile, the dyer led
me to a small room fitted up as a Buddhist chapel. Though
everything had had to be made on a reduced scale, I did
not remember to have seen a more artistic display in any
temple. He told me it had cost him about fifteen hundred

yen. I did not understand how even that sum could have sufficed. There were three elaborately carven altars,—a triple blaze of gold lacquer-work; a number of charming Buddhist images; many exquisite vessels; an ebony reading-desk; a mokugyō;[2] two fine bells,—in short, all the paraphernalia of a temple in miniature. My host had studied at a Buddhist temple in his youth, and knew the sutras, of which he had all that are used by the Jōdo sect. He told me that he could celebrate any of the ordinary services. Daily, at a fixed hour, the whole family assembled in the chapel for prayers; and he generally read the Kyō for them. But on extraordinary occasions a Buddhist priest from the neighboring temple would come to officiate.

He told me a queer story about robbers. Dyers are peculiarly liable to be visited by robbers; partly by reason of the value of the silks intrusted to them, and also because the business is known to be lucrative. One evening the family were robbed. The master was out of the city; his old mother, his wife, and a female servant were the only persons in the house at the time. Three men, having their faces masked and carrying long swords, entered the door. One asked the servant whether any of the apprentices were still in the building; and she, hoping to frighten the invaders away, answered that the young men were all still at work. But the robbers were not disturbed by this assurance. One posted himself at the entrance, the other two strode into the sleeping-apartment. The women started up in alarm, and the wife asked, "Why do you wish to kill us?" He who seemed to be the leader answered, "We do not wish to kill you; we want money only. But if we do not get it, then it will be this"—striking his sword into the matting. The old mother said, "Be so kind as not to frighten my daughter-in-law, and I will give you whatever money there is in the house. But you ought to know there cannot be much, as my son has gone to Kyōto." She handed them the money-drawer and her own purse. There were just twenty-seven yen and eighty-four sen. The head robber counted it, and said, quite gently, "We do not want to frighten you. We know you are a very devout believer in Buddhism, and we think you would not tell a lie. Is this all?" "Yes, it is all," she answered. "I am, as you say, a believer in the teaching of the Buddha, and if you come to rob me now, I believe it is only because I myself, in some former life, once robbed you. This is my punishment for that fault and so, instead of wishing to deceive you, I feel grateful at this opportunity to atone for the wrong which I did to you in my previous state of existence." The robber laughed, and said, "You are a good old woman, and we believe you. If you were poor, we would not rob you at all. Now we only want a couple of kimono and this,"—laying his hand on a very fine silk overdress. The old woman replied, "All my son's kimono I can give you, but I beg you will not take that, for it does not belong to my son, and was confided to us only for dyeing. What is ours I can give, but I cannot give what belongs to another." "That is quite right," approved the robber, "and we shall not take it."

After receiving a few robes, the robbers said good-night, very politely, but ordered the women not to look after them. The old servant was still near the door. As the chief robber passed her, he said, "You told us a lie,—so take that!"—and struck her senseless. None of the robbers were ever caught.

III

August 29. When a body has been burned, according to the funeral rites of certain Buddhist sects, search is made among the ashes for a little bone called the Hotoke-San, or "Lord Buddha," popularly supposed to be a little bone of the throat. What bone it really is I do not know, never having had a chance to examine such a relic.

According to the shape of this little bone when found after the burning, the future condition of the dead may be predicted. Should the next state to which the soul is destined be one of happiness, the bone will have the form of a small image of Buddha. But if the next birth is to be unhappy, then the bone will have either an ugly shape, or no shape at all.

A little boy, the son of a neighboring tobacconist, died the night before last, and to-day the corpse was burned. The little bone left over from the burning was discovered to have the form of three Buddhas,—San-Tai,—which may have afforded some spiritual consolation to the bereaved parents.[3]

IV

September 13. A letter from Matsue, Izumo, tells me that the old man who used to supply me with pipestems is dead. (A Japanese pipe, you must know, consists of three pieces, usually,—a metal bowl large enough to hold a pea, a metal mouthpiece, and a bamboo stem which is renewed at regular intervals.) He used to stain his pipestems very prettily: some looked like porcupine quills, and some like cylinders of snakeskin. He lived in a queer narrow little street at the verge of the city. I know the street because in it there is a famous statue of Jizō called Shiroko-Jizō,— "White-Child-Jizō,"—which I once went to see. They whiten its face, like the face of a dancing-girl, for some reason which I have never been able to find out.

The old man had a daughter, O-Masu, about whom a story is told. O-Masu is still alive. She has been a happy wife for many years; but she is dumb. Long ago, an angry mob sacked and destroyed the dwelling and the storehouses of a rice speculator in the city. His money, including a quantity of gold coin *(koban),* was scattered through the street. The rioters—rude, honest peasants—did not want it: they wished to destroy, not to steal. But O-Masu's father, the same evening, picked up a koban from the mud, and took it home. Later on a neighbor denounced him, and secured his arrest. The judge before whom he was summoned tried to obtain certain evidence by cross-questioning O-Masu, then a shy girl of fifteen. She felt that if she continued to answer she would be made, in spite of herself, to give testimony unfavorable to her father; that she was in the presence of a trained inquisitor, capable, without effort, of forcing her to acknowledge everything she knew. She ceased to speak, and a stream of blood gushed from her mouth. She had silenced herself forever by simply biting off her tongue. Her father was acquitted. A merchant who admired the act demanded her in marriage, and supported her father in his old age.

V

October 10. There is said to be one day—only one—in the life of a child during which it can remember and speak of its former birth.

On the very day that it becomes exactly two years old, the child is taken by its mother into the most quiet part of the house, and is placed in a *mi,* or rice-winnowing basket. The child sits down in the mi. Then the mother says, calling the child by name, *"Omae no zensé wa, nande attakane?—iute, gōran."*[4] Then the child always answers in one word. For some mysterious reason, no more lengthy reply is ever given. Often the answer is so enigmatic that some priest or fortune-teller must be asked to interpret it. For instance, yesterday, the little son of a coppersmith living near us answered only "Umé" to the magical question. Now umé might mean a plum-flower, a plum, or a girl's name,—"Flower-of-the-Plum." Could it mean that the boy remembered having been a girl? Or that he had been a plum-tree? "Souls of men do not enter plum-trees," said a neighbor. A fortune-teller this morning declared, on being questioned about the riddle, that the boy had probably been a scholar, poet, or statesman, because the plum-tree is the symbol of Tenjin, patron of scholars, statesmen, and men of letters.

VI

November 17. An astonishing book might be written about those things in Japanese life which no foreigner can understand. Such a book should include the study of certain rare but terrible results of anger.

As a national rule, the Japanese seldom allow themselves to show anger. Even among the common classes, any serious menace is apt to take the form of a smiling assurance that your favor shall be remembered, and that its recipient is grateful. (Do not suppose, however, that this is ironical, in our sense of the word: it is only euphemistic,—ugly things not being called by their real names.) But this smiling assurance may possibly mean death. When vengeance comes, it comes unexpectedly. Neither distance nor time, within the empire, can offer any obstacles to the avenger who can walk fifty miles a day, whose whole baggage can be tied up in a very small towel, and whose patience is almost infinite. He may choose a knife, but is much more likely to use a sword,—a Japanese sword. This, in Japanese hands, is the deadliest of weapons; and the killing of ten or twelve persons by one angry man may occupy less than a minute. It does not often happen that the murderer thinks of trying to escape. Ancient custom requires that, having taken another life, he should take his own; wherefore to fall into the hands of the police would be to disgrace his name. He has made his preparations beforehand, written his letters, arranged for his funeral, perhaps—as in one appalling instance last year—even chiseled his own tombstone. Having fully accomplished his revenge, he kills himself.

There has just occurred, not far from the city, at the village called Sugikamimura, one of those tragedies which are difficult to understand. The chief actors were, Narumatsu

Ichirō, a young shopkeeper; his wife, O-Noto, twenty years of age, to whom he had been married only a year; and O-Noto's maternal uncle, one Sugimoto Kasaku, a man of violent temper, who had once been in prison. The tragedy was in four acts.

ACT I. *Scene: Interior of public bathhouse. Sugimoto Kasaku in the bath. Enter Narumatsu Ichirō, who strips, gets into the smoking water without noticing his relative, and cries out,—*

"*Aa!* as if one should be in Jigoku, so hot this water is!"

(The word "Jigoku" signifies the Buddhist hell; but, in common parlance, it also signifies a prison,—this time an unfortunate coincidence.)

Kasaku (terribly angry). "A raw baby, you, to seek a hard quarrel! What do you not like?"

Ichirō (surprised and alarmed, but rallying against the tone of Kasaku). "Nay! What? That I said need not by you be explained. Though I said the water was hot, your help to make it hotter was not asked."

Kasaku (now dangerous). "Though for my own fault, not once, but twice in the hell of prison I had been, what should there be wonderful in it? Either an idiot child or a low scoundrel you must be!"

(Each eyes the other for a spring, but each hesitates, although things no Japanese should suffer himself to say have been said. They are too evenly matched, the old and the young.)

Kasaku (growing cooler as Ichirō becomes angrier). "A child, a raw child, to quarrel with me! What should a baby do with a wife? Your wife is my blood, mine,—the blood of the man from hell! Give her back to my house."

Ichirō (desperately, now fully assured Kasaku is physically

the better man). "Return my wife? You say to
return her? Right quickly shall she be returned, at
once!"

So far everything is clear enough. Then Ichirō hurries
home, caresses his wife, assures her of his love, tells her all,
and sends her, not to Kasaku's house, but to that of her
brother. Two days later, a little after dark, O-Noto is called
to the door by her husband, and the two disappear in the
night.

Act II. *Night scene. House of Kasaku closed: light appears
through chinks of sliding shutters. Shadow of a woman
approaches. Sound of knocking. Shutters slide back.*

Wife of Kasaku (recognizing O-Noto). "*Aa! aa!* Joyful it is
     to see you! Deign to enter, and some honorable tea
     to take."
O-Noto (speaking very sweetly). "Thanks indeed. But
     where is Kasaku San?"
Wife of Kasaku. "To the other village he has gone, but must
     soon return. Deign to come in and wait for him."
O-Noto (still more sweetly). "Very great thanks. A little,
     and I come. But first I must tell my brother."

*(Bows, and slips off into the darkness, and becomes a shad-
ow again, which joins another shadow. The two shadows
remain motionless.)*

Act III. *Scene: Bank of a river at night, fringed by pines.
Silhouette of the house of Kasaku far away. O-Noto and Ichirō
under the trees, Ichirō with a lantern. Both have white towels
tightly bound round their heads; their robes are girded well up,
and their sleeves caught back with tasuki cords, to leave the
arms free. Each carries a long sword.*

It is the hour, as the Japanese most expressively say,
"when the sound of the river is loudest." There is no other

sound but a long occasional humming of wind in the nee-
dles, of the pines; for it is late autumn, and the frogs are
silent. The two shadows do not speak, and the sound of the
river grows louder.

Suddenly there is the noise of a plash far off,—somebody crossing the shallow stream; then an echo of wooden
sandals,—irregular, staggering,—the footsteps of a drunkard, coming nearer and nearer. The drunkard lifts up his
voice: it is Kasaku's voice. He sings,—

> *"Suita okata ni suirarete;*
> *Ya-ton-ton!"*[5]

—a song of love and wine.

Immediately the two shadows start toward the singer at
a run,—a noiseless flitting, for their feet are shod with
waraji. Kasaku still sings. Suddenly a loose stone turns
under him; he wrenches his ankle, and utters a growl of
anger. Almost in the same instant a lantern is held close to
his face. Perhaps for thirty seconds it remains there. No one
speaks. The yellow light shows three strangely inexpressive
masks rather than visages. Kasaku sobers at once,—recognizing the faces, remembering the incident of the bath-
house, and seeing the swords. But he is not afraid, and
presently bursts into a mocking laugh.

"Hé! hé! The Ichirō pair! And so you take me, too, for a
baby? What are you doing with such things in your hands?
Let me show you how to use them."

But Ichirō, who has dropped the lantern, suddenly
delivers, with the full swing of both hands, a sword-slash
that nearly severs Kasaku's right arm from the shoulder;
and as the victim staggers, the sword of the woman cleaves
through his left shoulder. He falls with one fearful cry,
"Hitogoroshi!" which means "murder." But he does not cry
again. For ten whole minutes the swords are busy with
him. The lantern, still glowing, lights the ghastliness. Two
belated pedestrians approach, hear, see, drop their wooden

sandals from their feet, and flee back into the darkness without a word. Ichirō and O-Noto sit down by the lantern to take breath, for the work was hard.

The son of Kasaku, a boy of fourteen, comes running to find his father. He has heard the song, then the cry; but he has not yet learned fear. The two suffer him to approach. As he nears O-Noto, the woman seizes him, flings him down, twists his slender arms under her knees, and clutches the sword. But Ichirō, still panting, cries, "No! no! Not the boy! He did us no wrong!" O-Noto releases him. He is too stupefied to move. She slaps his face terribly, crying, "Go!" He runs,—not daring to shriek.

Ichirō and O-Noto leave the chopped mass, walk to the house of Kasaku, and call loudly. There is no reply;—only the pathetic, crouching silence of women and children waiting death. But they are bidden not to fear. Then Ichirō cries:—

"Honorable funeral prepare! Kasaku by my hand is now dead!"

"And by mine!" shrills O-Noto.

Then the footsteps recede.

ACT IV. *Scene: Interior of Ichirō's house. Three persons kneeling in the guest-room: Ichirō, his wife, and an aged woman, who is weeping.*

Ichirō. "And now, mother, to leave you alone in this world, though you have no other son, is indeed an evil thing. I can only pray your forgiveness. But my uncle will always care for you, and to his house you must go at once, since it is time we two should die. No common, vulgar death shall we have, but an elegant, splendid death,— *Rippana!* And you must not see it. Now go."

She passes away, with a wail. The doors are solidly barred behind her. All is ready.

O-Noto thrusts the point of the sword into her throat.

But she still struggles. With a last kind word Ichirō ends her pain by a stroke that severs the head.

And then?

Then he takes his writing-box, prepares the inkstone, grinds some ink, chooses a good brush, and, on carefully selected paper, composes five poems, of which this is the last:—

> *"Meido yori*
> *Yu dempō ga*
> *Aru naraba,*
> *Hayaku an chaku*
> *Mōshi okuran.*[6]

Then he cuts his own throat perfectly well.

Now, it was clearly shown, during the official investigation of these facts, that Ichirō and his wife had been universally liked, and had been from their childhood noted for amiability.

The scientific problem of the origin of the Japanese has never yet been solved. But sometimes it seems to me that those who argue in favor of a partly Malay origin have some psychological evidence in their favor. Under the submissive sweetness of the gentlest Japanese woman—a sweetness of which the Occidental can scarcely form any idea—there exist possibilities of hardness absolutely inconceivable without ocular evidence. A thousand times she can forgive, can sacrifice herself in a thousand ways unutterably touching; but let one particular soul-nerve be stung, and fire shall forgive sooner than she. Then there may suddenly appear in that frail-seeming woman an incredible courage, an appalling, measured, tireless purpose of honest vengeance. Under all the amazing self-control and patience of the man there exists an adamantine something very dangerous to reach. Touch it wantonly, and there can be no pardon. But resentment is seldom likely to be excited by mere hazard. Motives are keenly judged. An error can be forgiven; deliberate malice never.

In the house of any rich family the guest is likely to be shown some of the heirlooms. Among these are almost sure to be certain articles belonging to those elaborate tea ceremonies peculiar to Japan. A pretty little box, perhaps, will be set before you. Opening it, you see only a beautiful silk bag, closed with a silk running-cord decked with tiny tassels. Very soft and choice the silk is, and elaborately figured. What marvel can be hidden under such a covering? You open the bag, and see within another bag, of a different quality of silk, but very fine. Open that, and lo! a third, which contains a fourth, which contains a fifth, which contains a sixth, which contains a seventh bag, which contains the strangest, roughest, hardest vessel of Chinese clay that you ever beheld. Yet it is not only curious but precious: it may be more than a thousand years old.

Even thus have centuries of the highest social culture wrapped the Japanese character about with many priceless soft coverings of courtesy, of delicacy, of patience, of sweetness, of moral sentiment. But underneath these charming multiple coverings there remains the primitive clay, hard as iron;—kneaded perhaps with all the mettle of the Mongol,—all the dangerous suppleness of the Malay.

VII

December 28. Beyond the high fence inclosing my garden in the rear rise the thatched roofs of some very small houses occupied by families of the poorest class. From one of these little dwellings there continually issues a sound of groaning,—the deep groaning of a man in pain. I have heard it for more than a week, both night and day, but latterly the sounds have been growing longer and louder, as if every breath were an agony. "Somebody there is very sick," says Manyemon, my old interpreter, with an expression of extreme sympathy.

The sounds have begun to make me nervous. I reply, rather brutally, "I think it would be better for all concerned if that somebody were dead."

Manyemon makes three times a quick, sudden gesture with both hands, as if to throw off the influence of my wicked words, mutters a little Buddhist prayer, and leaves me with a look of reproach. Then, conscience-stricken, I send a servant to inquire if the sick person has a doctor, and whether any aid can be given. Presently the servant returns with the information that a doctor is regularly attending the sufferer, and that nothing else can be done.

I notice, however, that, in spite of his cob-webby gestures, Manyemon's patient nerves have also become affected by those sounds. He has even confessed that he wants to stay in the little front room, near the street, so as to be away from them as far as possible. I can neither write nor read. My study being in the extreme rear, the groaning is there almost as audible as if the sick man were in the room itself. There is always in such utterances of suffering a certain ghastly timbre by which the intensity of the suffering can be estimated; and I keep asking myself, How can it be possible for the human being making those sounds by which I am tortured, to endure much longer?

It is a positive relief, later in the morning, to hear the moaning drowned by the beating of a little Buddhist drum in the sick man's room, and the chanting of the *Namu myō ho renge kyō* by a multitude of voices. Evidently there is a gathering of priests and relatives in the house. "Somebody is going to die," Manyemon says. And he also repeats the holy words of praise to the Lotus of the Good Law.

The chanting and the tapping of the drum continue for several hours. As they cease, the groaning is heard again. Every breath a groan! Toward evening it grows worse—horrible. Then it suddenly stops. There is a dead silence of

minutes. And then we hear a passionate burst of weeping,—the weeping of a woman,—and voices calling a
name. "Ah! somebody is dead!" Manyemon says.

We hold council. Manyemon has found out that the
people are miserably poor; and I, because my conscience
smites me, propose to send them the amount of the funeral expenses, a very small sum. Manyemon thinks I wish to
do this out of pure benevolence, and says pretty things. We
send the servant with a kind message, and instructions to
learn if possible the history of the dead man. I cannot help
suspecting some sort of tragedy; and a Japanese tragedy is
generally interesting.

December 29. As I had surmised, the story of the dead
man was worth learning. The family consisted of four,—
the father and mother, both very old and feeble, and two
sons. It was the eldest son, a man of thirty-four, who had
died. He had been sick for seven years. The younger brother, a kurumaya, had been the sole support of the whole
family. He had no vehicle of his own, but hired one, paying five sen a day for the use of it. Though strong and a
swift runner, he could earn little: there is in these days too
much competition for the business to be profitable. It
taxed all his powers to support his parents and his ailing
brother; nor could he have done it without unfailing self-
denial. He never indulged himself even to the extent of a
cup of saké; he remained unmarried; he lived only for his
filial and fraternal duty.

This was the story of the dead brother:

> When about twenty years of age, and following
> the occupation of a fish-seller, he had fallen in
> love with a pretty servant at an inn. The girl
> returned his affection. They pledged themselves to
> each other. But difficulties arose in the way of
> their marriage. The girl was pretty enough to have
> attracted the attention of a man of some means,

who demanded her hand in the customary way. She disliked him; but the conditions he was able to offer decided her parents in his favor. Despairing of union, the two lovers resolved to perform jōshi. Somewhere or other they met at night, renewed their pledge in wine, and bade farewell to the world. The young man then killed his sweetheart with one blow of a sword, and immediately afterward cut his own throat with the same weapon. But people rushed into the room before he had expired, took away the sword, sent for the police, and summoned a military surgeon from the garrison. The would-be suicide was removed to the hospital, skillfully nursed back to health, and after some months of convalescence was put on trial for murder.

What sentence was passed I could not fully learn. In those days, Japanese judges used a good deal of personal discretion when dealing with emotional crime; and their exercise of pity had not yet been restricted by codes framed upon Western models. Perhaps in this case they thought that to have survived a jōshi was in itself a severe punishment. Public opinion is less merciful, in such instances, than law. After a term of imprisonment the miserable man was allowed to return to his family, but was placed under perpetual police surveillance. The people shrank from him. He made the mistake of living on. Only his parents and brother remained to him. And soon he became a victim of unspeakable physical suffering; yet he clung to life.

The old wound in his throat, although treated at the time as skillfully as circumstances permitted, began to cause terrible pain. After its apparent healing, some slow cancerous growth commenced to spread from it, reaching into the breathing-passages above and below where the sword-blade had passed. The surgeon's knife, the torture of the cautery, could only delay the end. But the man lingered through seven years of continually increasing agony. There are dark beliefs about the results of betraying the dead,— of breaking the mutual promise to travel together to the Meido. Men said that the hand of the murdered girl always reopened the wound,—undid by night all that the surgeon could accomplish by day. For at night the pain invariably increased, becoming most terrible at the precise hour of the attempted shinjū!

Meanwhile, through abstemiousness and extraordinary self-denial, the family found means to pay for medicines, for attendance, and for more nourishing food than they themselves ever indulged in. They prolonged by all possible means the life that was their shame, their poverty, their burden. And now that death has taken away that burden, they weep!

Perhaps all of us learn to love that which we train ourselves to make sacrifices for, whatever pain it may cause. Indeed, the question might be asked whether we do not love most that which causes us most pain.

女
の
髪

Of Women's Hair

I

The hair of the younger daughter of the family is very long; and it is a spectacle of no small interest to see it dressed. It is dressed once in every three days; and the operation, which costs four sen, is acknowledged to require one hour. As a matter of fact it requires nearly two. The hairdresser *(kamiyui)* first sends her maiden apprentice, who cleans the hair, washes it, perfumes it, and combs it with extraordinary combs of at least five different kinds. So thoroughly is the hair cleansed that it remains for three days, or even four, immaculate beyond our Occidental conception of things. In the morning, during the dusting time, it is carefully covered with a handkerchief or a little blue towel; and the curious Japanese wooden pillow, which supports the neck, not the head, renders it possible to sleep at ease without disarranging the marvelous structure.[1]

After the apprentice has finished her part of the work, the hairdresser herself appears, and begins to build the coiffure. For this task she uses, besides the extraordinary vari-

ety of combs, fine loops of gilt thread or colored paper
twine, dainty bits of deliciously tinted crape-silk, delicate
steel springs, and curious little basket-shaped things over
which the hair is moulded into the required forms before
being fixed in place.

The kamiyui also brings razors with her; for the
Japanese girl is shaved,—cheeks, ears, brows, chin, even
nose! What is there to shave? Only that peachy floss which
is the velvet of the finest human but which Japanese taste
removes. There is, however, another use for the razor. All
maidens bear the signs of their maidenhood in the form of
a little round spot, about an inch in diameter, shaven clean
upon the very top of the head. This is only partially concealed by a band of hair brought back from the forehead
across it, and fastened to the back hair. The girl-baby's head
is totally shaved. When a few years old the little creature's
hair is allowed to grow except at the top of the head, where
a large tonsure is maintained. But the size of the tonsure
diminishes year by year, until it shrinks after childhood to
the small spot above described; and this, too, vanishes after
marriage, when a still more complicated fashion of wearing
the hair is adopted.

II

Such absolutely straight dark hair as that of most
Japanese women might seem, to Occidental ideas at least,
ill-suited to the highest possibilities of the art of the *coiffeuse.*[2] But the skill of the kamiyui has made it tractable to
every æsthetic whim. Ringlets, indeed, are unknown, and
curling irons. But what wonderful and beautiful shapes the
hair of the girl is made to assume: volutes, jets, whirls,
eddyings, foliations, each passing into the other blandly as
a linking of brush-strokes in the writing of a Chinese master! Far beyond the skill of the Parisian *coiffeuse* is the art of
the kamiyui. From the mythical era[3] of the race, Japanese
ingenuity has exhausted itself in the invention and the

improvement of pretty devices for the dressing of woman's hair; and probably there have never been so many beautiful fashions of wearing it in any other country as there have been in Japan. These have changed through the centuries; sometimes becoming wondrously intricate of design, sometimes exquisitely simple,—as in that gracious custom, recorded for us in so many quaint drawings, of allowing the long black tresses to flow unconfined below the waist.[4] But every mode of which we have any pictorial record had its own striking charm. Indian, Chinese, Malayan, Korean ideas of beauty found their way to the Land of the Gods, and were appropriated and transfigured by the finer native conceptions of comeliness. Buddhism, too, which so profoundly influenced all Japanese art and thought, may possibly have influenced fashions of wearing the hair; for its female divinities appear with the most beautiful coiffures. Notice the hair of a Kwannon or a Benten, and the tresses of the Tennin,—those angel-maidens who float in azure upon the ceilings of the great temples.

III

The particular attractiveness of the modern styles is the way in which the hair is made to serve as an elaborate nimbus for the features, giving delightful relief to whatever of fairness or sweetness the young face may possess. Then behind this charming black aureole is a riddle of graceful loopings and weavings whereof neither the beginning nor the ending can possibly be discerned. Only the kamiyui knows the key to that riddle. And the whole is held in place with curious ornamental combs, and shot through with long fine pins of gold, silver, nacre, transparent tortoise-shell, or lacquered wood, with cunningly carven heads.[5]

IV

Not less than fourteen different ways of dressing the hair

are practiced by the *coiffeuses* of Izumo; but doubtless in the capital, and in some of the larger cities of eastern Japan, the art is much more elaborately developed. The hairdressers *(kamiyui)* go from house to house to exercise their calling, visiting their clients upon fixed days at certain regular hours. The hair of little girls from seven to eight years old is in Matsue dressed usually after the style called O-tabako-bon, unless it be simply "banged." In the O-tabako-bon ("honorable smoking-box" style) the hair is cut to the length of about four inches all round except above the fore-head, where it is clipped a little shorter; and on the summit of the head it is allowed to grow longer and is gathered up into a peculiarly shaped knot, which justifies the curious name of the coiffure. As soon as the girl becomes old enough to go to a female public day-school, her hair is dressed in the pretty simple style called katsurashita, or per-haps in the new, ugly, semi-foreign "bundle style" called sokuhatsu, which has become the regulation fashion in boarding-schools. For the daughters of the poor, and even for most of those of the middle classes, the public-school period is rather brief; their studies usually cease a few years before they are marriageable, and girls marry very early in Japan. The maiden's first elaborate coiffure is arranged for her when she reaches the age of fourteen or fifteen, at ear-liest. From twelve to fourteen her hair is dressed in the fashion called Omoyedzuki; then the style is changed to the beautiful coiffure called jorōwage. There are various forms of this style, more or less complex. A couple of years later, the jorōwage yields place in the turn to the shinjōchō[6] ("new-butterfly" style), or the shimada, also called takawage. The shinjōchō style is common, is worn by women of various ages, and is not considered very genteel. The shimada, exquisitely elaborate, is; but the more respectable the family, the smaller the form of this coiffure; geisha and jorō wear a larger and loftier variety of it, which properly answers to the name takawage, or "high coiffure." Between eighteen and twenty years of age the maiden again exchanges this style for another termed Tenjingaeshi; between twenty and twenty-four years of age she adopts the style called mitsuwage, or the "triple coiffure" of three loops; and a somewhat similar but still more complicated coiffure, called mitsuwakudzushi is worn by young women of from twenty-five to twenty-eight. Up to that age every change in the fashion of wearing the hair has been in the direction of elaborateness and complexity. But after twenty-eight a Japanese woman is no longer considered young, and there is only one more coiffure for her,—the mochiriwage or bobai, the simple and rather ugly style adopted by old women.

But the girl who marries wears her hair in a fashion quite different from any of the preceding. The most beautiful, the most elaborate, and the most costly of all modes is the bride's coiffure, called hanayome, a word literally signifying "flower-wife." The structure is dainty as its name, and must be seen to be artistically appreciated. Afterwards the wife wears her hair in the styles called kumesa or maruwage, another name for which is katsuyama. The kumesa style is not genteel, and is the coiffure of the poor; the maruwage or katsuyama is refined. In former times the samurai women wore their hair in two particular styles: the maiden's coiffure was ichōgaeshi, and that of the married folk katahajishi. It is still possible to see in Matsue a few katahajishi coiffures.

V

The family kamiyui, O-Koto-San, the most skillful of her craft in Izumo, is a little woman of about thirty, still quite attractive. About her neck there are three soft-pretty lines, forming what connoisseurs of beauty term "the necklace of Venus." This is a rare charm; but it once nearly proved the ruin of Koto. The story is a curious one.

Koto had a rival at the beginning of her professional

career,—a woman of considerable skill as a *coiffeuse,* but of malignant disposition, named Jin. Jin gradually lost all her respectable custom, and little Koto became the fashionable hairdresser. But her old rival, filled with jealous hate, invented a wicked story about Koto, and the story found root in the rich soil of old Izumo superstition, and grew fantastically. The idea of it had been suggested to Jin's cunning mind by those three soft lines about Koto's neck. She declared that Koto had a "NUKE-KUBI."

What is a nuke-kubi? "Kubi" signifies either the neck or head. "Nukeru" means to creep, to skulk, to prowl, to slip away stealthily. To have a nuke-kubi is to have a head that detaches itself from the body, and prowls about at night—by itself.

Koto has been twice married, and her second match was a happy one. But her first husband caused her much trouble, and ran away from her at last, in company with some worthless woman. Nothing was ever heard of him afterward,—so that Jin thought it quite safe to invent a nightmare-story to account for his disappearance. She said that he abandoned Koto because, on awaking one night, he saw his young wife's head rise from the pillow, and her neck lengthen like a great white serpent, while the rest of her body remained motionless. He saw the head, supported by the ever lengthening neck, enter the farther apartment and drink all the oil in the lamps, and then return to the pillow slowly,—the neck simultaneously contracting. "Then he rose up and fled away from the house in great fear," said Jin.

As one story begets another, all sorts of queer rumors soon began to circulate about poor Koto. There was a tale that some police-officer, late at night saw a woman's head without a body, nibbling fruit from a tree overhanging some garden-wall; and that, knowing it to be a nuke-kubi, he struck it with the flat of his sword. It shrank away as swiftly as a bat flies but not before he had been able to recognize the face of the kamiyui. "Oh! it is quite true!" declared Jin, the morning after the alleged occurrence; "and if you don't believe it, send word to Koto that you want to see her. She can't go out: her face is all swelled up." Now the last statement was fact,—for Koto had a very severe toothache at that time,—and the fact helped the falsehood. And the story found its way to the local newspaper, which published it—only as a strange example of popular credulity; and Jin said, "Am I a teller of the truth? See, the paper has printed it!"

Wherefore crowds of curious people gathered before Koto's little house, and made her life such a burden to her that her husband had to watch her constantly to keep her from killing herself. Fortunately she had good friends in the family of the Governor, where she had been employed for years a *coiffeuse;* and the Governor, hearing of the wickedness, wrote a public denunciation of it, and set his name to it, and printed it. Now the people of Matsue reverenced their old samurai Governor as if he were a god, and believed his least word; and seeing what he had written, they became ashamed, and also denounced the lie and the liar; and the little hairdresser soon became more prosperous than before through popular sympathy.

Some of the most extraordinary beliefs of old days are kept alive in Izumo and elsewhere by what are called in America "traveling side-shows"; and the inexperienced foreigner could never imagine the possibilities of a Japanese side-show. On certain great holidays the showmen make their appearance, put up their ephemeral theatres of rush-matting and bamboos in some temple court, surfeit expectation by the most incredible surprises, and then vanish as suddenly as they came. The Skeleton of a Devil, the Claws of Goblin, and "a Rat as large as a sheep," were some of the least extraordinary displays which I saw. The Goblin's Claws were remarkably fine shark's teeth; the Devil's

Skeleton had belonged to an orangoutang,—all except the horns ingeniously attached to the skull; and the wondrous Rat I discovered to be a tame kangaroo. What I could not fully understand was the exhibition of a nuke-kubi, in which a young woman stretched her neck, apparently, to a length of about two feet, making ghastly faces during the performance.

VI

There are also some strange old superstitions about women's hair. The myth of Medusa has many a counterpart in Japanese folk-lore: the subject of such tales being always some wondrously beautiful girl, whose hair turns to snakes only at night, and who is discovered at last to be either a dragon or a dragon's daughter. But in ancient times it was believed that the hair of any young woman might, under certain trying circumstances, change into serpents. For instance: under the influence of long-suppressed jealousy.

There were many men of wealth who, in the days of Old Japan, kept their concubines (*mekaké* or *aishō*) under the same roof with their legitimate wives *(okusama).* And it is told that, although the severest patriarchal discipline might compel the mekaké and the okusama to live together in perfect seeming harmony by day, their secret hate would reveal itself by night in the transformation of their hair. The long black tresses of each would uncoil and hiss and strive to devour those of the other;—and even the mirrors of the sleepers would dash themselves together;—for, saith an ancient proverb, *kagami onna-no tamashii,*—"a Mirror is the Soul of a Woman."[7] And there is a famous tradition of one Kato Sayemon Shigenji, who beheld in the night the hair of his wife and the hair of his concubine changed into vipers, writhing together and hissing and biting. Then Kato Sayemon grieved much for that secret bitterness of hatred which thus existed through his fault; and he shaved his head and became a priest in the great Buddhist monastery of Koya-San, where he dwelt until the day of his death under the name of Karukaya.

VII

The hair of dead women is arranged in the manner called tabanegami, somewhat resembling the shimada extremely simplified, and without ornaments of any kind. The name tabanegami signifies hair tied into a bunch, like a sheaf of rice. This style must also be worn by women during the period of mourning.

Ghosts, nevertheless, are represented with hair loose and long, falling weirdly over the face. And no doubt because of the melancholy suggestiveness of its drooping branches, the willow is believed to be the favorite tree of ghosts. Thereunder, it is said, they mourn in the night, mingling their shadowy hair with the long disheveled tresses of the tree.

Tradition says that Ōkyo Maruyama was the first Japanese artist who drew a ghost. The Shogun, having invited him to his palace, said: "Make a picture of a ghost for me." Ōkyo promised to do so; but he was puzzled how to execute the order satisfactorily. A few days later, hearing that one of his aunts was very ill, he visited her. She was so emaciated that she looked like one already long dead. As he watched by her bedside, a ghastly inspiration came to him: he drew the fleshless face and long disheveled hair, and created from that hasty sketch a ghost that surpassed all the Shogun's expectations. Afterwards Ōkyo became very famous as a painter of ghosts.

Japanese ghosts are always represented as diaphanous, and preternaturally tall,—only the upper part of the figure being distinctly outlined, and the lower part fading utterly away. As the Japanese say, "a ghost has no feet:" its appearance is like an exhalation, which becomes visible only at a certain distance above the ground; and it wavers and lengthens and undulates in the conceptions of artists, like vapor moved by the wind. Occasionally phantom women figure in picture-books in the likeness of living women but these are not true ghosts. They are fox-women or other goblins; and their supernatural character is suggested by a peculiar expression of the eyes and a certain impossible elfish grace.

Little children in Japan, like little children in all countries, keenly enjoy the pleasure of fear; and they have many games in which such pleasure forms the chief attraction. Among these is O-bake-goto, or Ghost-play. Some nurse-girl or elder sister loosens her hair in front, so as to let it fall over her face, and pursue the little folk with moans and weird gestures, miming all the attitudes of the ghosts of the picture-books.

VIII

As the hair of the Japanese woman is her richest ornament, it is of all her possessions that which she would most suffer to lose; and in other days the man too manly to kill an erring wife deemed it vengeance enough to turn her away with all her hair shorn off. Only the greatest faith or the deepest love can prompt a woman to the voluntary sacrifice of her entire *chevelure,* though partial sacrifice, offerings of one or two long thick cuttings, may be seen suspended before many an Izumo shrine.

What faith can do in the way of such sacrifice, he best knows who has seen the great cables, woven of women's hair, that hang in the vast Hongwanji temple at Kyōto. And love is stronger than faith, though much less demonstrative. According to ancient custom a wife bereaved sacrifices a portion of her hair to be placed in the coffin of her husband, and buried with him. The quantity is not fixed: in the majority of cases it is very small, so that the appearance of the coiffure is thereby nowise affected. But she who resolves to remain forever loyal to the memory of the lost yields up all. With her own hand she cuts off her hair, and lays the whole glossy sacrifice—emblem of her youth and beauty—upon the knees of the dead.

It is never suffered to grow again.

門つけ

A Street Singer

A woman carrying a samisen, and accompanied by a little boy seven or eight years old, came to my house to sing. She wore the dress of a peasant, and a blue towel tied round her head. She was ugly; and her natural ugliness had been increased by a cruel attack of smallpox. The child carried a bundle of printed ballads.

Neighbors then began to crowd into my front yard,— mostly young mothers and nurse girls with babies on their backs, but old women and men likewise—the *inkyō* of the vicinity. Also the jinrikisha-men came from their stand at the next street-corner; and presently there was no more room within the gate.

The woman sat down on my doorstep, tuned her samisen, played a bar of accompaniment,—and a spell descended upon the people; and they stared at each other in smiling amazement.

For out of those ugly disfigured lips there gushed and rippled a miracle of a voice—young, deep, unutterably touching in its penetrating sweetness. "Woman or wood-fairy?" queried a bystander. Woman only,—but a very, very great artist. The way she handled her instrument might have astounded the most skillful geisha; but no such voice had ever been heard from any geisha, and no such song. She sang as only a peasant can sing,—with vocal rhythms learned, perhaps, from the cicadæ and the wild nightingales,—and with fractions and semi-fractions and demi-semi-fractions of tones never written down in the musical language of the West.

And as she sang, those who listened began to weep silently. I did not distinguish the words; but I felt the sorrow and the sweetness and the patience of the life of Japan pass with her voice into my heart,—plaintively seeking for something never there. A tenderness invisible seemed to gather and quiver about us; and sensations of places and of times forgotten came softly back, mingled with feelings ghostlier,—feelings not of any place or time in living memory.

Then I saw that the singer was blind.

When the song was finished, we coaxed the woman into the house, and questioned her. Once she had been fairly well to do, and had learned the samisen when a girl. The little boy was her son. Her husband was paralyzed. Her eyes had been destroyed by smallpox. But she was strong, and able to walk great distances. When the child became tired, she would carry him on her back. She could support the little one, as well as the bed-ridden husband, because whenever she sang the people cried and gave her coppers and food. . . . Such was her story. We gave her some money and a meal; and she went away, guided by her boy.

I bought a copy of the ballad, which was about a recent double suicide: *"The Sorrowful Ditty of Tamayoné and Takejirō,—composed by Takenaka Yoné of Number Fourteen of the Fourth Ward of Nippon-bashi in the South District of the City of Ōsaka."* It had evidently been printed from a wooden block; and there were two little pictures. One showed a girl and boy sorrowing together. The other—a sort of tail-piece—represented a writing-stand, a dying lamp, an open letter, incense burning in a cup, and a vase containing *shikimi*,—that sacred plant used in the Buddhist ceremony of making offerings to the dead. The queer cursive text, looking like shorthand written perpendicularly, yielded to translation only lines like these:—

"In the First Ward of Nichi-Hommachi, in far-famed Ōsaka—*O the sorrow of this tale of shinjū!*

"Tamayoné, aged nineteen,—to see her was to love her, for Takejirō, the young workman.

"For the time of two lives they exchange mutual vows— *O the sorrow of loving a courtezan!*

"On their arms they tattoo a Raindragon, and the character 'Bamboo'—thinking never of the troubles of life. . . .

"But he cannot pay the fifty-five yen for her freedom— *O the anguish of Takejirō's heart!*

"Both then vow to pass away together, since never in this world can they become husband and wife.

"Trusting to her comrades for incense and for flowers— *O the pity of their passing like the dew!*

"Tamayoné takes the wine-cup filled with water only, in which those about to die pledge each other. . . .

"O the tumult of the lovers' suicide!—O the pity of their lives thrown away!"

In short, there was nothing very unusual in the story, and nothing at all remarkable in the verse. All the wonder of the performance had been in the voice of the woman. But long after the singer had gone that voice seemed still to stay,—making within me a sense of sweetness and of sadness so strange that I could not but try to explain to myself the secret of those magical tones.

And I thought that which is hereafter set down:—

All song, all melody, all music, means only some evolution of the primitive natural utterance of feeling,—of that untaught speech of sorrow, joy, or passion, whose words are tones. Even as other tongues vary, so varies this language of tone combinations. Wherefore melodies which move us deeply have no significance to Japanese ears; and melodies that touch us not at all make powerful appeal to the emotion of a race whose soul-life differs from our own as blue differs from yellow. . . . Still, what is the reason of the deeper feelings evoked in me—an alien—by this Oriental chant that I could never even learn,—by this common song of a blind woman of the people? Surely that in the voice of the singer there were qualities able to make appeal to something larger than the sum of the experience of one race,— to something wide as human life, and ancient as the knowledge of good and evil.

One summer evening, twenty-five years ago, in a London park, I heard a girl say "Good-night" to somebody passing by. Nothing but those two little words,—"Good-night." Who she was I do not know: I never even saw her face; and I never heard that voice again. But still, after the passing of one hundred seasons, the memory of her "Good-night" brings a double thrill incomprehensible of pleasure and pain,—pain and pleasure, doubtless, not of me, not of my own existence, but of pre-existences and dead suns.

For that which makes the charm of a voice thus heard but once cannot be of this life. It is of lives innumerable and forgotten. Certainly there never have been two voices having precisely the same quality. But in the utterance of affection there is a tenderness of timbre common to the myriad million voices of all humanity. Inherited memory makes familiar to even the newly-born the meaning of this tone of caress. Inherited, no doubt, likewise, our knowledge of the tones of sympathy, of grief, of pity. And so the chant of a blind woman in this city of the Far East may revive in even a Western mind emotion deeper than individual being,—vague dumb pathos of forgotten sorrows,—

dim loving impulses of generations unremembered. The dead die never utterly. They sleep in the darkest cells of tired hearts and busy brains,—to be startled at rarest moments only by the echo of some voice that recalls their past.

Kimiko

Wasuraruru
Mi naran to omō
Kokoro koso
Wasuré nu yori mo
Omoi nari-keré.[1]

I

The name is on a paper-lantern at the entrance of a house in the Street of the Geisha.

Seen at night the street is one of the queerest in the world. It is narrow as a gangway; and the dark shining woodwork of the house fronts, all tightly closed,—each having a tiny sliding door with paper-panes that look just like frosted glass,—make you think of first-class passenger-cabins. Really the buildings are several stories high; but you do not observe this at once,—especially if there be no moon,—because only the lower stories are illuminated up to their awnings, above which all is darkness. The illumination is made by lamps behind the narrow paper-paned doors, and by the paper-lanterns hanging outside,—one at every door. You look down the street between two lines of these lanterns,—lines converging far-off into one motionless bar of yellow light. Some of the lanterns are egg-shaped, some cylindrical; others four-sided or six-sided; and Japanese characters are beautifully written upon them. The street is very quiet,—silent as a display of cabinet-work in some great exhibition after closing-time. This is because the inmates are mostly away,—attending banquets and other festivities. Their life is of the night.

The legend upon the first lantern to the left as you go south is *"Kinoya: uchi O-Kata;"* and that means The House of Gold wherein O-Kata dwells. The lantern to the right tells of the House of Nishimura, and of a girl Miyotsuru,—which name signifies The Stork Magnificently Existing. Next upon the left comes the House of Kajita;—and in that house are Kohana, the Flower-Bud, and Hinako, whose face is pretty as the face of a doll. Opposite is the House Nagaye, wherein live Kimika and Kimiko. . . . And this luminous double litany of names is half-a-mile long.

The inscription on the lantern of the last-named house reveals the relationship between Kimika and Kimiko,—and yet something more; for Kimiko is styled *Ni-dai-me,* an honorary untranslatable title which signifies that she is only Kimiko No. 2. Kimika is the teacher and mistress: she has educated two geisha, both named, or rather renamed by her, Kimiko; and this use of the same name twice is proof positive that the first Kimiko—*Ichi-dai-me*—must have been celebrated. The professional appellation borne by an unlucky or unsuccessful geisha is never given to her successor.

If you should ever have good and sufficient reason to enter the house,—pushing open that lantern-slide of a door which sets a gong-bell ringing to announce visits,—you might be able to see Kimika, provided her little troupe be not engaged for the evening. You would find her a very intelligent person, and well worth talking to. She can tell, when she pleases, the most remarkable stories,—real flesh-and-blood stories,—true stories of human nature. For the Street of the Geisha is full of traditions,—tragic, comic, melodramatic;—every house has its memories;—and Kimika knows them all. Some are very, very terrible; and some would make you laugh; and some would make you think. The story of the first Kimiko belongs to the last class. It is not one of the most extraordinary; but it is one of the least difficult for Western people to understand.

II

There is no more Ichi-dai-me Kimiko: she is only a remembrance. Kimika was quite young when she called that Kimiko her professional sister.

"An exceedingly wonderful girl," is what Kimika says of Kimiko. To win any renown in her profession, a geisha must be pretty or very clever; and the famous ones are usually both,—having been selected at a very early age by their trainers according to the promise of such qualities. Even the commoner class of singing-girls must have some charm in their best years,—if only that *beauté du diable* which inspired the Japanese proverb that even a devil is pretty at eighteen.[2] But Kimiko was much more than pretty. She was according to the Japanese ideal of beauty; and that standard is not reached by one woman in a hundred thousand. Also she was more than clever: she was accomplished. She composed very dainty poems,—could arrange flowers exquisitely, perform tea-ceremonies faultlessly, embroider, make silk mosaic: in short, she was genteel. And her first public appearance made a flutter in the fast world of Kyōto. It was evident that she could make almost any conquest she pleased, and that fortune was before her.

But it soon became evident, also, that she had been perfectly trained for her profession. She had been taught how to conduct herself under almost any possible circumstances; for what she could not have known Kimika knew everything about: the power of beauty, and the weakness of passion; the craft of promises and the worth of indifference; and all the folly and evil in the hearts of men. So Kimiko made few mistakes and shed few tears. By and by she proved to be, as Kimika wished,—slightly dangerous. So a lamp is to night-fliers: otherwise some of them would put it out. The duty of the lamp is to make pleasant things visible: it has no malice. Kimiko had no malice, and was not too dangerous. Anxious parents discovered that she did not want to enter into respectable families, nor even to lend herself to any serious romances. But she was not particularly merciful to that class of youths who sign documents with their own blood, and ask a dancing-girl to cut off the extreme end of the little finger of her left hand as a pledge of eternal affection. She was mischievous enough with them to cure them of their folly. Some rich folks who offered her lands and houses on condition of owning her, body and soul, found her less merciful. One proved generous enough to purchase her freedom unconditionally, at a price which made Kimika a rich woman; and Kimiko was grateful,—but she remained a geisha. She managed her rebuffs with too much tact to excite hate, and knew how to heal despairs in most cases. There were exceptions, of course. One old man, who thought life not worth living unless he could get Kimiko all to himself, invited her to a banquet one evening, and asked her to drink wine with him. But Kimika, accustomed to read faces, deftly substituted tea (which has precisely the same color) for Kimiko's wine, and so instinctively saved the girl's precious life,—for only ten minutes later the soul of the silly host was on its way to the Meido alone, and doubtless greatly disappointed. . . . After that night Kimika watched over Kimiko as a wild cat guards her kitten.

The kitten became a fashionable mania, a craze,—a delirium,—one of the great sights and sensations of the period. There is a foreign prince who remembers her name: he sent her a gift of diamonds which she never wore. Other presents in multitude she received from all who could afford the luxury of pleasing her; and to be in her good graces, even for a day, was the ambition of the "gilded youth." Nevertheless she allowed no one to imagine himself a special favorite, and refused to make any contracts for perpetual affection. To any protests on the subject she answered that she knew her place. Even respectable women spoke not unkindly of her,—because her name never figured in any story of family unhappiness. She really kept her place. Time seemed to make her more charming. Other geisha grew into fame, but no one was even classed with her. Some manufacturer secured the sole right to use her photograph for a label; and that label made a fortune for the firm.

But one day the startling news was abroad that Kimiko had at last shown a very soft heart. She had actually said good-by to Kimika, and had gone away with somebody able to give her all the pretty dresses she could wish for,— somebody eager to give her social position also, and to silence gossip about her naughty past,—somebody willing to die for her ten times over, and already half-dead for love of her. Kimika said that a fool had tried to kill himself because of Kimiko, and that Kimiko had taken pity on him, and nursed him back to foolishness. Taiko Hideyoshi had said that there were only two things in this world which he feared,—a fool and a dark night. Kimika had always been afraid of a fool; and a fool had taken Kimiko away. And she added, with not unselfish tears, that Kimiko would never come back to her: it was a case of love on both sides for the time of several existences.

Nevertheless, Kimika was only half right. She was very shrewd indeed; but she had never been able to see into certain private chambers in the soul of Kimiko. If she could have seen, she would have screamed for astonishment.

III

Between Kimiko and other geisha there was a difference of gentle blood. Before she took a professional name, her name was Ai, which, written with the proper character, means love. Written with another character the same word-sound signifies grief. The story of Ai was a story of both grief and love.

She had been nicely brought up. As a child she had been sent to a private school kept by an old samurai,—where the little girls squatted on cushions before little writing-tables twelve inches high, and where the teachers taught without salary. In these days when teachers get better salaries than civil-service officials, the teaching is not nearly so honest or so pleasant as it used to be. A servant always accompanied the child to and from the school-house, carrying her books, her writing-box, her kneeling cushion, and her little table.

Afterwards she attended an elementary public school. The first "modern" text-books had just been issued,—containing Japanese translations of English, German, and French stories about honor and duty and heroism, excellently chosen, and illustrated with tiny innocent pictures of Western people in costumes never of this world. Those dear pathetic little text-books are now curiosities: they have long been superseded by pretentious compilations much less lovingly and sensibly edited. Ai learned well. Once a year, at examination time, a great official would visit the school, and talk to the children as if they were all his own, and stroke each silky head as he distributed the prizes. He is now a retired statesman, and has doubtless forgotten Ai;—and in the schools of to-day nobody caresses little girls, or gives them prizes.

Then came those reconstructive changes by which families of rank were reduced to obscurity and poverty; and Ai had to leave school. Many great sorrows followed, till there remained to her only her mother and an infant sister. The mother and Ai could do little but weave; and by weaving alone they could not earn enough to live. House and lands first,—then, article by article, all things not necessary to existence—heirlooms, trinkets, costly robes, crested lac-quer-ware—passed cheaply to those whom misery makes rich, and whose wealth is called by the people *Namida no kane,*—"the Money of Tears." Help from the living was scanty,—for most of the samurai-families of kin were in like distress. But when there was nothing left to sell,—not even Ai's little school-books,—help was sought from the dead.

For it was remembered that the father of Ai's father had been buried with his sword, the gift of a daimyō; and that the mountings of the weapon were of gold. So the grave was opened, and the grand hilt of curious workmanship exchanged for a common one, and the ornaments of the lacquered sheath removed. But the good blade was not taken, because the warrior might need it. Ai saw his face as he sat erect in the great red-clay urn which served in lieu of coffin to the samurai of high rank when buried by the ancient rite. His features were still recognizable after all those years of sepulture; and he seemed to nod a grim assent to what had been done as his sword was given back to him.

At last the mother of Ai became too weak and ill to work at the loom; and the gold of the dead had been spent. Ai said:—"Mother, I know there is but one thing now to do. Let me be sold to the dancing-girls." The mother wept, and made no reply. Ai did not weep, but went out alone.

She remembered that in other days, when banquets were given in her father's house, and dancers served the wine, a free geisha named Kimika had often caressed her. She went straight to the house of Kimika. "I want you to buy me," said Ai;—"and I want a great deal of money." Kimika laughed, and petted her, and made her eat, and heard her story,—which was bravely told, without one tear. "My child," said Kimika, "I cannot give you a great deal of money; for I have very little. But this I can do:—I can

promise to support your mother. That will be better than
to give her much money for you,—because your mother,
my child, has been a great lady, and therefore cannot know
how to use money cunningly. Ask your honored mother to
sign the bond,—promising that you will stay with me till
you are twenty-four years old, or until such time as you can
pay me back. And what money I can now spare, take home
with you as a free gift."

Thus Ai became a geisha; and Kimika renamed her
Kimiko, and kept the pledge to maintain the mother and
the child-sister. The mother died before Kimiko became
famous; the little sister was put to school. Afterwards those
things already told came to pass.

The young man who had wanted to die for love of a
dancing-girl was worthy of better things. He was an only
son; and his parents, wealthy and titled people, were willing to make any sacrifice for him,—even that of accepting
a geisha for daughter-in-law. Moreover they were not altogether displeased with Kimiko, because of her sympathy
for their boy.

Before going away, Kimiko attended the wedding of her
young sister, Umé, who had just finished school. She was
good and pretty. Kimiko had made the match, and used
her wicked knowledge of men in making it. She chose a
very plain, honest, old-fashioned merchant,—a man who
could not have been bad, even if he tried. Umé did not
question the wisdom of her sister's choice, which time
proved fortunate.

IV

It was in the period of the fourth moon that Kimiko was
carried away to the home prepared for her,—a place in
which to forget all the unpleasant realities of life,—a sort of
fairy-palace lost in the charmed repose of great shadowy
silent high-walled gardens. Therein she might have felt as

one reborn, by reason of good deeds, into the realm of Hōrai, But the spring passed, and the summer came,—and Kimiko remained simply Kimiko. Three times she had contrived, for reasons unspoken, to put off the wedding-day.

In the period of the eighth moon, Kimiko ceased to be playful, and told her reasons very gently but very firmly:— "It is time that I should say what I have long delayed saying. For the sake of the mother who gave me life, and for the sake of my little sister, I have lived in hell. All that is past; but the scorch of the fire is upon me, and there is no power that can take it away. It is not for such as I to enter into an honored family,—nor to bear you a son,—nor to build up your house. . . . Suffer me to speak; for in the knowing of wrong I am very, very much wiser than you. . . . Never shall I be your wife to become your shame. I am your companion only, your play-fellow, your guest of an hour,—and this not for any gifts. When I shall be no longer with you—nay! certainly that day must come!—you will have clearer sight. I shall still be dear to you, but not in the same way as now—which is foolishness. You will remember these words out of my heart. Some true sweet lady will be chosen for you, to become the mother of your children. I shall see them; but the place of a wife I shall never take, and the joy of a mother I must never know. I am only your folly, my beloved,—an illusion, a dream, a shadow flitting across your life. Somewhat more in later time I may become, but a wife to you never,—neither in this existence nor in the next. Ask me again—and I go."

In the period of the tenth moon, and without any reason imaginable, Kimiko disappeared,—vanished,—utterly ceased to exist.

V

Nobody knew when or how or whither she had gone.

Even in the neighborhood of the home she had left, none
had seen her pass. At first it seemed that she must soon
return. Of all her beautiful and precious things—her robes,
her ornaments, her presents: a fortune in themselves—she
had taken nothing. But weeks passed without word or sign;
and it was feared that something terrible had befallen her.
Rivers were dragged, and wells were searched. Inquiries
were made by telegraph and by letter. Trusted servants were
sent to look for her. Rewards were offered for any news—
especially a reward to Kimika, who was really attached to
the girl, and would have been only too happy to find her
without any reward at all. But the mystery remained a mystery. Application to the authorities would have been useless: the fugitive had done no wrong, broken no law; and
the vast machinery of the imperial police-system was not to
be set in motion by the passionate whim of a boy. Months
grew into years; but neither Kimika, nor the little sister in
Kyōto, nor any one of the thousands who had known and
admired the beautiful dancer, ever saw Kimiko again.

But what she had foretold came true;—for time dries all
tears and quiets all longing; and even in Japan one does not
really try to die twice for the same despair. The lover of
Kimiko became wiser; and there was found for him a very
sweet person for wife, who gave him a son. And other years
passed; and there was happiness in the fairy-home where
Kimiko had once been.

There came to that home one morning, as if seeking
alms, a traveling nun; and the child, hearing her Buddhist
cry of *"Ha-i! ha-i!"* ran to the gate. And presently a house-
servant, bringing out the customary gift of rice, wondered
to see the nun caressing the child, and whispering to him.
Then the little one cried to the servant, "Let me give!"—
and the nun pleaded from under the veiling shadow of her
great straw hat: "Honorably allow the child to give me." So
the boy put the rice into the mendicant's bowl. Then she
thanked him, and asked:—"Now will you say again for me
the little word which I prayed you to tell your honored

father?" And the child lisped:—*"Father, one whom you will never see again in this world, says that her heart is glad because she has seen your son."*

The nun laughed softly, and caressed him again, and passed away swiftly; and the servant wondered more than ever, while the child ran to tell his father the words of the mendicant.

But the father's eyes dimmed as he heard the words, and he wept over his boy. For he, and only he, knew who had been at the gate,—and the sacrificial meaning of all that had been hidden.

Now he thinks much, but tells his thought to no one.

He knows that the space between sun and sun is less than the space between himself and the woman who loved him.

He knows it were vain to ask in what remote city, in what fantastic riddle of narrow nameless streets, in what obscure little temple known only to the poorest poor, she waits for the darkness before the Dawn of the Immeasurable Light,—when the Face of the Teacher will smile upon her,—when the Voice of the Teacher will say to her, in tones of sweetness deeper than ever came from human lover's lips:— *"O my daughter in the Law, thou hast practiced the perfect way; thou hast believed and understood the highest truth;—therefore come I now to meet and to welcome thee!"*

Yuko: A Reminiscence

Meiji, XXIV, 5. May, 1891

> Who shall find a valiant woman?—far and from the
> uttermost coasts is the price of her.—*Vulgate.*

"Tenshi-Sama go-shimpai." The Son of Heaven augustly
sorrows.

Strange stillness in the city, a solemnity as of public
mourning. Even itinerant venders utter their street cries in
a lower tone than is their wont. The theatres, usually
thronged from early morning until late into the night, are
all closed. Closed also every pleasure-resort, every show—
even the flower-displays. Closed likewise all the banquet-
halls. Not even the tinkle of a samisen can be heard in the
silent quarters of the geisha. There are no revelers in the
great inns; the guests talk in subdued voices. Even the faces
one sees upon the street have ceased to wear the habitual
smile; and placards announce the indefinite postponement
of banquets and entertainments.

Such public depression might follow the news of some great calamity or national peril,—a terrible earthquake, the destruction of the capital, a declaration of war. Yet there has been actually nothing of all this,—only the announcement that the Emperor sorrows; and in all the thousand cities of the land, the signs and tokens of public mourning are the same, expressing the deep sympathy of the nation with its sovereign.

And following at once upon this immense sympathy comes the universal spontaneous desire to repair the wrong, to make all possible compensation for the injury done. This manifests itself in countless ways mostly straight from the heart, and touching in their simplicity. From almost everywhere and everybody, letters and telegrams of condolence, and curious gifts, are forwarded to the Imperial guest. Rich and poor strip themselves of their most valued heirlooms, their most precious household treasures, to offer them to the wounded Prince. Innumerable messages also are being prepared to send to the Czar,—and all this by private individuals, spontaneously. A nice old merchant calls upon me to request that I should compose for him a telegram in French, expressing the profound grief of all the citizens for the attack upon the Czarevitch,—a telegram to the Emperor of all the Russias. I do the best I can for him, but protest my total inexperience in the wording of telegrams to high and mighty personages. "Oh! that will not matter," he makes answer; "we shall send it to the Japanese Minister at St. Petersburg: he will correct any mistakes as to form." I ask him if he is aware of the cost of such a message. He has correctly estimated it as something over one hundred yen, a very large sum for a small Matsue merchant to disburse.

Some grim old samurai show their feelings about the occurrence in a less gentle manner. The high official intrusted with the safety of the Czarevitch at Otsu receives, by express, a fine sword and a stern letter bidding him

prove his manhood and his regret like a samurai, by performing harakiri immediately.

For this people, like its own Shintō gods, has various
souls: it has its Nigi-mi-tama and its Ara-mi-tama, its
Gentle and its Rough Spirit. The Gentle Spirit seeks only
to make reparation; but the Rough Spirit demands expiation. And now through the darkening atmosphere of the
popular life, everywhere is felt the strange thrilling of these
opposing impulses, as of two electricities.

Far away in Kanagawa, in the dwelling of a wealthy family, there is a young girl, a serving-maid, named Yuko, a
samurai name of other days, signifying "valiant."

Forty millions are sorrowing, but she more than all the
rest. How and why no Western mind could fully know.
Her being is ruled by emotions and by impulses of which
we can guess the nature only in the vaguest possible way.
Something of the soul of a good Japanese girl we can know.
Love is there—potentially, very deep and still. Innocence
also, insusceptible of taint—that whose Buddhist symbol is
the lotus-flower. Sensitiveness likewise, delicate as the earliest snow of plum-blossoms. Fine scorn of death is there—
her samurai inheritance—hidden under a gentleness soft as
music. Religion is there, very real and very simple,—a faith
of the heart, holding the Buddhas and the Gods for friends,
and unafraid to ask them for anything of which Japanese
courtesy allows the asking. But these, and many other feelings, are supremely dominated by one emotion impossible
to express in any Western tongue—something for which
the word "loyalty" were an utterly dead rendering, something akin rather to that which we call mystical exaltation:
a sense of uttermost reverence and devotion to the Tenshi-
Sama. Now this is much more than any individual feeling.
It is the moral power and will undying of a ghostly multitude whose procession stretches back out of her life into
the absolute night of forgotten time. She herself is but a

spirit-chamber, haunted by a past utterly unlike our own,—a past in which, through centuries uncounted, all lived and felt and thought as one, in ways which never were as our ways.

"Tenshi-Sama go-shimpai." A burning shock of desire to give was the instant response of the girl's heart—desire overpowering, yet hopeless, since she owned nothing, unless the veriest trifle saved from her wages. But the longing remains, leaves her no rest. In the night she thinks; asks herself questions which the dead answer for her. "What can I give that the sorrow of the August may cease?" "Thyself," respond voices without sound. "But can I?" she queries wonderingly. "Thou hast no living parent," they reply; "neither does it belong to thee to make the offerings. Be thou our sacrifice. To give life for the August One is the highest duty, the highest joy." "And in what place?" she asks. "Saikyō," answer the silent voices; "in the gateway of those who by ancient custom should have died."

Dawn breaks; and Yuko rises to make obeisance to the sun. She fulfills her first morning duties; she requests and obtains leave of absence. Then she puts on her prettiest robe, her brightest girdle, her whitest tabi, that she may look worthy to give her life for the Tenshi-Sama. And in another hour she is journeying to Kyōto. From the train window she watches the gliding of the landscapes. Very sweet the day is;—all distances, blue-toned with drowsy vapors of spring, are good to look upon. She sees the loveliness of the land as her fathers saw it, but as no Western eyes can see it, save in the weird, queer charm of the old Japanese picture-books. She feels the delight of life, but dreams not at all of the possible future preciousness of that life for herself. No sorrow follows the thought that after her passing the world will remain as beautiful as before. No Buddhist melancholy weighs upon her: she trusts herself utterly to the ancient gods. They smile upon her from the dusk of their holy groves, from their immemorial shrines upon the backward fleeing hills. And one, perhaps, is with her: he who makes the grave seem fairer than the palace to those who fear not; he whom the people call Shinigami, the lord of death-desire. For her the future holds no blackness. Always she will see the rising of the holy Sun above the peaks, the smile of the Lady-Moon upon the waters, the eternal magic of the Seasons. She will haunt the places of beauty, beyond the folding of the mists, in the sleep of the cedar-shadows, through circling of innumerable years. She will know a subtler life, in the faint winds that stir the snow of the flowers of the cherry, in the laughter of playing waters, in every happy whisper of the vast green silences. But first she will greet her kindred, somewhere in shadowy halls awaiting her coming to say to her: *"Thou hast done well,—like a daughter of samurai. Enter, child! because of thee to-night we sup with the Gods!"*

It is daylight when the girl reaches Kyōto. She finds a lodging, and seeks the house of a skillful female hair-dresser.

"Please to make it very sharp," says Yuko, giving the kamiyui a very small razor (article indispensable of a lady's toilet); "and I shall wait here till it is ready." She unfolds a freshly bought newspaper and looks for the latest news from the capital; while the shop-folk gaze curiously, wondering at the serious pretty manner which forbids familiarity. Her face is placid like a child's; but old ghosts stir restlessly in her heart, as she reads again of the Imperial sorrow. "I also wish it were the hour," is her answering thought. "But we must wait." At last she receives the tiny blade in faultless order, pays the trifle asked, and returns to her inn.

There she writes two letters: a farewell to her brother, an irreproachable appeal to the high officials of the City of Emperors, praying that the Tenshi-Sama may be petitioned to cease from sorrowing, seeing that a young life, even though unworthy, has been given in voluntary expiation of the wrong.

When she goes out again it is that hour of heaviest darkness which precedes the dawn; and there is a silence as of cemeteries. Few and faint are the lamps; strangely loud the sound of her little geta. Only the stars look upon her.

Soon the deep gate of the Government edifice is before her. Into the hollow shadow she slips, whispers a prayer, and kneels. Then, according to ancient rule, she takes off her long under-girdle of strong soft silk, and with it binds her robes tightly about her, making the knot just above her knees. For no matter what might happen in the instant of blind agony, the daughter of a samurai must be found in death with limbs decently composed. And then, with steady precision, she makes in her throat a gash, out of which the blood leaps in a pulsing jet. A samurai girl does not blunder in these matters: she knows the place of the arteries and the veins.

At sunrise the police find her, quite cold, and the two letters, and a poor little purse containing five yen and a few sen (enough, she had hoped, for her burial); and they take her and all her small belongings away.

Then by lightning the story is told at once to a hundred cities.

The great newspapers of the capital receive it; and cynical journalists imagine vain things, and try to discover common motives for that sacrifice: a secret shame, a family sorrow, some disappointed love. But no; in all her simple life there had been nothing hidden, nothing weak, nothing unworthy; the bud of the lotus unfolded were less virgin. So the cynics write about her only noble things, befitting the daughter of a samurai.

The Son of Heaven hears, and knows how his people love him, and augustly ceases to mourn.

The Ministers hear, and whisper to one another, within the shadow of the Throne: "All else will change; but the heart of the nation will not change."

Nevertheless, for high reasons of State, the State pretends not to know.

On a Bridge

My old kurumaya, Heishichi, was taking me to a famous temple in the neighborhood of Kumamoto.

We came to a humped and venerable bridge over the Shirakawa; and I told Heishichi to halt on the bridge, so that I could enjoy the view for a moment. Under the summer sky, and steeped in a flood of sunshine electrically white, the colors of the land seemed almost unreally beautiful. Below us the shallow river laughed and gurgled over its bed of grey stones, overshadowed by verdure of a hundred tints. Before us the reddish white road alternately vanished and re-appeared as it wound away, through grove or hamlet, toward the high blue ring of peaks encircling the vast Plain of Higo. Behind us lay Kumamoto,—a far bluish confusion of myriad roofs;—only the fine grey lines of its castle showing sharp against the green of further wooded hills. . . . Seen from within, Kumamoto is a shabby place; but seen as I beheld it that summer day, it is a fairy-city, built out of mist and dreams. . . .

"Twenty-two years ago," said Heishichi, wiping his fore-

205

head—"no, twenty-three years ago,—I stood here, and saw the city burn."

"At night?" I queried.

"No," said the old man, "it was in the afternoon—a wet day. . . . They were fighting; and the city was on fire."

"Who were fighting?"

"The soldiers in the castle were fighting with the Satsuma men. We dug holes in the ground and sat in them, to escape the balls. The Satsuma men had cannons on the hill; and the soldiers in the castle were shooting at them over our heads. The whole city was burned."

"But how did you happen to be here?"

"I ran away. I ran as far as this bridge,—all by myself. I thought that I could get to my brother's farm—about seven miles from here. But they stopped me."

"Who stopped you?"

"Satsuma men,—I don't know who they were. As I got to the bridge I saw three peasants—I thought they were peasants—leaning over the railing: men wearing big straw hats and straw rain-cloaks and straw sandals. I spoke to them politely; and one of them turned his head round, and said to me, 'You stay here!' That was all he said: the others did not say anything. Then I saw that they were not peasants; and I was afraid."

"How did you know that they were not peasants?"

"They had long swords hidden under their rain-cloaks,—very long swords. They were very tall men. They leaned over the bridge, looking down into the river. I stood beside them,—just there, by the third post to the left, and did as they did. I knew that they would kill me if I moved from there. None of them spoke. And we four stood leaning over the railing for a long time."

"How long?"

"I do not know exactly—it must have been a long time. I saw the city burning. All that while none of the men spoke to me or looked at me: they kept their eyes upon the water. Then I heard a horse; and I saw a cavalry officer coming at a trot,—looking all about him as he came. . . ."

"From the city?"

"Yes,—along that road behind you. . . . The three men watched him from under their big straw hats; but they did not turn their heads;—they pretended to be looking down into the river. But, the moment that the horse got on the bridge, the three men turned and leaped;—and one caught the horse's bridle; and another gripped the officer's arm; and the third cut off his head—all in a moment. . . ."

"The officer's head?"

"Yes—he did not even have time to shout before his head was off. . . . I never saw any thing done so quickly. Not one of the three men uttered a word."

"And then?"

"Then they pitched the body over the railing into the river; and one of them struck the horse,—hard; and the horse ran away. . . ."

"Back to the town?"

"No—the horse was driven straight out over the bridge, into the country. . . . The head was not thrown into the river: one of the Satsuma men kept it—under his straw cloak. . . . Then all of us leaned over the railing, as before,—looking down. My knees were shaking. The three samurai did not speak a single word. I could not even hear them breathing. I was afraid to look at their faces;—I kept looking down into the river. . . . After a little while I heard another horse,—and my heart jumped so that I felt sick; and I looked up, and saw a cavalry-soldier coming along the road, riding very fast. No one stirred till he was on the bridge: then—in one second—his head was off! The body was thrown into the river, and the horse driven away— exactly as before. Three men were killed like that. Then the samurai left the bridge."

"Did you go with them?"

"No: they left immediately after having killed the third

man,—taking the heads with them;—and they paid no attention to me. I stayed on the bridge, afraid to move, until they were very far away. Then I ran back to the burning town;—I ran quick, quick! There I was told that the Satsuma troops were retreating. Soon afterwards, the army came from Tōkyō; and I was given some work: I carried straw sandals for the soldiers."

"Who were the men that you saw killed on the bridge?"

"I don't know."

"Did you never try to find out?"

"No," said Heishichi, again mopping his forehead: "I said nothing about the matter until many years after the war."

"But why?" I persisted.

Heishichi gave me one astonished look, smiled in a pitying way, and answered,—

"Because it would have been wrong;—it would have been ungrateful."

I felt properly rebuked.

And we resumed our journey.

The Case of O-Dai

I

O-Dai pushed aside the lamplet and the incense-cup and the water vessel on the Buddha-shelf, and opened the little shrine before which they had been placed. Within were the *ihai*, the mortuary tablets of her people,—five in all; and a gilded figure of the Bodhisattva Kwannon stood smiling behind them. The *ihai* of the grandparents occupied the left side; those of the parents the right; and between them was a smaller tablet, bearing the *kaimyo* of a child-brother with whom she used to play and quarrel, to laugh and cry, in other and happier years. Also the shrine contained a *makémono,* or scroll, inscribed with the spirit-names of many ancestors. Before that shrine, from her infancy, O-Dai had been wont to pray.

The tablets and the scroll signified more to her faith in former time—very much more—than remembrance of a father's affection and a mother's caress;—more than any remembrance of the ever-loving, ever-patient, ever-smiling

209

elders who had fostered her babyhood, carried her pick-aback to every temple-festival, invented her pleasures, consoled her small sorrows, and soothed her fretfulness with song;—more than the memory of the laughter and the tears, the cooing and the calling and the running of the dear and mischievous little brother;—more than all the traditions of the ancestors.

For those objects signified the actual viewless presence of the lost,—the haunting of invisible sympathy and tenderness,—the gladness and the grief of the dead in the joy and the sorrow of the living. When, in other time, at evening dusk, she was wont to kindle the lamplet before them, how often had she seen the tiny flame astir with a motion not its own!

Yet the *ihai* is even more than a token to pious fancy. Strange possibilities of transmutation, transubstantiation, belong to it. It serves as temporary body for the spirit between death and birth: each fibre of its incense-penetrated wood lives with a viewless life-potential. The will of the ghost may quicken it. Sometimes, through power of love, it changes to flesh and blood. By help of the *ihai* the buried mother returns to suckle her babe in the dark. By help of the *ihai,* the maid consumed upon the funeral pyre may return to wed her betrothed,—even to bless him with a son. By power of the *ihai,* the dead servant may come back from the dust of his rest to save his lord from ruin. Then, after love or loyalty has wrought its will, the personality vanishes;—the body again becomes, to outward seeming, only a tablet.

All this O-Dai ought to have known and remembered. Maybe she did; for she wept as she took the tablets and the scroll out of the shrine, and dropped them from a window into the river below. She did not dare to look after them, as the current whirled them away.

II

O-Dai had done this by order of two English mission-ary-women who, by various acts of seeming kindness, had persuaded her to become a Christian. (Converts are always commanded to bury or to cast away their ancestral tablets.) These missionary-women—the first ever seen in the province—had promised O-Dai, their only convert, an allowance of three *yen* a month, as assistant,—because she could read and write. By the toil of her hands she had never been able to earn more than two *yen* a month; and out of that sum she had to pay a rent of twenty five *sen* for the use of the upper floor of a little house, belonging to a dealer in second-hand goods. Thither, after the death of her parents, she had taken her loom, and the ancestral tablets. She had been obliged to work very hard indeed in order to live. But with three *yen* a month she could live very well; and the missionary women had a room for her. She did not think that the people would mind her change of religion.

As a matter of fact they did not much care. They did not know anything about Christianity, and did not want to know: they only laughed at the girl for being so foolish as to follow the ways of the foreign women. They regarded her as a dupe, and mocked her without malice. And they continued to laugh at her, good-humoredly enough, until the day when she was seen to throw the tablets into the river. Then they stopped laughing. They judged the act in itself, without discussing its motives. Their judgment was instantaneous, unanimous, and voiceless. They said no word of reproach to O-Dai. They merely ignored her exis-tence.

The moral resentment of a Japanese community is not always a hot resentment,—not the kind that quickly burns itself out. It may be cold. In the case of O-Dai it was cold and silent and heavy like a thickening of ice. No one uttered it. It was altogether spontaneous, instinctive. But the universal feeling might have been thus translated into speech:—

"Human society, in this most eastern East, has been held together from immemorial time by virtue of that cult which exacts the gratitude of the present to the past, the reverence of the living for the dead, the affection of the descendant for the ancestor. Far beyond the visible world extends the duty of the child to the parent, of the servant to the master, of the subject to the sovereign. Therefore do the dead preside in the family council, in the communal assembly, in the high seats of judgment, in the governing of cities, in the ruling of the land.

"Against the Virtue Supreme of Filial Piety,—against the religion of the Ancestors,—against all faith and gratitude and reverence and duty,—against the total moral experience of her race,—O-Dai has sinned the sin that cannot be forgiven. Therefore shall the people account her a creature impure,—less deserving of fellowship than the Éta,—less worthy of kindness than the dog in the street or the cat upon the roof; since even these, according to their feebler light, observe the common law of duty and affection.

"O-Dai has refused to her dead the word of thankfulness, the whisper of love, the reverence of a daughter. Therefore, now and forever, the living shall refuse to her the word of greeting, the common salutation, the kindly answer.

"O-Dai has mocked the memory of the father who begot her, the memory of the mother whose breasts she sucked, the memory of the elders who cherished her childhood, the memory of the little one who called her Sister. She has mocked at love: therefore all love shall be denied her, all offices of affection.

"To the spirit of the father who begot her, to the spirit of the mother who bore her, O-Dai has refused the shadow of a roof, and the vapor of food, and the offering of water. Even so to her shall be denied the shelter of a roof, and the gift of food, and the cup of refreshment.

"And even as she cast out the dead, the living shall cast her out. As a carcass shall she be in the way,—as the small carrion that none will turn to look upon, that none will bury, that none will pity, that none will speak for in prayer to the Gods and the Buddhas. As a *Gaki* [1] she shall be,—as a *Shōjiki-Gaki,*—seeking sustenance in refuse-heaps. Alive into hell shall she enter;—yet shall her hell remain the single hell, the solitary hell, the hell *Kodoku,* that spheres the spirit accurst in solitude of fire. . . ."

III

Unexpectedly the missionary-women informed O-Dai that she would have to take care of herself. Perhaps she had done her best; but she certainly had not been to them of any use whatever, and they required a capable assistant. Moreover they were going away for some time, and could not take her with them. Surely she could not have been so foolish as to think that they were going to give her three *yen* per month merely for being a Christian! . . .

O-Dai cried; and they advised her to be brave, and to walk in the paths of virtue. She said that she could not find employment: they told her that no industrious and honest person need ever want for work in this busy world. Then, in desperate terror, she told them truths which they could not understand, and energetically refused to believe. She spoke of a danger imminent; and they answered her with all the harshness of which they were capable,—believing that she had confessed herself utterly depraved. In this they were wrong. There was no atom of vice in the girl: an amiable weakness and a childish trustfulness were the worst of her faults. Really she needed help,—needed it quickly,—needed it terribly. But they could understand only that she wanted money; and that she had threatened to commit sin if she did not get it. They owed her nothing, as she had always been paid in advance; and they imagined excellent reasons for denying her further aid of any sort.

So they put her into the street. Already she had sold her loom. She had nothing more to sell except the single robe upon her back, and a few pair of useless *tabi,* or cleft stockings, which the missionary-women had obliged her to buy, because they thought that it was immodest for a young girl to be seen with naked feet. (They had also obliged her to twist her hair into a hideous back-knot, because the Japanese style of wearing the hair seemed to them ungodly.)

What becomes of the Japanese girl publicly convicted of offending against filial piety? What becomes of the English girl publicly convicted of unchastity? . . .

Of course, had she been strong, O-Dai might have filled her sleeves with stones, and thrown herself into the river,—which would have been an excellent thing to do under the circumstances. Or she might have cut her throat,—which is more respectable, as the act requires both nerve and skill. But, like most converts of her class, O-Dai was weak: the courage of the race had failed in her. She wanted still to see the sun; and she was not of the sturdy type able to wrestle with the earth for that privilege. Even after fully abjuring her errors, there was left but one road for her to travel.

Said the person who bought the body of O-Dai at a third of the price prayed for:—

"My business is an exceedingly shameful business. But even into this business no woman can be received who is known to have done the thing that you have done. If I were to take you into my house, no visitors would come; and the people would probably make trouble. Therefore to Ōsaka, where you are not known, you shall be sent; and the house in Ōsaka will pay the money. . . ."

So vanished forever O-Dai,—flung into the furnace of a city's lust. . . . Perhaps she existed only to furnish one example of facts that every foreign missionary ought to try to understand.

Drifting

A typhoon was coming; and I sat on the sea-wall in a great wind to look at the breakers; and old Amano Jinsuké sat beside me. Southeast all was black-blue gloom, except the sea, which had a strange and tawny color. Enormous surges were already towering in. A hundred yards away they crumbled over with thunder and earthquake, and sent their foam leaping and sheeting up the slope, to spring at our faces. After each long crash, the sound of the shingle retreating was exactly like the roar of a railway train at full speed. I told Amano Jinuské that it made me afraid; and he smiled.

"I swam for two nights and two days," he said, "in a sea worse than this. I was nineteen years old at the time. Out of a crew of eight, I was the only man saved.

"Our ship was called the *Fukuju Maru*;[1] —she was owned by Mayéda Jingorō, of this town. All of the crew but one were Yaidzu men. The captain was Saito Kichiyëmon,—a man more than sixty years of age: he lived in Jō-no-Koshi,—the street just behind us. There was another old man on board, called Nito Shōshichi, who lived in the Araya quarter. Then there was Terao Kankichi, forty-two years old: his brother Minosuké, a lad of sixteen, was also with us. The Terao folk lived in Araya. Then there was Saito Heikichi, thirty years old; and there was a man called Matsushirō;—he came from Suō, but had settled in Yaidzu. Washino Otokichi was another of the crew: he lived in Jō-no-Koshi, and was only twenty-one. I was the youngest on board,—excepting Terao Minosuké.

"We sailed from Yaidzu on the morning of the tenth day of the seventh month of Manyen Gwannen,[2] —the Year of the Ape,—bound for Sanuki. On the night of the eleventh, in the Kishū offing, we were caught by a typhoon from the southeast. A little before midnight, the ship capsized. As I felt her going over, I caught a plank, and threw it out, and jumped. It was blowing fearfully at the time; and the night was so dark that I could see only a few feet away; but I was lucky enough to find that plank, and put it under me. In another moment the ship was gone. Near me in the water were Washino Otokichi and the Terao brothers and the man Matsushirō,—all swimming. There was no sign of the rest: they probably went down with the ship. We five kept calling to each other as we went up and down with the great seas; and I found that every one except Terao Kankichi had a plank or a timber of some sort. I cried to Kankichi:—'Elder brother, you have children, and I am very young;—let me give you this plank!' He shouted back:—'In this sea a plank is dangerous!—keep away from timber, Jinyō!—you may get hurt!' Before I could answer him, a wave like a black mountain burst over us. I was a long time under; and when I came up again, there was no sign of Kankichi. The younger men were still swimming; but they had been swept away to the left of me;—I could not see them: we shouted to each other. I tried to keep with the waves—the others called to me:—'Jinyō! Jinyō!—come this way,—this way!' But I knew that to go in their direction would be very dangerous; for every time that a wave struck me sideways, I was taken under. So I called back to them, 'Keep with the tide!—keep with the current!' But they did not seem to understand;—and they still called to me, *'Kocchi é koi!—kocchi é koi!'* —and their voices each time sounded more and more far away. I became afraid to answer. . . . The drowned call to you like that when they want company: *Kocchi é koi!—kocchi é koi!* . . .

"After a little time the calling ceased; and I heard only the sea and the wind and the rain. It was so dark that one could see the waves only at the moment they went by,— high black shadows,—each with a great pull. By the pull of them I guessed how to direct myself. The rain kept them from breaking much;—had it not been for the rain, no man could have lived long in such a sea. And hour after hour the wind became worse, and the swells grew high-er;—and I prayed for help to Jizō-Sama of Ogawa all that night. . . . Lights?—yes, there were lights in the water, but not many: the large kind, that shine like candles. . . .

"At dawn the sea looked ugly,—a muddy green; and the waves were like hills; and the wind was terrible. Rain and spray made a fog over the water; and there was no horizon. But even if there had been land in sight I could have done nothing except try to keep afloat. I felt hungry,—very hun-gry; and the pain of the hunger soon became hard to bear. All that day I went up and down with the great waves,— drifting under the wind and the rain; and there was no sign of land. I did not know where I was going: under that sky one could not tell east from west.

"After dark the wind lulled; but the rain still poured, and all was black. The pain of the hunger passed; but I felt weak,—so weak that I thought I must go under. Then I heard the voices calling me,—just as they had called me the night before:—*'Kocchi é koi!—kocchi é koi!'* . . . And, all at once, I saw the four men of the *Fukuju Maru*,—not swim-ming, but standing by me,—Terao Kankichi, and Terao Minosuké, and Washino Otokichi, and the man Matsushirō. All looked at me with angry faces; and the boy

Minosuké cried out, as in reproach:—'Here I have to fix the helm; and you, Jinsuké, do nothing but sleep!' Then Terao Kankichi—the one to whom I had offered the plank—bent over me with a *kakémono* in his hands, and half-unrolled it, and said:—'Jinyō! here I have a picture of Amida Buddha—see! Now indeed you must repeat the *Nembutsu!*' He spoke strangely, in a way that made me afraid: I looked at the figure of the Buddha; and I repeated the prayer in great fear,—*Namu Amida Butsu!—namu Amida Butsu!*'[4] In the same moment a pain, like the pain of fire, stung through my thighs and hips; and I found that I had rolled off the plank into the sea. The pain had been caused by a great *katsuo no-éboshi*. . . . You never saw a *katsuo-no-éboshi?* It is a jelly-fish shaped like the *éboshi,* or cap, of a Shinto priest; and we call it the *katsuo-no-éboshi* because the *katsuo*-fish [bonito] feed upon it. When that thing appears anywhere, the fishermen expect to catch many *katsuo.* The body is clear like glass; but underneath there is a kind of purple fringe, and long purple strings; and when those strings touch you, the pain is very great, and lasts for a long time. . . . That pain revived me; if I had not been stung I might never have awakened. I got on the plank again, and prayed to Jizō-Sama of Ogawa, and to Kompira-Sama; and I was able to keep awake until morning.

"Before daylight the rain stopped, and the sky began to clear; for I could see some stars. At dawn I got drowsy again; and I was awakened by a blow on the head. A large sea-bird had struck me. The sun was rising behind clouds; and the waves had become gentle. Presently a small brown bird flew by my face,—a coast-bird (I do not know its real name); and I thought that there must be land in sight. I looked behind me, and I saw mountains. I did not recognize the shapes of them: they were blue,—seemed to be nine or ten *ri* distant. I made up my mind to paddle towards them,—though I had little hope of getting to shore. I was feeling hungry again,—terribly hungry!

"I paddled towards the mountains, hour after hour. Once more I fell asleep; and once again a sea-bird struck me. All day I paddled. Towards evening I could tell, from the look of the mountains, that I was approaching them; but I knew that it would take me two days to reach the shore. I had almost ceased to hope when I caught sight of a ship,—a big junk. She was sailing towards me; but I saw that, unless I could swim faster, she would pass me at a great distance. It was my last chance: so I dropped the plank, and swam as fast as I could. I did get within about two chō of her: then I shouted. But I could see nobody on deck; and I got no answer. In another minute she had passed beyond me. The sun was setting; and I despaired. All of a sudden a man came on deck, and shouted to me:— 'Don't try to swim! don't tire yourself!—we are going to send a boat!' I saw the sail lowered at the same time; and I felt so glad that new strength seemed to come to me;—I swam on fast. Then the junk dropped a little boat; and as the boat came towards me, a man called out:—'Is there anybody else?—have you dropped anything?' I answered:—'I had nothing but a plank.' . . . In the same instant all my strength was gone: I felt the men in the boat pulling me up; but I could neither speak nor move, and everything became dark.

"After a time I heard the voices again,—the voices of the men of the *Fukuju Maru:*—'Jinyō! Jinyō!'—and I was frightened. Then somebody shook me, and said:— *'Oi! oi!'* [5] it is only a dream!'—and I saw that I was lying in the junk, under a hanging lantern (for it was night);—and beside me an old man, a stranger, was kneeling, with a cup of boiled rice in his hand. 'Try to eat a little,' he said, very kindly. I wanted to sit up, but could not: then he fed me himself, out of the cup. When it was empty I asked for more; but the old man answered:—'Not now;—you must sleep first.' I heard him say to someone else:—'Give him nothing more until I tell you: if you let him eat much, he will die.' I slept again; and twice more that night I was given rice—soft-boiled rice—one small cupful at a time.

"In the morning I felt much better; and the old man, who had brought me the rice, came and questioned me. When he heard about the loss of our ship, and the time that I had been in the water, he expressed great pity for me. He told me that I had drifted, in those two nights and days, more than twenty-five *ri*[6] 'We went after your plank,' he said, 'and picked it up. Perhaps you would like to present it some day to the temple of Kompira-Sama.' I thanked him, but answered that I wanted to offer it to the temple of Jizō-Sama of Ogawa, at Yaidzu; for it was to Jizō-Sama of Ogawa that I had most often prayed for help.

"The kind old man was the captain, and also the owner, of the junk. She was a Banshū ship, and was bound for the port of Kuki, in Kishū. . . . You write the name, *Ku-ki,* with the character for 'demon,'—so that it means the Nine Demons. . . . All the men of the ship were very good to me. I was naked, except for a loincloth, when I came on board; and they found clothes for me. One gave me an under-robe, and another an upper-robe, and another a girdle;—several gave me towels and sandals;—and all of them together made up a gift of money for me, amounting to between six and seven *ryō.*

"When we reached Kuki—a nice little place, though it has a queer name—the captain took me to a good inn; and after a few days' rest I got strong again. Then the governor of the district, the Jitō, as we called him in those days,—sent for me, and heard my story, and had it written down. He told me that he would have to send a report of the matter to the Jitō of the Yaidzu district, after which he would find means to send me home. But the Banshū captain, who had saved me, offered to take me home in his own ship, and also to act as messenger for the Jitō; and there was much argument between the two. At that time we had no telegraph and no post; and to send a special messenger *(hikyaku),* from Kuki to Yaidzu,[7] would have cost at least fifty *ryō*. But, on the other hand, there were particular laws and customs about such matters,—laws very different from those of to-day. Meanwhile a Yaidzu ship came to the neighboring port of Arasha; and a woman of Kuki, who happened to be at Arasha, told the Yaidzu captain that I was at Kuki. The Yaidzu ship then came to Kuki; and the Jitō decided to send me home in charge of the Yaidzu captain,—giving him a written order.

"Altogether, it was about a month from the time of the loss of the *Fukuju Maru* when I returned to Yaidzu. We reached the harbor at night; and I did not go home at once: it would have frightened my people. Although no certain news of the loss of our ship had then been received at Yaidzu, several things belonging to her had been picked up by fishing-craft; and as the typhoon had come very suddenly, with a terrible sea, it was generally believed that the *Fukuju Maru* had gone down, and that all of us had been drowned. . . . None of the other men were ever heard of again. . . . I went that night to the house of a friend; and in the morning I sent word to my parents and brother; and they came for me. . . .

"Once every year I go to the temple of Kompira in Sanuki: all who have been saved from shipwreck go there to give thanks. And I often go to the temple of Jizō-Sama of Ogawa. If you will come with me there to-morrow, I will show you that plank."

かけひき

Diplomacy

It had been ordered that the execution should take place in the garden of the *yashiki*. So the man was taken there, and made to kneel down in a wide sanded space crossed by a line of *tobi-ishi,* or stepping-stones, such as you may still see in Japanese landscape-gardens. His arms were bound behind him. Retainers brought water in buckets, and rice-bags filled with pebbles; and they packed the rice-bags round the kneeling man,—so wedging him in that he could not move. The master came, and observed the arrangements. He found them satisfactory, and made no remarks.

Suddenly the condemned man cried out to him:—

"Honored Sir, the fault for which I have been doomed I did not wittingly commit. It was only my very great stupidity which caused the fault. Having been born stupid, by reason of my Karma, I could not always help making mistakes. But to kill a man for being stupid is wrong,—and that wrong will be repaid. So surely as you kill me, so surely shall I be avenged;—out of the resentment that you pro-

223

voke will come the vengeance; and evil will be rendered for evil." . . .

If any person be killed while feeling strong resentment, the ghost of that person will be able to take vengeance upon the killer. This the samurai knew. He replied very gently,—almost caressingly:—

"We shall allow you to frighten us as much as you please—after you are dead. But it is difficult to believe that you mean what you say. Will you try to give us some sign of your great resentment—after your head has been cut off?"

"Assuredly I will," answered the man.

"Very well," said the samurai, drawing his long sword;—"I am now going to cut off your head. Directly in front of you there is a stepping-stone. After your head has been cut off, try to bite the stepping-stone. If your angry ghost can help you to do that, some of us may be frightened. . . . Will you try to bite the stone?"

"I will bite it!" cried the man, in great anger,—"I will bite it!—I will bite"—

There was a flash, a swish, a crunching thud: the bound body bowed over the rice sacks,—two long blood-jets pumping from the shorn neck;—and the head rolled upon the sand. Heavily toward the stepping-stone it rolled: then, suddenly bounding, it caught the upper edge of the stone between its teeth, clung desperately for a moment, and dropped inert.

None spoke; but the retainers stared in horror at their master. He seemed to be quite unconcerned. He merely held out his sword to the nearest attendant, who, with a wooden dipper, poured water over the blade from haft to point, and then carefully wiped the steel several times with sheets of soft paper. . . . And thus ended the ceremonial part of the incident.

For months thereafter, the retainers and the domestics

lived in ceaseless fear of ghostly visitation. None of them doubted that the promised vengeance would come; and their constant terror caused them to hear and to see much that did not exist. They became afraid of the sound of the wind in the bamboos,—afraid even of the stirring of shadows in the garden. At last, after taking counsel together, they decided to petition their master to have a *Ségaki*-service performed on behalf of the vengeful spirit.

"Quite unnecessary," the samurai said, when his chief retainer had uttered the general wish. . . . "I understand that the desire of a dying man for revenge may be a cause for fear. But in this case there is nothing to fear."

The retainer looked at his master beseechingly, but hesitated to ask the reason of this alarming confidence.

"Oh, the reason is simple enough," declared the samurai, divining the unspoken doubt. "Only the very last intention of that fellow could have been dangerous; and when I challenged him to give me the sign, I diverted his mind from the desire of revenge. He died with the set purpose of biting the stepping stone; and that purpose he was able to accomplish, but nothing else. All the rest he must have forgotten. . . . So you need not feel any further anxiety about the matter."

—And indeed the dead man gave no more trouble. Nothing at all happened.

悪因縁

A Passional Karma

One of the never-failing attractions of the Tōkyō stage is the performance, by the famous Kikugorō and his company, of the *Botan-Dōrō,* or "Peony-Lantern." This weird play, of which the scenes are laid in the middle of the last century, is the dramatization of a romance by the novelist Enchō, written in colloquial Japanese, and purely Japanese in local color, though inspired by a Chinese tale. I went to see the play; and Kikugorō made me familiar with a new variety of the pleasure of fear.

"Why not give English readers the ghostly part of the story?"—asked a friend who guides me betimes through the mazes of Eastern philosophy. "It would serve to explain some popular ideas of the supernatural which Western people know very little about. And I could help you with the translation."

I gladly accepted the suggestion; and we composed the following summary of the more extraordinary portion of Enchō's romance. Here and there we found it necessary to condense the original narrative; and we tried to keep close to the text only in the conversational passages,—some of which happen to possess a particular quality of psychological interest.

* * *

—This is the story of the Ghosts in the Romance of the Peony-Lantern:—

I

There once lived in the district of Ushigomé, in Yedo, a *hatamoto*[1] called Iijima Heizayémon, whose only daughter, Tsuyu, was beautiful as her name, which signifies "Morning Dew." Iijima took a second wife when his daughter was about sixteen; and, finding that O-Tsuyu could not be happy with her mother-in-law, he had a pretty villa built for the girl at Yanagijima, as a separate residence, and gave her an excellent maidservant, called O-Yoné, to wait upon her.

O-Tsuyu lived happily enough in her new home until one day when the family physician, Yamamoto Shijō, paid her a visit in company with a young samurai named Hagiwara Shinzaburō, who resided in the Nedzu quarter. Shinzaburō was an unusually handsome lad, and very gentle; and the two young people fell in love with each other at sight. Even before the brief visit was over, they contrived,—unheard by the old doctor,—to pledge themselves to each other for life. And, at parting, O-Tsuyu whispered to the youth,—*"Remember! if you do not come to see me again, I shall certainly die!"*

Shinzaburō never forgot those words; and he was only too eager to see more of O-Tsuyu. But etiquette forbade him to make the visit alone: he was obliged to wait for some other chance to accompany the doctor, who had promised to take him to the villa a second time. Unfortunately the old man did not keep this promise. He had perceived the sudden affection of O-Tsuyu; and he feared that her father would hold him responsible for any serious results. Iijima Heizayémon had a reputation for cutting off heads. And the more Shijō thought about the possible consequences of his introduction of Shinzaburō at the Iijima villa, the more he became afraid. Therefore he purposely abstained from calling upon his young friend.

Months passed; and O-Tsuyu, little imagining the true cause of Shinzaburō's neglect, believed that her love had been scorned. Then she pined away, and died. Soon afterwards, the faithful servant O-Yoné also died, through grief at the loss of her mistress; and the two were buried side by side in the cemetery of Shin-Banzui-In,—a temple which still stands in the neighborhood of Dango-Zaka, where the famous chrysanthemum-shows are yearly held.

II

Shinzaburō knew nothing of what had happened; but his disappointment and his anxiety had resulted in a prolonged illness. He was slowly recovering, but still very weak, when he unexpectedly received another visit from Yamamoto Shijō. The old man made a number of plausible excuses for his apparent neglect. Shinzaburō said to him:—

"I have been sick ever since the beginning of spring;— even now I cannot eat anything. . . . Was it not rather unkind of you never to call? I thought that we were to make another visit together to the house of the Lady Iijima; and I wanted to take to her some little present as a return for our kind reception. Of course I could not go by myself."

Shijō gravely responded,—

"I am very sorry to tell you that the young lady is dead."

"Dead!" repeated Shinzaburō, turning white,—"did you say that she is dead?"

The doctor remained silent for a moment, as if collecting himself: then he resumed, in the quick light tone of a man resolved not to take trouble seriously:—

"My great mistake was in having introduced you to her; for it seems that she fell in love with you at once. I am afraid that you must have said something to encourage this affection—when you were in that little room together. At all events, I saw how she felt towards you; and then I became uneasy,—fearing that her father might come to hear of the matter, and lay the whole blame upon me. So— to be quite frank with you,—I decided that it would be better not to call upon you; and I purposely stayed away for a long time. But, only a few days ago, happening to visit Iijima's house, I heard, to my great surprise, that his daughter had died, and that her servant O-Yoné had also died. Then, remembering all that had taken place, I knew that the young lady must have died of love for you. . . . [*Laughing*] Ah, you are really a sinful fellow! Yes, you are! [*Laughing*] Isn't it a sin to have been born so handsome that the girls die for love of you?[2] . . . [*Seriously*] Well, we must leave the dead to the dead. It is no use to talk further about the matter;—all that you now can do for her is to repeat the Nembutsu[3] . . . Good-bye."

And the old man retired hastily,—anxious to avoid further converse about the painful event for which he felt himself to have been unwittingly responsible.

III

Shinzaburō long remained stupefied with grief by the news of O-Tsuyu's death. But as soon as he found himself again able to think clearly, he inscribed the dead girl's name upon a mortuary tablet, and placed the tablet in the Buddhist shrine of his house, and set offerings before it, and recited prayers. Every day thereafter he presented offerings, and repeated the *Nembutsu;* and the memory of O-Tsuyu was never absent from his thought.

Nothing occurred to change the monotony of his solitude before the time of the Bon,—the great Festival of the Dead,—which begins upon the thirteenth day of the seventh month. Then he decorated his house, and prepared everything for the festival;—hanging out the lanterns that guide the returning spirits, and setting the food of ghosts on the *shōryōdana,* or Shelf of Souls. And on the first evening of the Bon, after sundown, he kindled a small lamp before the tablet of O-Tsuyu, and lighted the lanterns.

The night was clear, with a great moon,—and windless, and very warm. Shinzaburō sought the coolness of his veranda. Clad only in a light summer-robe, he sat there thinking, dreaming, sorrowing;—sometimes fanning himself; sometimes making a little smoke to drive the mosquitoes away. Everything was quiet. It was a lonesome neighborhood, and there were few passers-by. He could hear only the soft rushing of a neighboring stream, and the shrilling of night-insects.

But all at once this stillness was broken by a sound of women's *geta*[4] approaching—*kara-kon, kara-kon;*—and the sound drew nearer and nearer, quickly, till it reached the live-hedge surrounding the garden. Then Shinzaburō, feeling curious, stood on tiptoe, so as to look over the hedge; and he saw two women passing. One, who was carrying a beautiful lantern decorated with peony-flowers,[5] appeared to be a servant;—the other was a slender girl of about seventeen, wearing a long-sleeved robe embroidered with designs of autumn-blossoms. Almost at the same instant both women turned their faces toward Shinzaburō;—and to his utter astonishment, he recognized O-Tsuyu and her servant O-Yoné.

They stopped immediately; and the girl cried out,—

"Oh, how strange! . . . Hagiwara Sama !"

Shinzaburō simultaneously called to the maid:—

"O-Yoné! Ah, you are O-Yoné!—I remember you very well."

"Hagiwara Sama!" exclaimed O-Yoné in a tone of

supreme amazement. "Never could I have believed it possible! . . . Sir, we were told that you had died."

"How extraordinary!" cried Shinzaburō. "Why, I was told that both of you were dead!"

"Ah, what a hateful story!" returned O-Yoné. "Why repeat such unlucky words? . . . Who told you?"

"Please to come in," said Shinzaburō;—"here we can talk better. The garden-gate is open."

So they entered, and exchanged greeting; and when Shinzaburō had made them comfortable, he said:—

"I trust that you will pardon my discourtesy in not having called upon you for so long a time. But Shijō, the doctor, about a month ago, told me that you had both died."

"So it was he who told you?" exclaimed O-Yoné. "It was very wicked of him to say such a thing. Well, it was also Shijō who told us that *you* were dead. I think that he wanted to deceive you,—which was not a difficult thing to do, because you are so confiding and trustful. Possibly my mistress betrayed her liking for you in some words which found their way to her father's ears; and, in that case, O-Kuni—the new wife—might have planned to make the doctor tell you that we were dead, so as to bring about a separation. Anyhow, when my mistress heard that you had died, she wanted to cut off her hair immediately, and to become a nun. But I was able to prevent her from cutting off her hair; and I persuaded her at last to become a nun only in her heart. Afterwards her father wished her to marry a certain young man; and she refused. Then there was a great deal of trouble,—chiefly caused by O-Kuni;—and we went away from the villa, and found a very small house in Yanaka-no-Sasaki. There we are now just barely able to live, by doing a little private work. . . . My mistress has been constantly repeating the *Nembutsu* for your sake. To-day, being the first day of the Bon, we went to visit the temples; and we were on our way home—thus late—when this strange meeting happened."

"Oh, how extraordinary!" cried Shinzaburō. "Can it be

true?—or is it only a dream? Here I, too, have been constantly reciting the *Nembutsu* before a tablet with her name
upon it! Look!" And he showed them O-Tsuyu's tablet in
its place upon the Shelf of Souls.

"We are more than grateful for your kind remembrance," returned O-Yoné, smiling. . . . "Now as for my
mistress,"—she continued, turning towards O-Tsuyu, who
had all the while remained demure and silent, half hiding
her face with her sleeve,—"as for my mistress, she actually
says that she would not mind being disowned by her father
for the time of seven existences,⁶ or even being killed by
him, for your sake! . . . Come! will you not allow her to stay
here to-night?"

Shinzaburō turned pale for joy. He answered in a voice
trembling with emotion:—

"Please remain; but do not speak loud—because there is
a troublesome fellow living close by,—a *ninsomi*⁷ called
Hakuōdō Yusai, who tells people's fortunes by looking at
their faces. He is inclined to be curious; and it is better that
he should not know."

The two women remained that night in the house of the
young samurai, and returned to their own home a little
before daybreak. And after that night they came every
night for seven nights,—whether the weather were foul or
fair,—always at the same hour. And Shinzaburō became
more and more attached to the girl; and the twain were fet-
tered, each to each, by that bond of illusion which is
stronger than bands of iron.

IV

Now there was a man called Tomozō, who lived in a
small cottage adjoining Shinzaburō's residence. Tomozō
and his wife O-Miné were both employed by Shinzaburō
as servants. Both seemed to be devoted to their young master; and by his help they were able to live in comparative
comfort.

One night, at a very late hour, Tomozō heard the voice of a woman in his master's apartment; and this made him uneasy. He feared that Shinzaburō, being very gentle and affectionate, might be made the dupe of some cunning wanton,—in which event the domestics would be the first to suffer. He therefore resolved to watch; and on the following night he stole on tiptoe to Shinzaburō's dwelling, and looked through a chink in one of the sliding shutters. By the glow of a night-lantern within the sleeping-room, he was able to perceive that his master and a strange woman were talking together under the mosquito-net. At first he could not see the woman distinctly. Her back was turned to him;—he only observed that she was very slim, and that she appeared to be very young,—judging from the fashion of her dress and hair.[8] Putting his ear to the chink, he could hear the conversation plainly. The woman said:—

"And if I should be disowned by my father, would you then let me come and live with you?"

Shinzaburō answered:—

"Most assuredly I would—nay, I should be glad of the chance. But there is no reason to fear that you will ever be disowned by your father; for you are his only daughter, and he loves you very much. What I do fear is that some day we shall be cruelly separated."

She responded softly:—

"Never, never could I even think of accepting any other man for my husband. Even if our secret were to become known, and my father were to kill me for what I have done, still—after death itself—I could never cease to think of you. And I am now quite sure that you yourself would not be able to live very long without me." . . . Then clinging closely to him, with her lips at his neck, she caressed him; and he returned her caresses.

Tomozō wondered as he listened,—because the language of the woman was not the language of a common woman, but the language of a lady of rank.[9] Then he determined at all hazards to get one glimpse of her face; and he crept round the house, backwards and forwards, peering through every crack and chink. And at last he was able to see;—but therewith an icy trembling seized him; and the hair of his head stood up.

For the face was the face of a woman long dead,—and the fingers caressing were fingers of naked bone,—and of the body below the waist there was not anything: it melted off into thinnest trailing shadow. Where the eyes of the lover deluded saw youth and grace and beauty, there appeared to the eyes of the watcher horror only, and the emptiness of death. Simultaneously another woman's figure, and a weirder, rose up from within the chamber, and swiftly made toward the watcher, as if discerning his presence. Then, in uttermost terror, he fled to the dwelling of Hakuōdō Yusai, and, knocking frantically at the doors, succeeded in arousing him.

V

Hakuōdō Yusai, the *ninsomi,* was a very old man; but in his time he had travelled much, and he had heard and seen so many things that he could not be easily surprised. Yet the story of the terrified Tomozō both alarmed and amazed him. He had read in ancient Chinese books of love between the living and the dead; but he had never believed it possible. Now, however, he felt convinced that the statement of Tomozō was not a falsehood, and that something very strange was really going on in the house of Hagiwara. Should the truth prove to be what Tomozō imagined, then the young samurai was a doomed man.

"If the woman be a ghost,"—said Yusai to the frightened servant,"—if the woman be a ghost, your master must die very soon,—unless something extraordinary can be done to save him. And if the woman be a ghost, the signs of death will appear upon his face. For the spirit of the living is *yōki,* and pure;—the spirit of the dead is *inki,* and unclean: the one is Positive, the other Negative. He whose bride is a ghost cannot live. Even though in his blood there existed the force of a life of one hundred years, that force must quickly perish. . . . Still, I shall do all that I can to save Hagiwara Sama. And in the meantime, Tomozō, say nothing to any other person,—not even to your wife,—about this matter. At sunrise I shall call upon your master."

VI

When questioned next morning by Yusai, Shinzaburō at first attempted to deny that any women had been visiting the house; but finding this artless policy of no avail, and perceiving that the old man's purpose was altogether unselfish, he was finally persuaded to acknowledge what had really occurred, and to give his reasons for wishing to keep the matter a secret. As for the lady Iijima, he intended, he said, to make her his wife as soon as possible.

"Oh, madness!" cried Yusai,—losing all patience in the intensity of his alarm. "Know, sir, that the people who have been coming here, night after night, are dead! Some frightful delusion is upon you! . . . Why, the simple fact that you long supposed O-Tsuyu to be dead, and repeated the *Nembutsu* for her, and made offerings before her tablet, is itself the proof! . . . The lips of the dead have touched you!—the hands of the dead have caressed you! . . . Even at this moment I see in your face the signs of death—and you will not believe! . . . Listen to me now, sir,—I beg of you,— if you wish to save yourself: otherwise you have less than twenty days to live. They told you—those people—that they were residing in the district of Shitaya, in Yanaka-no-Sasaki. Did you ever visit them at that place? No!—of course you did not! Then go to-day,—as soon as you can,— to Yanaka-no-Sasaki, and try to find their home! . . ."

And having uttered this counsel with the most vehement earnestness, Hakuōdō Yusai abruptly took his departure.

Shinzaburō, startled though not convinced, resolved after a moment's reflection to follow the advice of the *nin-somi,* and to go to Shitaya. It was yet early in the morning when he reached the quarter of Yanaka-no-Sasaki, and began his search for the dwelling of O-Tsuyu. He went through every street and side-street, read all the names inscribed at the various entrances, and made inquiries whenever an opportunity presented itself. But he could not find anything resembling the little house mentioned by O-Yoné; and none of the people whom he questioned knew of any house in the quarter inhabited by two single women. Feeling at last certain that further research would be useless, he turned homeward by the shortest way, which happened to lead through the grounds of the temple Shin-Banzui-In.

Suddenly his attention was attracted by two new tombs, placed side by side, at the rear of the temple. One was a common tomb, such as might have been erected for a person of humble rank: the other was a large and handsome monument; and hanging before it was a beautiful peony-lantern, which had probably been left there at the time of the Festival of the Dead. Shinzaburō remembered that the peony-lantern carried by O-Yoné was exactly similar; and the coincidence impressed him as strange. He looked again at the tombs; but the tombs explained nothing. Neither bore any personal name,—only the Buddhist *kaimyō,* or posthumous appellation. Then he determined to seek information at the temple. An acolyte stated, in reply to his questions, that the large tomb had been recently erected for the daughter of Iijima Heizayémon, the *hatamoto* of Ushigomé; and that the small tomb next to it was that of her servant O-Yoné, who had died of grief soon after the young lady's funeral.

Immediately to Shinzaburō's memory there recurred, with another and sinister meaning, the words of O-Yoné:—*"We went away, and found a very small house in Yanaka-no-Sasaki. There we are now just barely able to live—*

by doing a little private work. . . ." Here was indeed the very small house,—and in Yanaka-no-Sasaki. But the little private work . . . ?

Terror-stricken, the samurai hastened with all speed to the house of Yusai, and begged for his counsel and assistance. But Yusai declared himself unable to be of any aid in such a case. All that he could do was to send Shinzaburō to the high-priest Ryōseki, of Shin-Banzui-In, with a letter praying for immediate religious help.

VII

The high-priest Ryōseki was a learned and a holy man. By spiritual vision he was able to know the secret of any sorrow, and the nature of the karma that had caused it. He heard unmoved the story of Shinzaburō, and said to him:—

"A very great danger now threatens you, because of an error committed in one of your former states of existence. The karma that binds you to the dead is very strong; but if I tried to explain its character, you would not be able to understand. I shall therefore tell you only this,—that the dead person has no desire to injure you out of hate, feels no enmity towards you: she is influenced, on the contrary, by the most passionate affection for you. Probably the girl has been in love with you from a time long preceding your present life,—from a time of not less than three or four past existences; and it would seem that, although necessarily changing her form and condition at each succeeding birth, she has not been able to cease from following after you. Therefore it will not be an easy thing to escape from her influence. . . . But now I am going to lend you this powerful *mamori*.[10] It is a pure gold image of that Buddha called the Sea-Sounding Tathâgata—*Kai-On Nyōrai,*—because his preaching of the Law sounds through the world like the sound of the sea. And this little image is especially a *shiryō-yoké,*[11]—which protects the living from the dead. This you must wear, in its covering, next to your body,—under the girdle. . . . Besides, I shall presently perform in the temple, a *segaki* service[12] for the repose of the troubled spirit. . . . And here is a holy sutra, called *Ubō-Darani-Kyō,* or "Treasure-Raining Sutra:"[13] you must be careful to recite it every night in your house—without fail. . . . Furthermore I shall give you this package of *o-fuda;*[14]—you must paste one of them over every opening of your house,—no matter how small. If you do this, the power of the holy texts will prevent the dead from entering. But—whatever may happen—do not fail to recite the sutra."

Shinzaburō humbly thanked the high-priest; and then, taking with him the image, the sutra, and the bundle of sacred texts, he made all haste to reach his home before the hour of sunset.

VIII

With Yusai's advice and help, Shinzaburō was able before dark to fix the holy texts over all the apertures of his dwelling. Then the *ninsomi* returned to his own house,—leaving the youth alone.

Night came, warm and clear. Shinzaburō made fast the doors, bound the precious amulet about his waist, entered his mosquito-net, and by the glow of a night-lantern began to recite the *Ubō-Darani-Kyō.* For a long time he chanted the words, comprehending little of their meaning;—then he tried to obtain some rest. But his mind was still too much disturbed by the strange events of the day. Midnight passed; and no sleep came to him. At last he heard the boom of the great temple-bell of Dentsu-In announcing the eighth hour.[15]

It ceased; and Shinzaburō suddenly heard the sound of *geta* approaching from the old direction,—but this time more slowly: *karan-koron, karan-koron!* At once a cold sweat broke over his forehead. Opening the sutra hastily, with trembling hand, he began again to recite it aloud. The steps came nearer and nearer,—reached the live hedge,—stopped! Then, strange to say, Shinzaburō felt unable to remain under his mosquito-net: something stronger even than his fear impelled him to look; and, instead of continuing to recite the *Ubō-Darani-Kyō,* he foolishly approached the shutters, and through a chink peered out into the night. Before the house he saw O-Tsuyu standing, and O-Yoné with the peony-lantern; and both of them were gazing at the Buddhist texts pasted above the entrance. Never before—not even in what time she lived—had O-Tsuyu appeared so beautiful; and Shinzaburō felt his heart drawn towards her with a power almost resistless. But the terror of death and the terror of the unknown restrained; and there went on within him such a struggle between his love and his fear that he became as one suffering in the body the pains of the *Shō-netsu* hell.[16]

Presently he heard the voice of the maid-servant, saying:—

"My dear mistress, there is no way to enter. The heart of Hagiwara Sama must have changed. For the promise that he made last night has been broken; and the doors have been made fast to keep us out. . . . We cannot go in to-night. . . . It will be wiser for you to make up your mind not to think any more about him, because his feeling towards you has certainly changed. It is evident that he does not want to see you. So it will be better not to give yourself any more trouble for the sake of a man whose heart is so unkind."

But the girl answered, weeping:—

"Oh, to think that this could happen after the pledges which we made to each other! . . . Often I was told that the heart of a man changes as quickly as the sky of autumn;—yet surely the heart of Hagiwara Sama cannot be so cruel that he should really intend to exclude me in this way! . . .

Dear Yoné, please find some means of taking me to him. . . . Unless you do, I will never, never go home again."

Thus she continued to plead, veiling her face with her long sleeves,—and very beautiful she looked, and very touching; but the fear of death was strong upon her lover.

O-Yoné at last made answer,—

"My dear young lady, why will you trouble your mind about a man who seems to be so cruel? . . . Well, let us see if there be no way to enter at the back of the house: come with me!"

And taking O-Tsuyu by the hand, she led her away toward the rear of the dwelling; and there the two disappeared as suddenly as the light disappears when the flame of a lamp is blown out.

IX

Night after night the shadows came at the Hour of the Ox; and nightly Shinzaburō heard the weeping of O-Tsuyu. Yet he believed himself saved,—little imagining that his doom had already been decided by the character of his dependents.

Tomozō had promised Yusai never to speak to any other person—not even to O-Miné—of the strange events that were taking place. But Tomozō was not long suffered by the haunters to rest in peace. Night after night O-Yoné entered into his dwelling, and roused him from his sleep, and asked him to remove the *o-fuda* placed over one very small window at the back of his master's house. And Tomozō, out of fear, as often promised her to take away the *o-fuda* before the next sundown; but never by day could he make up his mind to remove it,—believing that evil was intended to Shinzaburō. At last, in a night of storm, O-Yoné startled him from slumber with a cry of reproach, and stooped above his pillow, and said to him: "Have a care how you trifle with us! If, by to-morrow night, you do not take away that text, you shall learn how I can hate!" And she made her face so frightful as she spoke that Tomozō nearly died of terror.

O-Miné, the wife of Tomozō, had never till then known of these visits: even to her husband they had seemed like bad dreams. But on this particular night it chanced that, waking suddenly, she heard the voice of a woman talking to Tomozō. Almost in the same moment the talking ceased; and when O-Miné looked about her, she saw, by the light of the night-lamp, only her husband,—shuddering and white with fear. The stranger was gone; the doors were fast: it seemed impossible that anybody could have entered. Nevertheless the jealousy of the wife had been aroused; and she began to chide and to question Tomozō in such a manner that he thought himself obliged to betray the secret, and to explain the terrible dilemma in which he had been placed.

Then the passion of O-Miné yielded to wonder and alarm; but she was a subtle woman, and she devised immediately a plan to save her husband by the sacrifice of her master. And she gave Tomozō a cunning counsel,—telling him to make conditions with the dead.

They came again on the following night at the Hour of the Ox; and O-Miné hid herself on hearing the sound of their coming,—*karan-koron, karan-koron!* But Tomozō went out to meet them in the dark, and even found courage to say to them what his wife had told him to say:—

"It is true that I deserve your blame;—but I had no wish to cause you anger. The reason that the *o-fuda* has not been taken away is that my wife and I are able to live only by the help of Hagiwara Sama, and that we cannot expose him to any danger without bringing misfortune upon ourselves. But if we could obtain the sum of a hundred *ryō* in gold, we should be able to please you, because we should then

need no help from anybody. Therefore if you will give us a
hundred *ryō,* I can take the *o-fuda* away without being
afraid of losing our only means of support."

When he had uttered these words, O-Yoné and O-
Tsuyu looked at each other in silence for a moment. Then
O-Yoné said:—

"Mistress, I told you that it was not right to trouble this
man,—as we have no just cause of ill will against him. But
it is certainly useless to fret yourself about Hagiwara Sama,
because his heart has changed towards you. Now once
again, my dear young lady, let me beg you not to think any
more about him!"

But O-Tsuyu, weeping, made answer:—

"Dear Yoné, whatever may happen, I cannot possibly
keep myself from thinking about him! . . . You know that
you can get a hundred *ryō* to have the *o-fuda* taken off. . .
Only once more, I pray, dear Yoné!—only once more bring
me face to face with Hagiwara Sama,—I beseech you!" And
hiding her face with her sleeve, she thus continued to
plead.

"Oh! why will you ask me to do these things?" responded O-Yoné. "You know very well that I have no money. But
since you will persist in this whim of yours, in spite of all
that I can say, I suppose that I must try to find the money
somehow, and to bring it here to-morrow night. . . ." Then,
turning to the faithless Tomozō, she said:—"Tomozō, I
must tell you that Hagiwara Sama now wears upon his
body a *mamori* called by the name of *Kai-On-Nyōrai,* and
that so long as he wears it we cannot approach him. So you
will have to get that *mamori* away from him, by some
means or other, as well as to remove the *o-fuda.*"

Tomozō feebly made answer:—

"That also I can do, if you will promise to bring me the
hundred *ryō.*"

"Well, mistress," said O-Yoné, "you will wait,—will you
not,—until tomorrow night?"

"Oh, dear Yoné!" sobbed the other,—"have we to go

back to-night again without seeing Hagiwara Sama? Ah! it is cruel!"

And the shadow of the mistress, weeping, was led away by the shadow of the maid.

X

Another day went, and another night came, and the dead came with it. But this time no lamentation was heard without the house of Hagiwara; for the faithless servant found his reward at the Hour of the Ox, and removed the *o-fuda.* Moreover he had been able, while his master was at the bath, to steal from its case the golden *mamori,* and to substitute for it an image of copper; and he had buried the *Kai-On-Nyōrai* in a desolate field. So the visitants found nothing to oppose their entering. Veiling their faces with their sleeves they rose and passed, like a streaming of vapor, into the little window from over which the holy text had been torn away. But what happened thereafter within the house Tomozō never knew.

The sun was high before he ventured again to approach his master's dwelling, and to knock upon the sliding-doors. For the first time in years he obtained no response; and the silence made him afraid. Repeatedly he called, and received no answer. Then, aided by O-Miné, he succeeded in effecting an entrance and making his way alone to the sleeping-room, where he called again in vain. He rolled back the rumbling shutters to admit the light; but still within the house there was no stir. At last he dared to lift a corner of the mosquito-net. But no sooner had he looked beneath than he fled from the house, with a cry of horror.

Shinzaburō was dead—hideously dead;—and his face was the face of a man who had died in the uttermost agony of fear;—and lying beside him in the bed were the bones of a woman! And the bones of the arms, and the bones of the hands, clung fast about his neck.

XI

Hakuōdō Yusai, the fortune-teller, went to view the corpse at the prayer of the faithless Tomozō. The old man was terrified and astonished at the spectacle, but looked about him with a keen eye. He soon perceived that the *o-fuda* had been taken from the little window at the back of the house; and on searching the body of Shinzaburō, he discovered that the golden *mamori* had been taken from its wrapping, and a copper image of Fudō put in place of it. He suspected Tomozō of the theft; but the whole occurrence was so very extraordinary that he thought it prudent to consult with the priest Ryōseki before taking further action. Therefore, after having made a careful examination of the premises, he betook himself to the temple Shin-Banzui-In, as quickly as his aged limbs could bear him.

Ryōseki, without waiting to hear the purpose of the old man's visit, at once invited him into a private apartment.

"You know that you are always welcome here," said Ryōseki. "Please seat yourself at ease. . . . Well, I am sorry to tell you that Hagiwara Sama is dead."

Yusai wonderingly exclaimed:—"Yes, he is dead;—but how did you learn of it?"

The priest responded:—

"Hagiwara Sama was suffering from the results of an evil karma; and his attendant was a bad man. What happened to Hagiwara Sama was unavoidable;—his destiny had been determined from a time long before his last birth. It will be better for you not to let your mind be troubled by this event."

Yusai said:—

"I have heard that a priest of pure life may gain power to see into the future for a hundred years; but truly this is the first time in my existence that I have had proof of such power. . . . Still, there is another matter about which I am very anxious. . . ."

"You mean," interrupted Ryōseki, "the stealing of the holy *mamori*, the *Kai-On-Nyōrai*. But you must not give yourself any concern about that. The image has been buried in a field; and it will be found there and returned to me during the eighth month of the coming year. So please do not be anxious about it."

More and more amazed, the old *ninsomi* ventured to observe:—

"I have studied the *In-Yō*,[17] and the science of divination; and I make my living by telling peoples' fortunes;— but I cannot possibly understand how you know these things."

Ryōseki answered gravely:—

"Never mind how I happen to know them. . . . I now want to speak to you about Hagiwara's funeral. The House of Hagiwara has its own family-cemetery, of course; but to bury him there would not be proper. He must be buried beside O-Tsuyu, the Lady Iijima; for his karma-relation to her was a very deep one. And it is but right that you should erect a tomb for him at your own cost, because you have been indebted to him for many favors."

Thus it came to pass that Shinzaburō was buried beside O-Tsuyu, in the cemetery of Shin-Banzui In, in Yanaka-no-Sasaki.

—*Here ends the story of the Ghosts in the Romance of the Peony-Lantern.*

* * *

My friend asked me whether the story had interested me; and I answered by telling him that I wanted to go to the cemetery of Shin-Banzui-In,—so as to realize more definitely the local color of the author's studies.

"I shall go with you at once," he said. "But what did you think of the personages?"

"To Western thinking," I made answer, "Shinzaburō is a despicable creature. I have been mentally comparing him with the true lovers of our old ballad-literature. They were only too glad to follow a dead sweetheart into the grave; and nevertheless, being Christians, they believed that they had only one human life to enjoy in this world. But Shinzaburō was a Buddhist,—with a million lives behind him and a million lives before him; and he was too selfish to give up even one miserable existence for the sake of the girl that came back to him from the dead. Then he was even more cowardly than selfish. Although a samurai by birth and training, he had to beg a priest to save him from ghosts. In every way he proved himself contemptible; and O-Tsuyu did quite right in choking him to death."

"From the Japanese point of view, likewise," my friend responded, "Shinzaburō is rather contemptible. But the use of this weak character helped the author to develop incidents that could not otherwise, perhaps, have been so effectively managed. To my thinking, the only attractive character in the story is that of O-Yoné: type of the old-time loyal and loving servant,—intelligent, shrewd, full of resource,—faithful not only unto death, but beyond death. . . . Well, let us go to Shin-Banzui-In."

We found the temple uninteresting, and the cemetery an abomination of desolation. Spaces once occupied by graves had been turned into potato-patches. Between were tombs leaning at all angles out of the perpendicular, tablets made illegible by scurf, empty pedestals, shattered water tanks, and statues of Buddhas without heads or hands. Recent rains had soaked the black soil,—leaving here and there small pools of slime about which swarms of tiny frogs were hopping. Everything—excepting the potato-patches—seemed to have been neglected for years. In a shed just within the gate, we observed a woman cooking; and my companion presumed to ask her if she knew anything about the tombs described in the Romance of the Peony-Lantern.

"Ah! the tombs of O-Tsuyu and O-Yoné?" she responded, smiling;—"you will find them near the end of the first row at the back of the temple—next to the statue of Jizō."

Surprises of this kind I had met with elsewhere in Japan.

We picked our way between the rain pools and between the green ridges of young potatoes,—whose roots were doubtless feeding on the substance of many another O-Tsuyu and O-Yoné;—and we reached at last two lichen-eaten tombs of which the inscriptions seemed almost obliterated. Beside the larger tomb was a statue of Jizō, with a broken nose.

"The characters are not easy to make out," said my friend—"but wait!" . . . He drew from his sleeve a sheet of soft white paper, laid it over the inscription, and began to rub the paper with a lump of clay. As he did so, the characters appeared in white on the blackened surface.

" *'Eleventh day, third month—Rat, Elder Brother, Fire—Sixth year of Horéki* [A.D. 1756].' . . . This would seem to be the grave of some innkeeper of Nedzu, named Kichibei. Let us see what is on the other monument."

With a fresh sheet of paper he presently brought out the text of a *kaimyō*, and read,—

"*'En-myō-In, Hō-yō-I-tei-ken-shi, Hō-ni':*—'Nun-of-the-Law, Illustrious, Pure-of-heart-and-will, Famed-in-the-Law,—inhabiting the Mansion-of-the-Preaching-of-Wonder.' . . . The grave of some Buddhist nun."

"What utter humbug!" I exclaimed. "That woman was only making fun of us."

"Now," my friend protested, "you are unjust to the woman! You came here because you wanted a sensation; and she tried her very best to please you. You did not suppose that ghost story was true, did you?"

前代の遺物

Survivals

In the gardens of certain Buddhist temples there are trees which have been famous for centuries,—trees trained and clipped into extraordinary shapes. Some have the form of dragons; others have the form of pagodas, ships, umbrellas. Supposing that one of these trees were abandoned to its own natural tendencies, it would eventually lose the queer shape so long imposed upon it; but the outline would not be altered for a considerable time, as the new leafage would at first unfold only in the direction of least resistance: that is to say, within limits originally established by the shears and the pruning-knife. By sword and law the old Japanese society had been pruned and clipped, bent and bound, just like such a tree; and after the reconstructions of the Meiji period,—after the abolition of the daimiates, and the suppression of the military class,—it still maintained its former shape, just as the tree would continue to do when first abandoned by the gardener. Though delivered from the bonds of feudal law, released from the shears of military rule, the great bulk of the social structure preserved its ancient aspect; and the rare spectacle bewildered and

248

delighted and deluded the Western observer. Here indeed was Elf-land,—the strange, the beautiful, the grotesque, the very mysterious,—totally unlike aught of strange and attractive ever beheld elsewhere. It was not a world of the nineteenth century after Christ, but a world of many centuries before Christ: yet this fact—the wonder of wonders—remained unrecognized; and it remains unrecognized by most people even to this day.

Fortunate indeed were those privileged to enter this astonishing fairyland thirty odd years ago, before the period of superficial change, and to observe the unfamiliar aspects of its life: the universal urbanity, the smiling silence of crowds, the patient deliberation of toil, the absence of misery and struggle. Even yet, in those remoter districts where alien influence has wrought but little change, the charm of the old existence lingers and amazes; and the ordinary traveller can little understand what it means. That all are polite, that nobody quarrels, that everybody smiles, that pain and sorrow remain invisible, that the new police have nothing to do, would seem to prove a morally superior humanity. But for the trained sociologist it would prove something different, and suggest something very terrible. It would prove to him that this society had been moulded under immense coercion, and that the coercion must have been exerted uninterruptedly for thousands of years. He would immediately perceive that ethics and custom had not yet become dissociated, and that the conduct of each person was regulated by the will of the rest. He would know that personality could not develop in such a social medium,—that no individual superiority dare assert itself, that no competition would be tolerated. He would understand that the outward charm of this life—its softness, its smiling silence as of dreams—signified the rule of the dead. He would recognize that between those minds and the minds of his own epoch no kinship of thought, no community of sentiment, no sympathy whatever could exist,— that the separating gulf was not to be measured by thousands of leagues, but only by thousands of years,—that the psychological interval was hopeless as the distance from planet to planet. Yet this knowledge probably would not— certainly should not—blind him to the intrinsic charm of things. Not to feel the beauty of this archaic life is to prove oneself insensible to all beauty. Even that Greek world, for which our scholars and poets profess such loving admiration, must have been in many ways a world of the same kind, whose daily mental existence no modern mind could share.

Now that the great social tree, so wonderfully clipped and cared for during many centuries, is losing its fantastic shape, let us try to see how much of the original design can still be traced.

Under all the outward aspects of individual activity that modern Japan presents to the visitor's gaze, the ancient conditions really persist to an extent that no observation could reveal. Still the immemorial cult rules all the land. Still the family-law, the communal law, and (though in a more irregular manner) the clan-law, control every action of existence. I do not refer to any written law, but only to the old unwritten religious law, with its host of obligations deriving from ancestor worship. It is true that many changes—and, in the opinion of the wise, too many changes—have been made in civil legislation; but the ancient proverb, "Government-laws are only seven-day laws," still represents popular sentiment in regard to hasty reforms. The old law, the law of the dead, is that by which the millions prefer to act and think. Though ancient social groupings have been officially abolished, re-groupings of a corresponding sort have been formed, instinctively, throughout the country districts. In theory the individual is free; in practice he is scarcely more free than were his forefathers. Old penalties for breach of custom have been abrogated; yet communal opinion is able to compel the ancient obedience. Legal enactments can nowhere effect immediate change of sentiment and long-established usage,—least of all among a people of such fixity of character as the Japanese. Young persons are no more at liberty now, than were their fathers and mothers under the Shogunate, to marry at will, to invest their means and efforts in undertakings not sanctioned by family approval, to consider themselves in any way enfranchised from family authority; and it is probably better for the present that they are not. No man is yet complete master of his activities, his time, or his means.

Though the individual is now registered, and made directly accountable to the law, while the household has been relieved from its ancient responsibility for the acts of its members, still the family practically remains the social unit, retaining its patriarchal organization and its particular cult. Not unwisely, the modern legislators have protected this domestic religion: to weaken its bond at this time were to weaken the foundations of the national moral life,—to introduce disintegrations into the most deeply seated structures of the social organism. The new codes forbid the man who becomes by succession the head of a house to abolish that house: he is not permitted to suppress a cult. No legal presumptive heir to the headship of a family can enter into another family as adopted son or husband; nor can he abandon the paternal house to establish an independent family of his own.[1] Provision has been made to meet extraordinary cases; but no individual is allowed, without good and sufficient reason, to free himself from those traditional obligations which the family-cult imposes. As regards adoption, the new law maintains the spirit of the old, with fresh provision for the conservation of the family religion,—permitting any person of legal age to adopt a son, on the simple condition that the person adopted shall be younger than the adopter. The new divorce-laws do not permit the dismissal of a wife for sterility alone (and divorce for such cause had long been condemned by Japanese sentiment); but, in view of the facilities given for adoption, this reform does not endanger the continuance of the cult. An interesting example of the manner in which the law still protects ancestor-worship is furnished by the fact that an aged and childless widow, last representative of her family, is not permitted to remain without an heir. She must adopt a son if she can: if she cannot, because of poverty, or for other reasons, the local authorities will provide a son for her,—that is to say, a male heir to maintain the family worship. Such official interference would seem to us tyrannical: it is simply paternal, and represents the continuance of an ancient regulation intended to protect the bereaved against what Eastern faith still deems the supreme misfortune,—the extinction of the home-cult. . . . In other respects the later codes allow of individual liberty unknown in previous generations. But the ordinary person would not dream of attempting to claim a legal right opposed to common opinion. Family and public sentiment are still more potent than law. The Japanese newspapers frequently record tragedies resulting from the prevention or dissolution of unions; and these tragedies afford strong proof that most young people would prefer even suicide to the probable consequence of a successful appeal to law against family decision.

The communal form of coercion is less apparent in the large cities; but everywhere it endures to some extent, and in the agricultural districts it remains supreme. Between the new conditions and the old there is this difference, that the man who finds the yoke of his district hard to bear can flee from it: he could not do so fifty years ago. But he can flee from it only to enter into another state of subordination of nearly the same kind. Full advantage, nevertheless, has been taken of this modern liberty of movement: thousands yearly throng to the cities; other thousands travel over the country, from province to province; working for a year or a season in one place, then going to another, with little more to hope for than experience of change. Emigration also has been taking place upon an extensive scale; but for the common class of emigrants, at least, the advantage of emigration is chiefly represented by the chance of earning larger wages. A Japanese emigrant community abroad organizes itself upon the home-plan;[2] and the individual emigrant probably finds himself as much under communal coercion in Canada, Hawaii, or the Philippine Islands, as he could ever have been in his native province. Needless to say that in foreign countries such coercion is more than compensated by the aid and protection which the communal organization insures. But with the constantly increasing number of restless spirits at home, and the ever widening experience of Japanese emigrants abroad, it would seem likely that the power of the commune for compulsory coöperation must become considerably weakened in the near future.

As for the tribal or clan law, it survives to the degree of remaining almost omnipotent in administrative circles, and in all politics. Voters, officials, legislators, do not follow principles in our sense of the word: they follow men, and obey commands. In these spheres of action the penalties of disobedience to orders are endless as well as serious: by a single such offence one may array against oneself powers that will continue their hostile operation for years and years,—unreasoningly, implacably, blindly, with the weight and persistence of natural forces,—of winds or tides. Any comprehension of the history of Japanese politics during the last fifteen years is not possible without some knowledge of clan-history. A political leader, fully acquainted with the history of clan-parties, and their offshoots, can accomplish marvellous things; and even foreign residents, with long experience of Japanese life, have been able, by pressing upon clan-interests, to exercise a very real power in government circles. But to the ordinary foreigner, Japanese contemporary politics must appear a chaos, a disintegration, a hopeless flux. The truth is that most things remain, under varying outward forms, "as all were ordered, ages since,"—though the shiftings have become more rapid, and the results less obvious, in the haste of an era of steam and electricity.

The greatest of living Japanese statesmen, the Marquis Ito, long ago perceived that the tendency of political life to agglomerations, to clan-groupings, presented the most serious obstacle to the successful working of constitutional government. He understood that this tendency could be opposed only by considerations weightier than clan-interests, considerations worthy of supreme sacrifice. He therefore formed a party of which every member was pledged to pass over clan-interests, clique-interests, personal and every other kind of interests, for the sake of national interests. Brought into collision with a hostile cabinet in 1903, this party achieved the feat of controlling its animosities even to the extent of maintaining its foes in power; but large fragments broke off in the process. So profoundly is the grouping-tendency, the clan-sentiment, identified with national character, that the ultimate success of Marquis Ito's policy must still be considered doubtful. Only a national danger—the danger of war,—has yet been able to weld all parties together, to make all wills work as one.

Not only politics, but nearly all phases of modern life, yield evidence that the disintegration of the old society has been superficial rather than fundamental. Structures dissolved have recrystallized, taking forms dissimilar in aspect to the original forms, but inwardly built upon the same plan. For the dissolutions really effected represented only a separation of masses, not a breaking up of substance into independent units; and these masses, again cohering, continue to act only as masses. Independence of personal action, in the Western sense, is still almost inconceivable. The individual of every class above the lowest must continue to be at once coercer and coerced. Like an atom within a solid body, he can vibrate; but the orbit of his vibration is fixed. He must act and be acted upon in ways differing little from those of ancient time.

As for being acted upon, the average man is under three kinds of pressure: pressure from above, exemplified in the will of his superiors; pressure about him, represented by the common will of his fellows and equals; pressure from below, represented by the general sentiment of his inferiors. And this last sort of coercion is not the least formidable.

Individual resistance to the first kind of pressure—that represented by authority—is not even to be thought of; because the superior represents a clan, a class, an exceedingly multiple power of some description; and no solitary individual, in the present order of things, can strive against a combination. To resist injustice he must find ample support, in which case his resistance does not represent individual action.

Resistance to the second kind of pressure—communal coercion—signifies ruin, loss of the right to form a part of the social body.

Resistance to the third sort of pressure, embodied in the common sentiment of inferiors, may result in almost anything,—from momentary annoyance to sudden death,—according to circumstances.

In all forms of society these three kinds of pressure are exerted to some degree; but in Japanese society, owing to inherited tendency, and traditional sentiment, their power is tremendous.

Thus, in every direction, the individual finds himself confronted by the despotism of collective opinion: it is impossible for him to act with safety except as one unit of a combination. The first kind of pressure deprives him of moral freedom, exacting unlimited obedience to orders; the second kind of pressure denies him the right to use his best faculties in the best way for his own advantage (that is to say, denies him the right of free competition); the third kind of pressure compels him, in directing the actions of others, to follow tradition, to forbear innovations, to avoid making any changes, however beneficial, which do not find willing acceptance on the part of his inferiors.

These are the social conditions which, under normal circumstances, make for stability, for conservation; and they represent the will of the dead. They are inevitable to a militant state; they make the strength of that state; they render facile the creation and maintenance of formidable armies. But they are not conditions favourable to success in the future international competition,—in the industrial struggle for existence against societies incomparably more plastic, and of higher mental energy.

Notes

Strangeness and Charm (from *Japan: An Attempt at Interpretation*, 1904)

The Chief City of the Province of the Gods (*Glimpses of Unfamiliar Japan*, 1894)

1. Thick solid sliding shutters of unpainted wood, which in Japanese houses serve both as shutters and doors.

2. *Tanabiku.*

3. *Ama-terasu-oho-mi-Kami* literally signifies "the Heaven-Shining-Great-August-Divinity." (See Professor Chamberlain's translation of the *Kojiki.*)

4. "The gods who do harm are to be appeased, so that they may not punish those who have offended them." Such are the words of the great Shintō teacher, Hirata, as translated by Mr. Satow in his article, *The Revival of Pure Shintau.*

5. *Machi,* a stiff piece of pasteboard or other material sewn into the waist of the hakama at the back, so as to keep the folds of the garment perpendicular and neat-looking.

6. Kushi-no-ki-Matsuhira-Inari-Daimyōjin.

7. From an English composition by one of my Japanese students.

8. *Rin,* one tenth of one cent. A small round copper coin with a square hole in the middle.

9. An inn where soba is sold.

10. According to the mythology of the *Kojiki* the Moon-Deity is a male divinity. But the common people know nothing of the *Kojiki*, written in an archaic Japanese which only the learned can read; and they address the moon as O-Tsuki-San, or "Lady Moon," just as the old Greek idylists did.

In a Japanese Garden (*Glimpses of Unfamiliar Japan,* 1894)

1. Such as the garden attached to the abbot's palace at Tokuwamonji, cited by Mr. Conder, which was made to commemorate the legend of stones which bowed themselves in assent to the doctrine of Buddha. At Togo-ike, in Tottori-ken, I saw a very large garden consisting almost entirely of stones and sand. The impression which the designer had intended to convey was that of approaching the sea over a verge of dunes, and the illusion was beautiful.

2. The *Kojiki*, translated by Professor B. H. Chamberlain, p. 254.

3. Since this paper was written, Mr. Conder has published a beautiful illustrated volume,—"Landscape Gardening in Japan. By Josiah Conder, F. R. I., B. A. Tōkyō: 1893." A photographic supplement to the work gives views of the most famous gardens in the capital and elsewhere.

4. The observations of Dr. Rein on Japanese gardens are not to be recommended, in respect either to accuracy or to comprehension of the subject. Rein spent only two years in Japan, the larger part of which time he devoted to the study of the lacquer industry, the manufacture of silk and paper, and other practical matters. On these subjects his work is justly valued. But his chapters on Japanese manners and customs, art, religion, and literature show extremely little acquaintance with those topics.

5. This attitude of the shachihoko is somewhat *de rigueur*, whence the common expression *shachihoko dai*, signifying "to stand on one's head."

6. The magnificent perch called tai *(Serranus marginalis)*, which is very common along the Izumo coast, is not only justly prized as the most delicate of Japanese fish, but is also held to be an emblem of good fortune. It is a ceremonial gift at weddings and on congratulatory occasions. The Japanese call it also "the king of fishes."

7. *Nandina domestica.*

8. The most lucky of all dreams, they say in Izumo, is a dream of Fuji, the Sacred Mountain. Next in order of good omen is dreaming of a falcon *(taka)*. The third best subject for a dream is the eggplant *(nasubi)*. To dream of the sun or of the moon is very lucky; but it is still more so to dream of stars. For a young wife it is most fortunate to dream of *swallowing a star:* this signifies that she will become the mother of a beautiful child. To dream of a cow is a good omen; to dream of a horse is lucky, but it signifies traveling. To dream of rain or fire is good. Some dreams are held in Japan, as in the West, "to go by contraries." Therefore to dream of having one's house burned up, or of funerals, or of being dead, or of talking to the ghost of a dead person, is good. Some dreams which are good for women mean the reverse when dreamed by men; for example, it is good for a woman to dream that her nose bleeds, but for a man this is very bad. To dream of much money is a sign of loss to come. To dream of the *koi*, or of any fresh-water fish, is the most unlucky of all. This is curious, for in other parts of Japan the koi is a symbol of good fortune.

9. *Tebushukan: Citrus sarkodactilis.*

10. *Yuzuru* signifies to resign in favor of another; *ha* signifies a leaf. The botanical name, as given in Hepburn's dictionary, is *Daphniphilum macropodum.*

11. *Cerasus pseudo-cerasus* (Lindley).

12. About this mountain cherry there is a humorous saying which illustrates the Japanese love of puns. In order fully to appreciate it, the reader should know that Japanese nouns have no distinction of singular and plural. The word *ha*, as pronounced, may signify either "leaves" or "teeth"; and the word *hana*, either "flowers" or "nose." The yamazakura puts forth its ha (leaves) before its hana (flowers). Wherefore a man whose ha (teeth) project in advance of his hana (nose) is called a yamazakura. Prognathism is not uncommon in Japan, especially among the lower classes.

13. "If one should ask you concerning the heart of a true Japanese, point to the wild cherry flower glowing in the sun."

14. There are three noteworthy varieties: one bearing red, one pink and white, and one pure white flowers.

15. The expression *yanagi-goshi,* "a willow-waist," is one of several in common use comparing slender beauty to the willow-tree.

16. *Peonia albiflora.* The name signifies the delicacy of beauty.

The simile of the *botan* (the tree peony) can be fully appreciated only by one who is acquainted with the Japanese flower.

17. Some say keshiyuri (poppy) instead of himeyuri. The latter is a graceful species of lily, *Lilium callosum*.

18. "Standing, she is a shakuyaku; seated, she is a botan; and the charm of her figure in walking is the charm of a himeyuri."

19. In the higher classes of Japanese society to-day, the honorific *O* is not, as a rule, used before the names of girls, and showy appellations are not given to daughters. Even among the poor respectable classes, names resembling those of geisha, etc., are in disfavor. But those above cited are good, honest, every-day names.

20. Mr. Satow has found in Hirata a belief to which this seems to some extent akin,—the curious Shintō doctrine "according to which a divine being throws off portions of itself by a process of fissure, thus producing what are called waki-mi-tama,—parted spirits, with separate functions." The great god of Izumo, Oho-kuni-nushi-no-Kami, is said by Hirata to have three such "parted spirits:" his rough spirit *(ara-mi-tama)* that punishes, his gentle spirit *(nigi-mi-tama)* that pardons, and his benedictory or beneficent spirit *(saki-mi-tama)* that blesses. There is a Shintō story that the rough spirit of this god once met the gentle spirit without recognizing it.

21. Perhaps the most impressive of all the Buddhist temples in Kyōto. It is dedicated to Kwannon of the Thousand Hands, and is said to contain 33,333 of her images.

22. *Daidaimushi* in Izumo. The dictionary word is *dedemushi*. The snail is supposed to be very fond of wet weather; and one who goes out much in the rain is compared to a snail,—*dedemushi no yona*.

23. "Snail, snail, put out your horns a little: it rains and the wind is blowing, so put out your horns, just for a little while."

24. A Buddhist divinity, but within recent times identified by Shintō with the god Kotohira.

25. See Professor Chamberlain's version of it in the Japanese Fairy-Tale Series, with charming illustrations by a native artist.

26. "Butterfly, little butterfly, light upon the *na* leaf. But if thou dost not like the *na* leaf, light, I pray thee, upon my hand."

27. *Bōshi* means "a hat"; *tsukeru*, "to put on." But this etymology is more than doubtful.

28. Some say *"Choko-choko-uisu."* "Uisu" would be pronounced in English very much like "weece," the final *u* being silent. "Uiōsu" would be something like "we-oce."

29. Pronounced almost as "geece."

30. Contraction of *kore naru*.

31. A kindred legend attaches to the shiwan, a little yellow insect, which preys upon cucumbers. The shiwan is said to have been once a physician, who, being detected in an amorous intrigue, had to fly for his life. But as he went his foot caught in a cucumber vine, so that he fell and was overtaken and killed, and his ghost became an insect, the destroyer of cucumber vines.

In the zoölogical mythology and plant mythology of Japan there exist many legends offering a curious resemblance to the old Greek tales of metamorphoses. Some of the most remarkable bits of such folk-lore have originated, however, in comparatively modern time. The legend of the crab called heikegani, found at Nagato, is an example. The souls of the Taira warriors who perished in the great naval battle of Dan-no-ura (now Seto-Naikai), 1185, are supposed to have been transformed into heikegani. The shell of the heikegani is certainly surprising. It is wrinkled into the likeness of a grim face, or rather into exact semblance of one of those black iron visors, or masks, which feudal warriors wore in battle, and which were shaped like frowning visages.

32. "Come, firefly, I will give you water to drink. The water of that place is bitter; the water here is sweet."

33. By *honzon* is here meant the sacred kakemono, or picture, exposed to public view in the temples only upon the birthday of the Buddha, which is the eighth day of the old fourth month. *Honzon* also signifies the principal image in a Buddhist temple.

34. "A solitary voice! / Did the moon cry? / 'Twas but the hoto-togisu."

35. "When I gaze towards the place where I heard the hototogisu cry, lo! there is naught save the wan morning moon."

36. "Save only the morning moon, none heard the heart's-blood cry of the hototogisu."

37. A sort of doughnut made of bean flour, or tofu.

38. "Kite, kite, let me see you dance, and to-morrow evening, when the crows do not know, I will give you a rat."

39. "O tardy crow, hasten forward! Your house is all on fire. Hurry to throw water upon it. If there be no water, I will give you. If you have too much, I will give it to your child. If you have no child, then give it back to me."

40. The words *papa* and *mamma* exist in Japanese baby language, but their meaning is not at all what might be supposed. *Mamma,* or, with the usual honorific, *O-mamma,* means "boiled rice." *Papa* means "tobacco."

Three Popular Ballads (*Kokoro,* 1896)

1. Read before the Asiatic Society of Japan, October 17, 1894.

2. Since the time this letter to the *Mail* was written, a primary school has been established for the *yama-no-mono,* through the benevolence of Matsué citizens superior to prejudice. The undertaking did not escape severe local criticism, but it seems to have proved successful.

3. Daikoku is the popular God of Wealth. Ebisu is the patron of labor. See, for the history of these deities, an article (translated) entitled "The Seven Gods of Happiness," by Carlo Puini, vol. iii. *Transactions of the Asiatic Society.* See, also, for an account of their place in Shintō worship, *Glimpses of Unfamiliar Japan,* vol. i.

In the Cave of the Children's Ghosts (*Glimpses of Unfamiliar Japan,* 1894)

1. Such are the names given to the water-vessels or cisterns at which Shintō worshipers must wash their hands and rinse their mouths ere praying to the Kami. A mitarashi or ō-chōzubachi is placed before every Shintō temple. The pilgrim to Shin-Kukedo-San should perform this ceremonial ablution at the little rock-spring above described, before entering the sacred cave. Here even the gods of the cave are said to wash after having passed through the sea-water.

2. "The August Fire-Lady;" or, "the August Sun-Lady," Ama-tera-su-oho-mi-Kami.

A Letter from Japan (*The Romance of the Milky Way,* 1905)

Horai (*Kwaidan,* 1904)

Bits of Life and Death (*Out of the East,* 1895)

1. A sort of small silver carp.

2. A hollow wooden block shaped like a dolphin's head. It is tapped in accompaniment to the chanting of the Buddhist sutras.

3. At the great temple of Tennōji, at Ōsaka, all such bones are dropped into a vault; and according *to the sound each makes in falling,* further evidence about the Gōsho is said to be obtained. After a hundred years from the time of beginning this curious collection, all these bones are to be ground into a kind of paste, out of which a colossal statue of Buddha is to be made.

4. "Thy previous life as for,—what was it? Honorably look [or, *please look*] and tell."

5. The meaning is, "Give to the beloved one a little more [wine]." The *"Ya-ton-ton"* is only a burden, without exact meaning, like our own *"With a hey! and a ho!"* etc.

6. The meaning is about as follows: "If from the Meido it be possible to send letters or telegrams, I shall write and forward news of our speedy safe arrival there."

Of Women's Hair (*Glimpses of Unfamiliar Japan,* 1894)

1. Formerly both sexes used the same pillow for the same reason. The long hair of a samurai youth, tied up in an elaborate knot, required much time to arrange. Since it has become the almost universal custom to wear the hair short, the men have adopted a pillow shaped like a small bolster.

2. It is an error to suppose that all Japanese have blue-black hair. There are two distinct racial types. In one the hair is a deep brown instead of a pure black, and is also softer and finer. Rarely, but very rarely, one may see a Japanese *chevelure* having a natural tendency to ripple. For curious reasons, which cannot be stated here, an Izumo woman is very much ashamed of having wavy hair—more ashamed than she would be of a natural deformity.

3. Even in the time of the writing of the *Kojiki* the art of arranging the hair must have been somewhat developed. See Professor Chamberlain's introduction to translation, p. xxxi.; also vol. i. section ix.; vol. vii section xii; vol. ix. section xviii., *et passim.*

4. An art expert can decide the age of an unsigned kakemono or

other work of art in which human figures appear, by the style of the coiffure of the female personages.

5. The principal and indispensable hairpin *(kanzashi)*, usually about seven inches long, is split, and its well-tempered double shaft can be used like a small pair of chopsticks for picking up small things. The head is terminated by a tiny spoon-shaped projection, which has a special purpose in the Japanese toilette.

6. The shinjōchō is also called ichōgaeshi by old people, although the original Ichōgaeshi was somewhat different. The samurai girls used to wear their hair in the true ichōgaeshi manner; the name is derived from the ichō-tree *(Salisburia andiantifolia)*, whose leaves have a queer shape, almost like that of a duck's foot. Certain bands of the hair in this coiffure bore a resemblance in form to ichō-leaves.

7. The old Japanese mirrors were made of metal, and were extremely beautiful. *Kagami ga kumoru to tamashii ga kumoru* ("When the Mirror is dim, the Soul is unclean") is another curious proverb relating to mirrors. Perhaps the most beautiful and touching story of a mirror in any language is that called "Matsuyama-no-kagami," which has been translated by Mrs. James.

A Street Singer (*Kokoro,* 1896)

Kimiko (*Kokoro,* 1896)
1. "To wish to be forgotten by the beloved is a soul-task harder far than trying not to forget."—*Poem by* Kimiko.
2. *Oni mo jiuhachi, azami no hana.* There is a similar saying of a dragon: *ja mo hatachi* ("even a dragon at twenty").

Yuko: A Reminiscence (*Out of the East,* 1898)

On a Bridge (*A Japanese Miscellany,* 1901)

The Case of O-Dai (*A Japanese Miscellany,* 1901)
1. Prêta.

Drifting (*A Japanese Miscellany,* 1901)
1. The word *Fukuju* signifies "Fortunate Longevity."

2. That is to say the first, or coronation-year, of the Period Manyen,—1860–1861.

3. "Come this way!"

4. This invocation, signifying "Salutation to the Buddha Amitâbha," is commonly repeated as a prayer for the dead.

5. As we should say, "Hey! hey!"—to call attention.

6. That is to say, about sixty-three English miles.

7. The distance is more than one hundred and fifty miles.

Drifting (*A Japanese Miscellany,* 1901)

Diplomacy (*Kwaidan,* 1904)

A Passional Karma (*In Ghostly Japan,* 1899)

1. The *hatamoto* were samurai forming the special military force of the Shōgun. The name literally signifies "Banner-Supporters." These were the highest class of samurai,—not only as the immediate vassals of the Shōgun, but as a military aristocracy.

2. Perhaps this conversation may seem strange to the Western reader; but it is true to life. The whole of the scene is characteristically Japanese.

3. The invocation *Namu Amida Butsu!* ("Hail to the Buddha Amitâbha!"),—repeated, as a prayer, for the sake of the dead.

4. *Komageta* in the original. The geta is a wooden sandal, or clog, of which there are many varieties,—some decidedly elegant. The *komageta,* or "pony-geta," is so-called because of the sonorous hoof-like echo which it makes on hard ground.

5. The sort of lantern here referred to is no longer made. It was totally unlike the modern domestic hand-lantern, painted with the owner's crest; but it was not altogether unlike some forms of lanterns still manufactured for the Festival of the Dead, and called *Bon-dōrō.* The flowers ornamenting it were not painted: they were artificial flowers of crêpe-silk, and were attached to the top of the lantern.

6. "For the time of seven existences,"—that is to say, for the time of seven successive lives. In Japanese drama and romance it is not uncommon to represent a father as disowning his child "for the time of seven lives." Such a disowning is called *shichi-shō madé no mandō,*

a disinheritance for seven lives,—signifying that in six future lives after the present the erring son or daughter will continue to feel the parental displeasure.

7. The profession is not yet extinct. The *ninsomi* uses a kind of magnifying glass (or magnifying-mirror sometimes), called *tengankyō* or *ninsomégané*.

8. The color and form of the dress, and the style of wearing the hair, are by Japanese custom regulated according to the age of the woman.

9. The forms of speech used by the samurai, and other superior classes, differed considerably from those of the popular idiom; but these differences could not be effectively rendered into English.

10. The Japanese word *mamori* has significations at least as numerous as those attaching to our own term "amulet." It would be impossible, in a mere footnote, even to suggest the variety of Japanese religious objects to which the name is given. In this instance, the *mamori* is a very small image, probably enclosed in a miniature shrine of lacquerwork or metal, over which a silk cover is drawn. Such little images were often worn by *samurai* on the person. I was recently shown a miniature figure of Kwannon, in an iron case, which had been carried by an officer through the Satsuma war. He observed, with good reason, that it had probably saved his life; for it had stopped a bullet of which the dent was plainly visible.

11. From *shiryō,* a ghost, and *yokeru,* to exclude. The Japanese have two kinds of ghosts proper in their folk-lore: the spirits of the dead, *shiryō;* and the spirits of the living, *ikiryō.* A house or a person may be haunted by an *ikiryō* as well as by a *shiryō.*

12. A special service,—accompanying offerings of food, etc., to those dead having no living relatives or friends to care for them,—is thus termed. In this case, however, the service would be of a particular and exceptional kind.

13. The name would be more correctly written *Uhō-Darani-Kyō.* It is the Japanese pronunciation of the title of a very short sutra translated out of Sanscrit into Chinese by the Indian priest Amoghavajra, probably during the eighth century. The Chinese text contains transliterations of some mysterious Sanscrit words,—apparently talismanic words,—like those to be seen in Kern's translation of the Saddharma-Pundarika, ch. xxvi.

14. *O-fuda* is the general name given to religious texts used as charms or talismans. They are sometimes stamped or burned upon wood, but more commonly written or printed upon narrow strips of paper. *O-fuda* are pasted above house-entrances, on the walls of rooms, upon tablets placed in household shrines, etc., etc. Some kinds are worn about the person;—others are made into pellets, and swallowed as spiritual medicine. The text of the larger *o-fuda* is often accompanied by curious pictures or symbolic illustrations.

15. According to the old Japanese way of counting time, this *yat-sudoki* or eighth hour was the same as our two o'clock in the morning. Each Japanese hour was equal to two European hours, so that there were only six hours instead of our twelve; and these six hours were counted backwards in the order,—9, 8, 7, 6, 5, 4. Thus the ninth hour corresponded to our midday, or midnight; half-past nine to our one o'clock; eight to our two o'clock. Two o'clock in the morning, also called "the Hour of the Ox," was the Japanese hour of ghosts and goblins.

16. *En-netsu* or *Shō-netsu* (Sanscrit "Tapana") is the sixth of the Eight Hot Hells of Japanese Buddhism. One day of life in this hell is equal in duration to thousands (some say millions) of human years.

17. The Male and Female principles of the universe, the Active and Passive forces of Nature. Yusai refers here to the old Chinese nature-philosophy,—better known to Western readers by the name Feng-shui.

Survivals (*Japan: An Attempt at Interpretation,* 1904)

1. That is to say, he cannot separate himself from the family in law; but he is free to live in a separate house. The tendency to further disintegration of the family is shown by a custom which has been growing of late years,—especially in Tōkyō: the custom of demanding, as a condition of marriage, that the bride shall not be obliged to live in the same house with the parents of the bridegroom. This custom is yet confined to certain classes, and has been adversely criticised. Many young men, on marrying, leave the parental home to begin independent housekeeping,—though remaining legally attached to their parents' families, of course. . . . It will perhaps be asked, What becomes of the cult in such cases? The cult remains in

the parental home. When the parents die, then the ancestral tablets
are transferred to the home of the married son.

2. Except as regards the communal cult, perhaps. The domestic
cult is transplanted; emigrants who go abroad, accompanied by their
families, take the ancestral tablets with them. To what extent the
communal cult may have been established in emigrant communities,
I have not yet been able to learn. It would appear, however, that the
absence of Ujigami in certain emigrant settlements is to be account-
ed for solely by the pecuniary difficulty of constructing such temples
and maintaining competent officials. In Formosa, for example,
though the domestic ancestor-cult is maintained in the homes of the
Japanese settlers, Ujigami have not yet been established. The government, however, has erected several important Shintō temples; and I
am told that some of these will probably be converted into Ujigami
when the Japanese population has increased enough to justify the
measure.

Chronology

1850	Born in Greece, the son of a Greek woman and an Anglo-Irish surgeon in the British army.
April 1890	Arrives in Yokohama.
August 1890	Arrives in Matsue.
September 1890	Begins teaching at Matsue Jinjō Chūgakkō (Ordinary Middle School) and Shihan Gakkō (Normal School).
January 1891	Marries Koizumi Setsuko.
June 1891	Moves to house in Kitabori in Matsue.
November 1891	Leaves Matsue for Kumamoto. Begins teaching at Kumamoto Kōtō Chūgakkō (Higher Middle School).
January 1893	Completes first book, *Glimpses of Unfamiliar Japan*.
October 1894	Arrives in Kobe, writing for the *Kobe Chronicle*.
December 1894	Resigns from the *Kobe Chronicle*, claiming failing eyesight.

1895	Becomes Japanese citizen, Koizumi Yakumo.
Summer 1896	Visits Matsue.
September 1896	Begins teaching in the College of Literature at Tokyo Imperial University.
1903	Contract with Tokyo Imperial University expires.
August 1904	With family at Yaizu.
September 26, 1904	Dies at the age of 54.

Glossary

Note: Entries in the glossary follow modern Romanized spelling. Terms within brackets are written in Hearn's original Romanization.

ama-zake: sweet saké
ame: candy
ameya: sweets shop
azukimeshi [adzukimeshi]: rice and red beans

bake-mono ki: literally, ghost tree
bokkuri: girl's clogs
butsu-ma: room with a Buddhist altar

chō: 1. distance of about 120 yards 2. town
chōzu-bachi [chodzu-bachi]: basin for washing the hands

daimyō: feudal lord
dohyō-ba: wrestling ring
dōshin bōzu: priest

enoki: (Chinese) nettle tree

271

eta: outcast class

fukusa: square cloth for wrapping a small gift
fumi-bako: lacquered box for keeping letters

gaki: hungry ghost; famished devil
geta: wooden clogs
gohei: hanging white paper strip in a Shinto shrine
goshō: the future life; the life to come

hachiya: outcast class
haka: tomb
hakaba: cemetery
hakama: man's formal divided skirt
hanashi-ka: storyteller
hara-kiri: ritual suicide by cutting the abdomen
hashira [bashira]: pillar
hata-moto: direct vassal of the shogun
heike-gani: mask crab
heimin: commoner
hibachi: charcoal brazier
hijō: inanimate nature
hiki-gaeru: toad
hinoki: Japanese cypress
hotaru: firefly
hotoke: the Buddha
hototogisu: cuckoo

ihai: mortuary tablet; memorial tablet
inki: gloom; melancholy
inkyo [inkyō]: retired person

Jizō: bodhisattva usually shown with a jewel in one hand and a staff
    in the other, commonly regarded as the patron of children
jorō: prostitute
jorōya: brothel
jōshi: lovers' suicide

jūjutsu: judo

kachū yashiki [katchiū yashiki]: house of a retainer of a *daimyō*
kaimyō: posthumous Buddhist name
kake-mono: hanging scroll
kakitsubata: rabbit-ear iris
kamakake: praying mantis
kami: god; gods
kami-yui: hairdresser
kannushi: Shinto priest
katsuo-no-eboshi: Portuguese man-of-war
kawarake: unglazed earthenware
kazari: ornament; decoration
ken: prefecture
koku: unit of dry measure equivalent to about 5.1 US bushels
koniwa: small garden
kura: storehouse; godown
kuruma: ricksha
kuruma-ya: ricksha man
Kwannon: the bodhisattva Kannon; goddess of mercy
kyō: sutra

mamori: amulet; charm
meido: hades; the underworld
minmin-zemi: robust cicada
mi-tarashi: holy washing trough
mizu-ame [midzu-ame]: thick clear syrup
mokugyo [mokyogyō]: hollow wooden block shaped like a dolphin's
    head, which is tapped to accompany the chanting of a Buddhist
    sutra

ninsō-mi [ninsomi]: physiognomist
nobori: banner; streamer

o-bake: monster; ghost
obi: sash
o-chōzu-bachi: wash basin for washing the hands

o-fuda: holy text; holy charm
oni: goblin; fiend

ri: distance of about 2.44 miles
rin: unit of currency equal to one-thousandth of a yen
rokushaku: loincloth

sakura-no-hana: cherry blossom
sakura-no-ki: cherry tree
sanbō [sambo]: small wooden stand for an offering at a Buddhist temple or Shinto shrine
segaki: mass for the dead
semi: cicada
sen: unit of currency equal to one-hundredth of a yen
shachihoko: dolphin-like ornament on the roof of a castle
shikimi: sacred plant used for offerings in Buddhist ceremonies for the dead; Japanese star anise
shime-nawa: sacred rope of twisted rice straw
shinjū: lovers' suicide
shiryō-yoke: charm used as protection against a ghost
shizoku: person of samurai descent
shōji: paper-covered wooden sliding door
shōkonsha: Shinto shrine for the spirits of war dead
shōryō-bune: straw boat for the spirit of a dead person
shōryō-dana: shelf to welcome the souls of the departed at O-Bon, the Buddhist observance for the spirits of ancestors
shū: sect
soba: buckwheat noodles
sobaya: shop selling buckwheat noodles
suiban [suïbon]: shallow container for flowers

tabi: Japanese sock with the big toe separated from the other toes
tai: sea bream
taka-geta: clogs with high supports
tanabiku: to hang or lie over, as of clouds
tasuki: sash cord for holding up tucked kimono sleeves

tegashiwa: kind of oak

tengu: creature in Japanese folklore with a long beak, feared as an abductor of humans

to: door

toko: toko-no-ma

tokoniwa: miniature garden within a *toko-no-ma*

toko-no-ma: wall niche in a Japanese home for displaying a scroll, flowers, etc.

torii: gatelike structure at a shrine or on a path leading to a shrine

tōrō: 1. lantern 2. praying mantis

tsukutsuku-bōshi: kind of cicada

uguisu: Japanese nightingale

ujigami: tutelary god of a place; patron saint

ujiko: person living under the patronage of a local god

ujō: animate thing

ume-no-hana: plum blossom

ume-no-ki: plum tree

waraji: straw sandals

yama: mountain

yama-bato: turtledove

yama-no-mono: outcast class

yashiki: mansion; estate

yōki: loveliness; vivacity

yuzuri-ha: kind of evergreen used for New Year's decoration

zashiki: room

zuihitsu: light essay; random notes

Bibliography

Writings on Japan by Hearn

Glimpses of Unfamiliar Japan, 1894. Reprint. Tokyo: Charles E. Tuttle, 1976.

Out of the East: Reveries and Studies in New Japan, 1895. Reprint. Tokyo: Charles E. Tuttle, 1972.

Kokoro: Hints and Echoes of Japanese Inner Life, 1896. Reprint. Tokyo: Charles E. Tuttle, 1972.

Gleanings in Buddha Fields: Studies of Hand and Soul in the Far East, 1897. Reprint. Tokyo: Charles E. Tuttle, 1971.

Exotics and Retrospectives, 1898. Reprint. Tokyo: Charles E. Tuttle, 1971.

Japanese Fairytales, 1898 through 1922, five volumes.

In Ghostly Japan, 1899. Reprint. Tokyo: Charles E. Tuttle, 1971.

Shadowings, 1900. Reprint. Tokyo: Charles E. Tuttle, 1971.

A Japanese Miscellany: Strange Stories, Folklore Gleanings, Studies Here and There, 1901. Reprint. Tokyo: Charles E. Tuttle, 1967.

Kottō: Being Japanese Curios, with Sundry Cobwebs, 1902. Reprint. Tokyo: Charles E. Tuttle, 1971.

Kwaidan: Stories and Studies of Strange Things, 1904. Reprint. Tokyo: Charles E. Tuttle, 1971.

Japan: An Attempt at Interpretation, 1904. Reprint. Tokyo: Charles E. Tuttle, 1955.

The Romance of the Milky Way and Other Studies and Stories, 1904. Reprint. Tokyo: Charles E. Tuttle, 1974.

Uncollected Pieces:

"A Winter's Journey in Japan." *Harper's Monthly,* November, 1890.

"From My Japanese Diary." *Atlantic Monthly,* November, 1894.

"The Ballad of Shun Toku Maru." *The Chrysanthemum,* vol. 2, no. 1, 1897.

"Notes on a Trip to Izumo." *Atlantic Monthly,* May, 1897.

"The Nun Ryone." London: *Transactions of the Japan Society,* vol. VI, part 3.

Writings on Hearn

Allen, Louis, and Jean Wilson. *Lafcadio Hearn: Japan's Great Interpreter—A New Anthology of His Writings.* Folkestone, Kent: The Japan Library, 1992.

Barel, Leona. *The Idyll: My Personal Reminiscences of Lafcadio Hearn.* Tokyo: Hokuseido Press, 1933.

Bellair, John. *In Hearn's Footsteps.* Huntington University Editions, 1994.

Beong-cheon Yu. *An Ape of the Gods: The Art and Thought of Lafcadio Hearn.* Detroit: Wayne State University Press, 1964.

Bisland, Elizabeth. *Life and Letters of Lafcadio Hearn.* Boston: Houghton Mifflin, 1906.

Chamberlain, B. H. *Letters.* Tokyo: Hokuseido Press, 1936.

———. *More Letters.* Tokyo: Hokuseido Press, 1937.

Chisolm, Lawrence. *Fenollosa: The Far East and American Culture.* New Haven: Yale University Press, 1963.

Cott, Jonathan. *Wandering Ghost: The Odyssey of Lafcadio Hearn.* New York: Alfred Knopf, 1991.

Dawson, Carl. *Lafcadio Hearn and the Vision of Japan.* Baltimore & London: Johns Hopkins University Press, 1922.

Goebel, Rolf J. "Japan Was Western Text: Roland Barthes, Richard Gordon Smith, and Lafcadio Hearn." Pennsylvania State University: *Comparative Literature Studies,* vol. 30, no. 2, 1993.

Goodman, Henry, ed. *The Selected Writings of Lafcadio Hearn.* New York: Citadel Press, 1949.

Hasegawa Yoji. *Lafcadio Hearn's Japanese Wife: Her Memoirs.* Tokyo: Micro Printing Co., 1988.

_____ . *Walk in Kumamoto: The Life and Times of Setsu Koizumi, Lafcadio Hearn's Japanese Wife. With a New Translation of Her Memoir, "Reminiscences."* Folkestone, Kent, UK, Global Oriental, 1997.

Hearn Centennial Committee. *Selected Writings of Lafcadio Hearn.* Tokyo: Kenkyusha, 1953.

Hirakawa Sukihiro, ed. *Rediscovering Lafcadio Hearn.* Kent: Global Oriental, 1997.

Hughes, George. "Lafcadio Hearn: Between Britain and Japan." *Poetica* 44. Tokyo: Shubun, Int., 1996.

Jansen, Marius. "Lafcadio in Japan." *Princeton University Papers.* Princeton University, no. 19, Winter, 1963–64.

Kennard, Nina. *Lafcadio Hearn.* 1912. Reprint. Port Washington, N.Y.: Kennikat Press, 1967.

King, Francis. *Writings from Japan: An Anthology.* London: Penguin, 1984.

Kirkwood, Kenneth. *Unfamiliar Lafcadio Hearn.* Tokyo: Hokuseido Press, 1935.

Koizumi Kazuo. *Father and I: Memories of Lafcadio Hearn.* Boston & New York: Houghton Mifflin, 1935.

Koizumi Setsuko. *Reminiscences of Lafcadio Hearn.* Boston: Houghton Mifflin, 1918.

Kurihara Motoi. "My Teacher, Lafcadio Hearn." *Today's Japan,* vol. 4, no. 1, January, 1959.

Lazar, Margaret. *The Art of Lafcadio Hearn: A Study of His Literary Development.* Ann Arbor: University Microfilms, 1977.

Lewis, Oscar. *Hearn and His Biographers.* San Francisco: Westgate Press, 1930.

Lovell, Patrick. "Koizumi Yakumo: Beyond the Romantic Haze." Tokyo: *The Journal,* British Chamber of Commerce, Japan, vol. 4, no. 6, 1990.

McAdow, Margaret. *Lafcadio Hearn: A Study of his Literary Development.* Ann Arbor: University Microfilms, 1984.

McIvor, Peter. "Lafcadio Hearn's First Day in the Orient." *Japan Quarterly*, vol. 43, no. 2, April–June, 1996.

McWilliams, Vera. *Lafcadio Hearn*. 1946. Reprint. New York: Cooper Square Publishers, 1970.

Miner, Earl. *The Japanese Tradition in British and American Literature*. Princeton: Princeton University Press, 1958.

Mordell, Albert. *Lafcadio Hearn: An American Miscellany*. New York: Dodd, Mead, and Co., 1924.

Murray, Paul. "Lafcadio Hearn, 1850–1904." In *Britain & Japan: Biographical Portraits*, Vol. II, ed. Ian Nish. Richmond, Surrey, UK, Japan Library, 1997.

Noguchi Yone et al. *Lafcadio Hearn in Japan*. 1910. Reprint. Rye, NY: Folcroft Library Editions, 1978.

Rexroth, Kenneth, ed. *The Buddhist Writings of Lafcadio Hearn*. Santa Barbara: Ross-Erikson, Inc., 1977.

Richie, Donald. "Lafcadio Hearn: An Attempt at Interpretation." *Far East Stars and Stripes Weekly Review*, Sunday, March 21, 1948.

Robert, Marcel. *Lafcadio Hearn*. Tokyo: Hokuseido Press, 1950.

Rosenstone, Robert. *Mirror in the Shrine: American Encounters with Meiji Japan*. Cambridge: Harvard University Press, 1988.

Sanga Makoto. "Lafcadio Hearn in Japan." *Today's Japan*, vol. 4, no. 1, January, 1959.

Stevenson, Elizabeth. *Lafcadio Hearn*. New York: Macmillan, 1961.

Temple, Jean. *Blue Ghost: A Study of Lafcadio Hearn*. New York: Smith & Cape, 1931.

Thomas, Carl. *Lafcadio Hearn*. Boston & New York: Houghton Mifflin, 1912.

Zenimoto Kenji. *A General Catalogue of Hearn Collections in Japan and Overseas*. Matsue: The Hearn Society, 1991.